THE SLENDER BALANCE

The
SLENDER BALANCE:

Causes and Cures for Bulimia, Anorexia & the Weight-Loss/Weight-Gain Seesaw

Susan Squire

G. P. PUTNAM'S SONS
NEW YORK

Library of Congress Cataloging in Publication Data

Squire, Susan.
 The slender balance.

 Includes bibliographical references.
  1. Bulimarexia.   2. Anorexia nervosa.   3. Reducing—
Psychological aspects.   I. Title.
RC552.B84S68   1983   616.85′2   82-23139
ISBN 0-399-12781-X

Printed in the United States of America

Third Impression

To Jim Rahman

With thanks to those members of the staff of UCLA's Neuro-psychiatric Institute who are involved in the Eating Disorders Clinic, particularly Joel Yager, Karen Lee-Benner, Sandy Perlo and Charles Portney, for their patience with my endless questions. Thanks also to Adele Cygelman, Steven Benes and Debbie Michel for their help, and to Geoff Miller and Lew Harris of *Los Angeles* Magazine for their understanding.

CONTENTS

THE SLENDER BALANCE

PREFACE

by Joel Yager, M.D., director, UCLA Eating Disorders Clinic

It's remarkable how many of us choose to spend so much time concerned with our weight and physical appearance, time that would be better spent on truly threatening problems such as the nuclear threat, the unemployment crisis, pollution, drugs in the schools and crime in the streets. But then, these problems seem overwhelming, uncontrollable; improving our physical appearance seems more within our grasp. Indeed, surveys repeatedly show that among all of the hassles we contend with in life, the one that's very often uppermost in our minds is the issue of weight, diet and appearance—to a degree that surpasses a concern with simple physical health. The extent of our preoccupation suggests that some very basic, deep social or biological need is being met by it—perhaps even our very survival.

Is it possible today that being slim and attractive does in fact offer us an adaptive advantage? Certainly, social pressures for thinness are intense. As Susan Squire points out in her remarkably comprehensive overview of this major American problem, the popular magazines are increasing the rate at which they publish articles on dieting and appearance, and the women who are held up as physical ideals for teenagers all across the nation have grown progressively slimmer over recent decades. Increasingly, it seems that the packaging, the veneer, is more important than what's inside.

Though Western society has gradually evolved into a more and more visual one, with images on film and tape commanding our attention more insistently than words on paper, it's still not entirely clear why the voluptuous female idols of the past—Mae West, Jane Russell, Marilyn Monroe—have been replaced by icons of almost boylike slimness. For many generations and in many cultures, the pressures, particularly upon women, to fulfill their societies' expectations of physical beauty have given rise to devices and systems meant to help the woman along her way to the "ideal" form, but often these devices and systems have been dangerous and even life-threatening. Consider, for example, foot-binding in ancient China, which led to discomfort, disfigurement and crippling, yet was demanded by the culture for centuries. Is unwarranted slimness—requiring relentless dieting that in turn can lead to anorexia, bulimia and, at the very least, daily misery—contemporary America's version of foot-binding?

In our society, preoccupation with appearance and diet has become part of the common social currency. For women, talking diets may be the male equivalent of talking sports. The subject provides an easily understood vocabulary, a comfortable language of well-defined social chitchat that everyone can get involved in without getting to know one another on anything but a superficial level. But this diet-talk, and certainly the practice of chronic dieting itself, allows a dangerous avoidance of intimacy and the deeper exploration of feelings, frustrations and needs between people. Diet-talk, diet-thought, diet-action are increasingly insidious substitutes for true interaction as they have become the newest device to fill time.

Is the mounting prevalence of eating disorders, particularly among American women, a sign of the increasing social strain of changing roles? Is it the only way that women thrust into the superwife-superlover-supermother-superworker maze can say they need feeding? Is it a tool used to bury anger by "stuffing it" instead of expressing it, since being direct with anger is an uneasy state for many women? Numerous psychological explanations are currently being offered to such questions, and undoubtedly many of them are valid. But there's no pat answer.

For some people, eating or not eating is a way to exert control or influence over a life that otherwise seems uncontrollable. For others, feeling unappreciated may lead to feeling "unfed" and uncared for, and so they turn to feeding themselves. But again, such reasoning—that we strive for "fixes" of love and affection through chocolate when we can't get it from others—is far too simple. It doesn't take into account, for example, the many people who leave their lovers' beds in the middle of the night and sneak to the refrigerator to binge eat.

Very primitive tensions are handled by binge eating. People wolf down food in an atavistic way, with a fearful gulping, almost to insure that the morsels, the sustenance, will be safely inside before someone comes and steals them. Food is a cure for the existential blues, a fix, a hit. Yet so many of us today find ourselves caught in a tight squeeze between the opiate of the calories and the need to adhere to the rigid social code of being undersized. Clearly, some of us were intended to be squat or pear-shaped or round, just as others were designed to be tall or flat-chested or curly haired or brown-eyed.

There is really no way around it for those of us who have been genetically programmed to be chubby, yet many chubby people spend their lives in an endless battle with nature. And when you try to fight nature, you inevitably lose. If you try to squelch your body's hunger, an imp from within emerges to lead the hand automatically to food in spite of your protestations and horror. You starve yourself in the morning and at lunch, but by evening the imp catches up and demands its due.

Do people need something to be miserable about? Does everyone need a vice or an addiction, a way to comfort oneself when there's nobody else to do the comforting and caretaking? For some, food addiction and binge eating will be the least serious way of instant compensation for stress and alienation, whether the stress stems from being fearful about sex or loneliness or being overwhelmed by a job or lack of success in friendships. Some feel that if it weren't for binge eating, intolerable depression or alcoholism or drug use or some other form of self-destruction would surface. For others, food abuse is simply a habit that has taken on a life of its own and just won't go away. In such cases, the mindless time taken up by bingeing is frequently cherished by the binger. He or she feels that the time devoted to thinking about food and eating is, somehow, a relaxation, a time out from life's other worries. Why are some of us able to think very little about food or to deal with an occasional overindulgence by relatively painless attention to diet for a few days, while others feel completely locked into the up-and-down weight seesaw? It may be that people who are either overly impulsive or overly rigid have difficulty moderating their lives in all areas, not just in the food-and-weight area.

In this excellent book, Susan Squire thoroughly reviews the cultural, psychological and biological influences contributing to the rise of eating disorders, so far as they are currently understood, in language that is completely understandable by the nonprofessional reader. Yet she is comprehensive in her review of the most up-to-date scientific literature. Everyone except for the lucky few who have never worried about weight will find themselves somewhere along the Eating Arc described in the first chapter, and they will identify with the wide-ranging case histories narrated throughout the book. Many responsive chords will be struck by seeing ourselves or people close to us in print, and readers will benefit from the sense of connection to others with similar problems.

Many people who are excessively preoccupied with food and weight have found self-help groups to be very effective in getting them past these issues and on to more rewarding and productive areas of life. Others have been able to work within themselves and move on to fulfillment without the aid of anything beyond their inner resources.

But, as Susan Squire emphasizes, the degree of food addiction varies greatly along the Arc. The suffering of those with serious eating disorders is far from trivial; for them, the food issue is the tip of an iceberg—underneath lies tremendous emotional distress, often associated with great self-destructiveness and high costs to physical health. For these people, additional professional evaluation and treatment are necessary. We must acknowledge that, although will and determination go a long way in successfully grappling with these problems, the extent of depression or enslavement by habit is too great for some people to be fought alone, and seeking expert help from psychiatrists, other physicians, psychologists and professionals who are knowledgeable about eating disorders is essential. Sometimes, treatment in a hospital setting may even be advisable as a first place to begin intervention for serious problems.

What if someone in your family is suffering from an eating disorder? It's most important to acknowledge the problem and not ignore or minimize it. I suggest that family members be open and sympathetic; it's of little help to simply berate or ridicule the sufferer. Since people with eating disorders ordinarily tend to be secretive about them, the best approach is to acknowledge the problem sympathetically, offer to help and encourage sufferers to seek help on their own

On the bottom line, the current epidemic of eating disorders results from tremendous cultural and psychological forces impacting on human biology. In the area of eating, as in most other areas of life, we are reminded of Aristotle's golden maxim: A life of moderation may be more effective than striving after some unrealistic "ideal" form. A certain self-acceptance, of both our appearance and our psyche, may be necessary before we can begin to make the most of who we are.

THE EATING ARC

The world can be divided into two types of people: The ones
who stop eating under stress—and the ones who don't.
Joel Yager, M.D., director, UCLA Eating Disorders Clinic

If you have gone on more than one weight-loss diet in your life;
if you feel that being thin will solve your problems; if you're
terrified of gaining 5 pounds; if you have ever lost weight and
kept it off, but still think of yourself as fat; if you regularly binge
and try to compensate for the calories by strict dieting or fasting,
by making yourself vomit, by dosing yourself with laxatives,
diuretics, amphetamines or enemas, by exercising like a maniac;
if you've ever had anorexia nervosa; if you need to watch other
people eat in order to know how to eat yourself—then you will
benefit from reading this book.

"My weight decides just what kind of day I will have,"
declares a college student, 5'3", weight range from 100 to 120.

"I am forty-four years old and I have gone from diets to binges
since I was seventeen. I weigh a hundred and twenty-five and I
am five-foot-four and feel I am fat and fear I will gain weight
every time I eat," worries a midwestern housewife.

"After dieting to lose weight and succeeding, I find I no
longer know how to eat sensibly. I either eat nothing or I eat too
much. I feel guilty either way," confides a 32-year-old female
advertising executive.

It has nothing to do with how much you weigh. You can be so
thin that your friends and family urge you to gain weight. You
can have such a perfect figure that your friends tell you they're
insecure around you in a bathing suit. You can be, oh, 5 or 10 or

15 pounds heavier than some chart tells you is right for your height and build. In fact, the more normal you appear, the more panicked you may be about gaining weight and the more confused you may be about when, what and how much to eat.

From the already thin teen-age girl who mistakenly believes that happiness would be hers if she lost just a few pounds, to the attractive college student with an overly critical opinion of herself, to the fortyish housewife who noshes all day out of boredom, most sufferers of what could be called the "dieting disease" are at or near normal weight. They represent a new and increasingly mounting population of food abusers and point to an alarming fact of contemporary American life: Our cultural obsession with weight has blurred and in many cases erased the line between simple dieting and having an "eating disorder"—a distorted pattern of thinking about and behaving around food.

This modern dilemma is cyclical in nature, and potentially dangerous. Everything around us tells us that thinness is not only desirable but crucial to social, sexual, even professional success. Constant policing of our food intake—dieting—therefore seems essential. But the more we police ourselves, the more we want to eat. That denial/desire seesaw, whether or not we give in to it, is fueled by the ever-present fear of fat. For some of us, the conflict becomes a central, if not *the* central, life preoccupation, ultimately draining our energy and attention away from more enriching and important challenges.

Believe me—I know. I was a normal-looking 18-year-old who spent several years feeling like a freak inside, because all I could think about was food and whether I looked fat, and all I could do was either starve myself or stuff myself in desperate secret sessions and wonder why. I didn't know then that I was one of millions who feel trapped by one form or another of this seemingly uncontrollable behavior, disturbed and confused by a Jekyll-and-Hyde pattern of a good self and a bad self clashing repeatedly over the issues of food and fat, defining my own worth by a number on a scale, using that number as the criterion of self-rejection or self-acceptance. Most often, it was the former.

Psychiatrists tell us that the range of odd eating behaviors and attitudes currently held by countless American men and women, spawned at least partially by the cultural demand for slimness, exists on a sort of overlapping continuum. We'll call this continuum the "Eating Arc."

Picture, if you will, the arc: a quarter-moon-shaped crescent. At one end of it are people with *anorexia nervosa:* They have lost at least 25 percent of original body weight according to official diagnostic criteria (though many experts will settle for 15 percent), have no known physical illness to account for the weight loss, and "feel fat" though they are obviously emaciated. (For the official description of anorexia nervosa, see chapter 11.) About half of these are called *restrictor anorexics*—they maintain their emaciation by simple denial of food. The other half are called *bulimic anorexics*.

Bulimia is the official psychiatric term (see chapter 11) for an eating disorder in which one recurrently consumes a large amount of food in a short period of time, usually in secret; ends the binge by either abdominal pain, sleep, social interruption or self-induced vomiting; knows the behavior is abnormal, fears not being able to stop and feels depressed and self-disgusted afterward; tries repeatedly to lose weight by dieting, vomiting, using laxatives or diuretics; and may often fluctuate 10 pounds or more in weight due to alternating binges and fasts.

The behavior of the bulimic anorexic is more complicated than the restrictor's. Bulimic anorexics practice food denial, but regularly lose control of their hunger and binge, then choose one or more compensatory methods for getting rid of the food, such as self-induced vomiting, laxatives, diuretics, amphetamines and excessive exercise. Bulimic anorexics tend to be a little older; a little heavier; more sexually active; more prone to other impulsive behaviors, such as drinking, drug abuse or stealing; more psychologically disturbed; and more difficult to treat than restrictors. Bulimic anorexics are also more likely than restrictors to have been overweight before they became anorexic, or to come from families with a pattern of overweight and, possibly, alcoholism or depression in certain members.

Following the two types of anorexics on the Eating Arc are bulimics, or bingers, of basically ideal weight—within 10 percent, up or down, of the weight at which you can be expected to live the longest as calculated on life-insurance charts. Like the bulimic anorexics, normal-weight bulimics regularly go on eating binges and use the same combination of compensations to avoid gaining weight, most commonly vomiting, laxatives and, to a lesser degree, diuretics. Members of this group can be called *normal-weight bulimic purgers.* (We'll use the word "purge" to refer to all instant-evacuation methods such as vomiting, laxatives, enemas or diuretics.) Obviously, normal-weight bulimic purgers consume more food and practice less compensation than the bulimic anorexic group, because their weights are higher.

Then there are the *situational purgers* (also called *occasional* or *episodic purgers*) who may use instant-compensation methods (usually self-induced vomiting) for a specific reason, but who are not particularly obsessed with the fear of weight gain and don't hate themselves for their behavior. This group would include the wrestler, jockey, dancer, stewardess, actor or model who goes out and celebrates the night before a match, a race, a weigh-in or a photo session and eats too much, but must be at a certain weight or flatness of stomach for the next day's work; a young woman who needs to fit into a certain dress for a special occasion; the sorority girl who goes out on a dinner date Saturday night, eats a lot and feels uncomfortably bloated; the gymnastic team that practices a postmeet Romanesque ritual of pigging out and then make themselves vomit as a group in the name of camaraderie.

Next on the arc, approaching midpoint, are normal-weight people who also binge but who don't use instant-compensation methods to avoid weight gain; instead, they diet, fast or use exercise as their methods. They are *bulimic dieters.* As with most bulimics, whatever their weight, the urge to binge and the act itself is at first a direct response to the constant hunger of rigid dieting, but over time its function broadens to become an all-purpose tension releaser as well as a hunger reliever.

At midpoint on the arc are the *chronic dieters*. Their behavior is not as extreme as that of any of the groups preceding them. They overeat, but not in the same manner as the bulimics; instead of consuming a pint of ice cream in a half-hour, the chronic dieter may take all day to do it. The chronic dieter is more likely to nibble constantly. She never sits down to a whole dessert but instead eats from her dining companions' plates or "evens out" a pan of brownies in the kitchen, slowly consuming much more than she should and then wondering where it all went. When she's not nibbling, she's on a diet, usually a fad diet. She's probably done the Grapefruit Diet, the High-Protein Diet, the Scarsdale Diet, the Beverly Hills Diet, even the Pritikin Diet; she may have gone on and off Weight Watchers and attends occasional meetings; instead of regular exercise, she goes all out once or twice a year at a health spa, or takes a sporadic exercise class. The typical chronic dieter is married with a family, has always been a little overweight, and continues to lose and gain the same 10 or 15 pounds.

Following the chronic dieters, heading down the other side of the arc, are the *noncompensatory bulimics:* overweight-to-obese people who may go on binges but don't try to compensate by any consistent methods. Their weight, though high, remains relatively stable. They are disturbed about their weight and their compulsive eating, and are often drawn to self-help groups such as Overeaters Anonymous. An extreme faction of this group is the morbidly obese—their weight is 100 percent or more over ideal, and they constantly eat thousands of calories but don't try to compensate.

Descending on, there is the *occasional dieter*, who sensibly cuts back on food intake following, say, a gourmet vacation tour of France or the feast-filled holiday season. Occasional dieters watch their weight, but are not unusually preoccupied with it and avoid extreme dieting or overeating. On special occasions, they may go a bit overboard and complain about putting on weight, but that's it.

The occasional dieters sit next to the *normal eaters*, who oppose the anorexics at the other end of the arc. The normals are perfectly content with their bodies as they are, regardless of weight. They think about food—and eat it—only when they're hungry, stop eating when they feel full, and maintain the same weight for years without thinking about it. If you happen to recognize this spot as yours on the arc and you're a woman between puberty and old age in America, you are in a very small and very lucky minority. This book does not concern itself with you.

For everyone else, there is much overlap and interchange in eating behaviors along the arc. For example, as a teen-ager you may have been an occasional dieter, possibly overweight. You played at dieting with your friends in high school, but didn't get serious about it until you entered college. There, you went on a strict diet and dropped down from a size 12 to a size 6, but then you lost control of your eating and became bulimic. Not wanting to gain all the weight back but unable to recapture your control, you may have begun to make yourself vomit, and now you are a bulimic purger. Or maybe you were very heavy as a child, went on a rigid diet as a teen-ager and became anorexic, were forced to gain weight by your parents and physician, then became bulimic and ultimately overweight once again. By the time you were 30, you'd become a chronic dieter.

In addition to the behavioral overlap, there are also many interchangeable psychological traits along the arc. How extreme these traits are relates directly to how extreme your eating behavior is. They include: *Symptoms*

—High self-doubt, low self-esteem and low self-confidence.
—A passionate desire to be thin for reasons beyond health.
—A distorted body image—you see yourself as being much heavier than an objective observer would judge.
—A tendency to be overly concerned with the opinions of others and to try to please them—to give them what you think they want from you—at the expense of pleasing yourself.
—A drive to be the perfect mother, daughter, student, worker or wife, and a constant fear of failing at the task.

—The feeling that you are both special and inferior at the same time.

—A compulsion beyond logic to always feel responsible when something or someone goes wrong in your life.

—A difficulty in identifying and expressing your feelings to others, particularly anger.

You may also feel helpless, hopeless or ineffective in many situations and thus frustrated, resentful and often depressed. You probably assume that being assertive is the same as being selfish, and have at least one "significant other" in your life who is very critical of you.

Demographically speaking, you are female; probably white and possibly Oriental but very unlikely to be black; fairly well educated, middle-class or higher financially; not an only child; and more likely to be Catholic or Jewish than Protestant. You can become a dieter at any age, but you are unlikely to become officially bulimic or anorexic if you're over 25.[1]

If you're a chronic dieter who's 5'3", 40 years old and weighs 130, it may at first seem absurd to think that you have anything in common, other than your height, with an anorexic who's 5'3", 14 years old and weighs 80. But in fact there are probably more similarities than differences between anorexics, bulimics and dieters, regardless of weight, at least if you're female. The differences in behavior—and the psychology that drives the behavior—may be just a matter of degree.

"Anorexia nervosa, rather than a rare psychiatric disorder, may represent an extreme form of an *increasingly common mode of life organization* and psychological self-control in women," (emphasis added) concluded Michael G. Thompson, Ph.D., and Donald M. Schwartz, Ph.D., in the *International Journal of Eating Disorders*.[2]

In the following chapters, you'll enter the lives of a variety of real people—men and women, ranging in age from 14 to 53 and in occupation from student to physician to housewife. (Their names and certain identifying details have been changed.) They are all in conflict, to one degree or another, with themselves over their approach to food. You'll get an idea of the thoughts and emotions that underlie their behavior, in relationship to both their time of life and their places on the arc. Finally, you'll learn how to go about getting your eating, your thinking and your life in balance—and how to put the issues of food and weight back where they belong.

Tommy
Reader

2

LEAVING CHILDHOOD

Debbie

Although Debbie was very athletic, on the soccer and lacrosse teams at school, she was also chunky. Five-four and 135 was gross, but worse than the weight were her awful thighs. She'd hated them ever since she was 11 and first got her period. She wasn't sure why she connected those things, getting her period and hating her thighs, but there must be a reason. She had never worried about her weight before then.

She went on her first real diet when she was 14, after Christmas vacation, which was spent as always at a ski resort with her parents, her aunt and uncle and her three male cousins, who were 15, 17 and 18. They always ate a lot on these vacations, and Debbie certainly didn't eat any more than her cousins did, but they kept teasing her and telling her she'd get fat if she ate so much. It made her really self-conscious. They also told her about college girls they knew who would make themselves throw up to lose weight; and after they told her, Debbie sneaked off to the bathroom and tried to make herself do it, but it didn't work.

When she returned home, she started a 1000-calorie balanced diet that her mother had managed to lose 40 pounds on, but Debbie broke it over Chinese food after only a week. It seemed as though all the women in Debbie's family had trouble with weight. Her grandmother, and her aunt, and her mother, and even now her 20-year-old sister, Kathie, who gained 30 pounds her first year at college. Her oldest sister, Dana, who was 23 and taught art in a rural community up north, was neither fat nor thin, luckily for her.

Then it was finals week at Debbie's private prep school in Pennsylvania. When even ninth-graders are subjected to three-hour exams and all-nighters to prepare for them, you know the school is tough. It was during this week of intense pressure that Debbie's dog, Freddie, got really sick and had to go to the vet. Debbie made herself sit at the oak desk in her wonderful bedroom, its canopied four-poster alive with stuffed animals, the sitting-area couch covered in the same cheerful floral print that the draperies were made of, and an adjoining bathroom all her own. She'd concentrate really hard on her textbooks for an hour or two, then pick up her white Princess phone and call the vet to see how Freddie was. The nurse, who had known her forever, was patient with her insistent phone calls: "Don't worry, Deb, he's fine." Debbie's mother had instructed the nurse to say that. Freddie had been put to sleep earlier that week, but no one wanted to upset Debbie until exams were over.

Just a month after Freddie died, Debbie and her family moved from the house they'd lived in since Debbie was 2, the same year she'd gotten Freddie. So, with the loss of her dog and of the house she'd grown up in all at the same time, Debbie felt that double blows had been dealt to her childhood. She had so loved being a little kid in that house, and Freddie had been her substitute brother and best friend, especially when her two sisters left for college. Now Debbie had no sisters, no dog and no house; her parents had purchased a condominium instead. It was roomy and comfortable, and she had her very own suite decorated just the way she wanted it, but it wasn't the same. And though she'd always been close to her parents and used to be able to tell them everything, that was changing too.

All those things—her cousins teasing her, Freddie's death, and moving—added up to Debbie's decision: It was a very good time to get skinny. So before she got to school, she would throw away the bag lunch her mother had packed in the morning. At lunchtime she'd tell her friends that she'd eaten early so they wouldn't ask questions. Not only was skipping lunch a good way to lose weight, but she was mad at her mother for not telling her about Freddie and letting her call the vet when Freddie was already dead. Throwing away the lunch her mother made seemed a kind of revenge.

Debbie was still eating a normal dinner although she was skipping lunch, and one night she had some ice cream for dessert. Not that much, but enough so that later she lay in bed and, for the first time since Christmas vacation, thought about throwing up. She knew she'd have to wait until her parents went to bed, because she didn't want anyone to suspect anything. She lay in the dark and waited, and listened to them settle in, and then she got up and she did it. She felt proud of herself afterward, as if she'd discovered a secret. It gave her a pattern to follow for the next few weeks: Debbie would eat a croissant for breakfast, throw away her lunch, eat an orange before soccer practice and later a normal dinner. And then she'd throw up.

One day, not long after Debbie had first made herself throw up, her friend Tracy was over and they were pigging out on brownies and ice cream. Debbie was able to do such things now without worrying about getting fat. In the middle of the feast, Tracy said, "We should make ourselves throw up." Debbie made believe she didn't know what Tracy was talking about, though inside she was wondering if this was Tracy's way of tricking her—could she have guessed? Tracy went into the bathroom to try, but couldn't do it, and then Debbie went in and closed the door. Tracy heard her flushing the toilet and asked Debbie if she'd done it. Debbie was so proud that she could do it and Tracy couldn't—and besides, if Tracy was trying, it was probably okay to admit it. So Debbie said, "Just a little." She felt so pleased: She had the secret and Tracy didn't. Tracy showed Debbie how she'd tried to do it—by leaning against the toilet and pushing her stomach in. That was all wrong; Debbie showed her how it was done, and then they both started laughing like it was all a big joke. Neither of them ever mentioned that day again. It was as if it had never happened.

Then Debbie's rituals began. She would take half a bagel, break it into little pieces and put them on her lap. Or she'd peel a whole grapefruit, turn the sections upside down, put them one at a time in her mouth to squish them, and then put them back on her plate so they'd look eaten. She'd go to a school carnival and buy $15 worth of junk food so her friends would think she was eating, and when they weren't looking she'd drop the food on the street. She was so proud that they didn't guess. It was like a game: How many people could she fool?

But Debbie felt there were two people in her head, especially when she was in the bathroom throwing up. One would say, "Throw up, throw up," and the other would say, "Stop this, you're sick." In school sometimes she'd examine the skin of her hands and think how fat it was. But even though Debbie was throwing up just about every day, she wasn't getting that skinny, because on the weekends she'd eat tons and wouldn't throw all of it up. Her weight would go up and down 12 pounds during some weeks.

One night that spring, there was a movie on TV about a girl around Debbie's age who had anorexia nervosa. It was called *The Best Little Girl in the World*. That night, before the movie, Debbie had eaten at a Japanese restaurant with her mother and sister Kathie, home from college for a visit. Debbie had picked at her food, and when no one was looking, she'd sneaked it into a plastic bag hidden in her purse. Later, she threw the bag away in the rest room. On their way home, they'd stopped for ice cream, but Debbie didn't have any.

Debbie cried through the whole movie. As soon as it was over, she started exercising madly, like the girl in the movie, and for the next week she didn't eat anything. She wanted to be that girl in the movie. She wanted to be anorexic. If she were, she figured she could eat anything she wanted, because she'd have to gain weight. The girl in the movie had started her anorexia when she made the cheerleading squad. The week following the movie, Debbie tried out for cheerleading and made it.

Now she weighed 118, but she still pictured her body exactly as it had been at 135. No one else could tell she'd lost weight, because she always wore sweat pants or overalls at home, and at school everyone wore uniforms so unflattering that even the skinniest kids could look fat in them. The few times someone asked if she'd lost weight, she said no. She began to fight a lot with her friends. She knew she was acting differently—doing homework at lunch instead of socializing, or off in the bathroom throwing up, not being with them anymore—but she couldn't stand them bugging her, asking what was wrong. She stopped getting her period, but that had happened to the girl in the movie and so it was expected. At most, she was throwing up once a week—that wasn't so much.

It was sometime in late spring, between seeing the TV movie and the beginning of summer vacation, that something clicked in Debbie's head. She'd made cheerleading; she'd made student council; she'd lettered in softball; she'd gotten almost all A's. She was getting ready to go to camp, which she loved. And suddenly she was frightened that she could mess up her life and wind up in a hospital instead of at camp, instead of on the cheerleading squad or on student council next year.

Why are you doing this? she thought to herself one night in her room, after throwing up the few bites she'd had for dinner. Kathie was home for the weekend. Debbie had always thought Kathie was perfect. She was homecoming queen, head cheerleader, Miss Everything in high school, with tons of boyfriends. Debbie was madly jealous of her. She was even jealous of the fact that her mom confided more in Kathie than she did in Debbie, though that was probably natural since Kathie was six years older, more of an adult. And Debbie had to admit that Kathie was just about the best person in the world to talk to if you had a problem and needed advice or sympathy. No matter what it was, Kathie was able to make it seem less bad.

Debbie went into her sister's room and told her everything, about her food game and the lying and the vomiting. They talked for a long time, and each of them cried a little. Debbie admitted to Kathie that she was jealous of her; and to Debbie's surprise, Kathie said that she was jealous of Debbie—she'd always felt Debbie was smarter. It was a shock to Debbie to learn that her sister didn't like herself all that much. It made her feel they really had something in common. Finally, at 2:00 A.M.,

they decided to wake their parents and tell them what Debbie
had been doing and ask for their help. Debbie got really mad at
her father because he said, "Let's talk about it in the morning."
The next morning, Debbie regretted her confession. Nothing
had really changed—she still wanted to be thin and she still
thought she was fat—but now everyone knew about her game.
Her parents didn't seem to understand too much about what
Debbie had been doing—it almost seemed that they didn't want
to hear about it. They thought it was just some kind of phase.
But then, maybe it was. Debbie hoped it was, anyway. She was
going off to camp in a week, for the whole summer, and she
would forget about throwing up.

The summer was great and Debbie didn't throw up once, but
by the time school started, she had gained 25 pounds, everything she'd lost that spring. She went to a nutritionist for a diet
plan, but she was miserable not eating sweets and broke the
diet. She went on the Scarsdale Diet and lost about 15 pounds,
but then gained it back. Same for a bunch of other diets. She just
couldn't get back into that anorexic mood. A few nights before
Christmas vacation, when she was worrying about gaining even
more weight at the ski resort, she made herself throw up for the
first time since before camp.

The next day there was an assembly at school. The subject was
anorexia nervosa. A nurse was giving the lecture, and when she
finished, she asked the class if there were any examples. Debbie
found herself raising her hand and telling the whole audience
about losing weight and vomiting (though she didn't mention
the night before and made it sound like it was all in the past) and
throwing away her food and lying to her friends and family. The
class was surprised; they'd never thought of Debbie with these
problems because she didn't look anorexic. No one else volun-
teered to speak, though Debbie knew she probably wasn't the
only one. She thought back to the day after *The Best Little Girl
in the World* had been on TV and how just about everyone in
school had seen it and been really affected by it. It couldn't have
just been she who'd tried to behave like the girl in the movie.

Debbie wondered why she still wanted to lose weight. She

wasn't obese, and people liked her just as well when she was 15 pounds overweight (even better, in fact, because she wasn't acting separate and strange with her friends as she had during her anorexic phase), and losing weight had caused as many problems as it solved, maybe more. It had made her throw up, and work hard to get her eating to be *abnormal*, and made her feel like a split personality. But she still couldn't help thinking that life would be perfect if she were thin, even though she knew that couldn't be true.

That Christmas vacation was like a repeat of the last one, her cousins teasing her about eating too much and Debbie feeling self-conscious. Her cousins had never seen her when her weight was down; now she weighed just about what she had last Christmas. So what was the point? She wished people would realize that their little comments could really hurt. She knew her cousins liked her and even admired her for being able to keep up with them on the ski slopes, and she knew they didn't mean to upset her with their teasing. She never let on that they made her feel bad, just tossed off their comments with what she hoped was a casual shrug, or else tried to kid them back about potbellies. She didn't want to seem too sensitive, or babyish. If her cousins ever knew that she still liked her parents to tuck her in at night . . .

After vacation, Debbie returned home to face another round of finals. She decided not to think about losing weight until finals were over. But the night before her history exam, she made herself throw up, though she'd vowed that night before the school assembly never to do it again. She realized there was a connection between throwing up and the pressure of exams—this time it didn't seem to have anything to do with weight. But it didn't help relieve the pressure at all; instead, it made her terribly upset and disturbed her concentration.

She picked up a copy of *Seventeen* with Brooke Shields on the cover and stared at it: Did Brooke ever make herself throw up? Was that how she stayed so thin? If she did, Debbie hoped that Brooke would never admit it, because millions of teen-age girls would start doing it, too. It was bad enough that all the magazines showed girls so skinny that nobody could ever look like them.

Debbie didn't do as well as usual on the history exam—she got a B instead of an A. She told herself that that was the price she paid for throwing up, and that it was a good lesson because she would never throw up again. She really believed that—until the weekend after the new term began, when she went to a football game with her best friend, Maureen, and Maureen's parents, and ate too much: a couple of hot dogs, and popcorn, and an ice-cream bar, and a bag of peanuts. At the point where she'd eaten only one hot dog and was contemplating another, she said to herself that if she was going to eat a second one, she'd have to throw up. And that's just what she did.

Why? Debbie didn't understand why throwing up sometimes had nothing to do with overeating. She tried to think about what was going on in her head when she did it, and it seemed that it happened when she was feeling bad about herself—the way she imagined people must think when they're about to commit suicide. Did that mean that throwing up was a way of punishing yourself? Maybe she wanted to punish herself for feeling bad in the first place. There were so many things she could do to feel better besides throwing up: She had her friends and her family to talk to; she could play her guitar. So why did she choose to throw up?

What did she feel bad about? It had to do with the way she always compared herself to others. She knew she had good qualities—she cared about people, she didn't give in to peer pressure, she knew that if she worked hard she had the ability to do anything she wanted. But she also had all these visions of ideal characteristics that other people had, and she fantasized putting them all together into one single perfect person, and that person would be Debbie. These characteristics weren't usually physical; they had more to do with personality. Debbie thought that if she didn't compare herself to others, she wouldn't get depressed or jealous. She suspected that maybe she really *wanted* to be depressed, dumb as that sounded.

When she was depressed, she knew she was not a perfect person, because a perfect person wouldn't be depressed, and that thought made her more depressed. Which in some weird way gave her pleasure, let her feel sorry for herself. And there was no better way to feel sorry for herself and be depressed than by making herself throw up.

Debbie's biggest fear was that someone very close to her would die, but it hadn't happened so far. She knew how lucky she was—her mom was always there when she needed her, always came early to pick her up from school or a friend's, and she could really talk to both of her parents, which most of her friends couldn't do. She was afraid it would all be taken away because it wasn't fair to be so lucky. Come to think of it, that feeling was exactly what made her throw up the last time, a few days ago. She was having dinner at a Chinese restaurant with her grandmother, and asked her grandmother about how her father had reacted when his father died. Her grandmother described it, and Debbie kept saying, "It's not fair that I'm so lucky." And that night she made herself throw up.

Maybe it all connected to the fact that she still wanted to be thought of as a little kid, to *be* a little kid; and once they moved from the old house, she knew it was the end of being a kid. She tried to get it back by having her stuffed animals all around, by having her parents tuck her in, and even by acting naïve and immature sometimes, though she really knew better. Sometimes she carried it too far, to the point where people thought of her as being loud and not very serious about anything.

When you're a little kid, people don't expose you to bad things. Debbie pretended not to know anything about drugs, for example (it was true she'd never tried them, but her sisters had), and asked an older friend why people take drugs. "Everyone needs an escape," explained the friend.

That made perfect sense—it was like throwing up or acting like a little kid. But Debbie pretended she was too naïve to understand. She just hated to give up all the old, childhood ways of being.

Jennifer

Jennifer blamed it all on her mom. Everything. It was because of her mom that Brian never asked her out again. It was because of her mom that she was fat. And it was because of her mom that she was destroying her own body. Every single day. She hated herself, she hated her mom, she hated her life. She wished she were someone else. She wished she were dead. She headed straight for the bathroom. She hated these *feelings*.

Now she lay facedown on the bright red-and-yellow quilt that contrasted so boldly with her mood of late. She was exhausted from one of her rituals. As usual, it started off as her mother's fault—she'd accused Jennifer of stealing $10 off her dresser, and she wouldn't believe Jennifer's denial. In a rage, Jennifer began stuffing herself with huge gulps of the apple pie her mom had planned to serve to dinner guests that night. After devouring the pie, Jennifer began shoveling in vanilla ice cream, dripping it all over the kitchen floor, while her mother alternately screamed at her and watched helplessly in silence. Her mother's helplessness made Jennifer feel powerful.

When her mother screamed that Jennifer was "disgusting," Jennifer countered with a string of four-letter insults and threw the spoon dramatically onto the floor. Her mother stormed out of the kitchen, trying not to let Jennifer see her tears, while Jennifer made her way upstairs to her room and slammed the door, hateful thoughts crowding her. That's when she went into the adjoining bathroom and vomited until she'd gotten all the pie and ice cream up. Then she weighed herself. Oh, God: 115. In May she'd sworn to herself that she would never let herself hit three digits—99 was her maximum, and even that was too high. Now it was August and she was a pig.

She hugged her pillow, trying in vain to stave off the guilt she always felt about her mom after they went through one of these scenes together. It was true that she hadn't taken the money—this time. But Jennifer had to admit that she'd done it often enough to seem like "the boy who cried wolf" to her mother.

Yeah, she was a pretty big failure as a daughter. Even to the point of eating everyone else's dessert before they'd had even one bite. What was she trying to prove, anyway? That she could make her mother hysterical? That she really *was* disgusting? Both of those things were already obvious. If she had only been able to stay thin . . .

Jennifer's original plan had been to lose 10 pounds so that she would look better. By stepping up all her exercises, taking more ballet classes and cutting way, way back on food—a piece of fruit for breakfast, yogurt or salad for lunch and as little as she could get away with at dinner—she had been down to 105 by the end of January. Her mother had begun making noises about her getting too skinny, but Jennifer was elated. She was dancing so much better with less weight—her ballet teacher had complimented her on her willpower. She finally was starting to look really good in jeans, and her friends were envious. They kept asking her how she did it. Even her older brother noticed.

Best of all, boys were paying attention to her, and not just ninth-grade boys, either. She had gone to a Valentine's Day party—she weighed 101 that day—and was rushed by a high-school *junior*, who had a car and everything, plus he was totally cute. His name was Brian, and he had asked her out for the following weekend. Jennifer's mother wasn't too thrilled with the idea. She thought Jennifer was too young to be going out with a boy who was old enough to drive. But she agreed to it as long as Jennifer was home by 11:00 P.M.

Jennifer had practically starved herself all week so she'd look really thin for Brian. By Saturday morning, she'd gotten down to 99, her first time under 100. That gave her some confidence. But she was nervous all day, and when Brian picked her up and they got in his car, she couldn't think of anything to say and felt stupid. Luckily, they went to a movie, which gave them something to talk about. Afterward, they went to Burger King. Brian ordered a hamburger and fries and couldn't believe it when Jennifer ordered only a Tab. "You're too skinny to be on a diet," he said. "Aren't you hungry?" Jennifer loved him for that.

In the parking lot of the restaurant, inside the car, Brian

pulled Jennifer over to him and started kissing her and pretty soon had his hand under her sweater. She'd French-kissed boys at parties, but so far no one had touched her breasts except on top of her clothes. She wasn't sure if she minded or not, except she definitely didn't like doing it in the parking lot. Still, she let him continue because he wouldn't ask her out again if she was uncool. She wanted him to like her. It freaked her out when he put her hand on him, over his zipper. She let it lie there while she tried to think what to do, and she noticed on his watch that it was already 10:50.

"I've got to get home," she whispered, but he paid no attention, so she had to say it again. "You're kidding." Brian was not pleased. "It's not even midnight. Why?" She was completely embarrassed. "Oh, you know. Curfew." It didn't help when he said, "That's right, you're just a kid." But when he dropped her off, he said, "Hey, talk your mom into letting you out later next time," and Jennifer thought maybe he'd ask her out again. Especially if she lost just a few more pounds.

But he didn't call, even though she lost a few more pounds by eating no more than 500 calories a day. She decided it was because she had such a stupid, babyish curfew. When her mother asked her one night at the dinner table why she was moping around, Jennifer told her it was her fault; here was this great possible boyfriend and her mother had ruined it all.

Her older brother looked at Jennifer's dinner of lettuce, spinach and carrots (she'd told her mother that she'd become a vegetarian) and suggested that "the guy probably thought you were too scrawny."

"Better than too fat!" Jennifer spit out, and jumped up from the table.

In her room, agitated, Jennifer did her exercise routine for the third time that day—first the ballet stretches, then aerobics to music, then jumping rope, then the leg workouts meant to slim her thighs. The whole thing took about an hour. By her calculations, she had definitely burned up whatever calories were in the lettuce, spinach and carrots. She got on the scale: 97. The best news she'd had all day. Suddenly, she felt contented with herself. That allowed her to feel bad about her behavior at the dinner table. Filled with a sudden warmth for her mother, she decided to go downstairs and apologize.

Jennifer's mother, Eve, was in the den, reading. On the coffee table next to her was her usual straight vodka with a splash of club soda (no tonic water—"There's enough calories in the vodka," her mother used to say to her father before they split up). When Jennifer appeared, her mother tensed, waiting for a new call to arms. Instead, Jennifer went over and kissed her on the cheek. "Sorry, mom," she said. "I was upset."

"Oh, that's okay. I'm sorry, too," Eve said. "But, honey, I am a little worried about the way you eat, or don't eat." Jennifer could feel her hostility returning as her mother launched into the lecture. "You're a growing girl. You need more food. And your brother's right—you don't look good. Your face is so thin."

"God, mom, I come down to apologize and you start in on me. I don't hassle you about your drinking, so do me a favor and leave me alone about my eating, okay? It's my business, not yours. Give me a break!" She's probably jealous that she never will and never was able to wear tight jeans and miniskirts like me, Jennifer thought (though she had been wearing baggy clothes more often lately to avoid comments from her mother about looking too thin).

She studied her mother, curled up in her favorite chair with the book on her lap and the drink in her hand now, wearing one of the hostess gowns that she collected by the dozens. Jennifer didn't want to be like her—lumpy, not exercising, not active. "I'm going to bed," Jennifer finally said, now feeling depressed. She took with her the *Gourmet Cookbook*, volume 2. She'd become quite a cook lately, ever since she realized that she loved to make other people eat while she didn't. It was as good as eating—better, because it didn't make you fat.

Jennifer's diet was going great until that awful night that was supposed to be her fifteenth-birthday celebration. Her mother had decided to surprise her and had made reservations at Leo's Grotto, which used to be Jennifer's favorite restaurant before she decided she didn't eat "that stuff" (pasta, veal, garlic bread) anymore. Eve told Jennifer they were going to the movies and that Caroline, Jennifer's best friend, was joining them. Caroline knew about the surprise and had been sworn to secrecy.

Jennifer was none too thrilled about going to a movie; she didn't like to see all that junk food there. Though she found the idea of bonbons and popcorn and candy disgusting, she often imagined eating it just the same. It had been so long since she'd had any of that stuff. Also, she had been sort of growing away from her old friends, including Caroline. The two of them had been inseparable ever since fourth grade, but the last couple of months Jennifer had felt—different from Caroline. In some ways, she felt superior: Caroline lacked her discipline. Caroline didn't dance or exercise much, just what she had to do for gym classes; and though she often talked about going on a diet, her determination was short-lived. Caroline wasn't fat, but she wasn't as thin as Jennifer was now.

Since the beginning of their friendship years ago, Jennifer and Caroline used to polish off a Sara Lee cake practically every day after school. But once Jennifer had begun her diet, she'd sworn off all that. Soon she found herself making up excuses, like too much homework, whenever Caroline wanted to get together with her. Jennifer decided she liked some of the girls in her ballet school better. At least they understood about exercise, and calories, and the importance of weighing as little as possible.

Eve and Jennifer picked up Caroline on their way to the "movies." Jennifer was so distracted by her own thoughts, which involved a calculation of calories burned that day, that she didn't notice where they were going until they pulled up in front of the restaurant. "Mom, what are we doing here?" The parking valet was opening the door, and Caroline and Eve were getting out.

"It's a surprise—for your birthday," Eve said.

Jennifer didn't move. The valet held out his hand.

"Jenny, come on," her mother said. Jennifer got out; she had no choice. She was furious at her mother and at Caroline for such a nasty trick. They were smiling at her, expecting her to be happy about the whole thing—and it was *her* birthday, not theirs.

Inside the restaurant, the smell of garlic floated over Jennifer and she realized she was starving. Starving for real food. Starving and panicked. She had to eat, she had to. Her head was spinning with fear and delight. The delight came from the fantasy of eating anything she wanted. The fear came from what would happen to her if she did. It wasn't just that she'd gain weight. No, her real fear was that *she would never be able to stop*. She envisioned herself passing out, bloated, on top of the table. Or dying from the shock of eating, with her stomach so shrunken. She imagined that once she ate she would continue to eat forever until she was completely obese. But, oh, to taste some real food! What should she do? Suddenly something clicked. She had the solution.

"Hey, wake up, Jen, you daydreaming or something?" Caroline was waving her hand in front of Jennifer's face. Jennifer blinked. She'd almost forgotten, in her turmoil, that her mother and Caroline had been sitting there with her. She smiled broadly at both of them. "Mom, this really is a great idea. I'm glad you thought of it," Jennifer said. Eve looked relieved. She proposed a toast "to Jenny's fifteenth year." Caroline and Jennifer clinked water glasses with her.

A waiter came by with menus and a basket of garlic bread. Jennifer took a piece of bread and ate it without doing her usual number of discarding the soft part, picking off all the crust and making breadcrumbs out of it, then putting one crumb at a time on her fork and counting to ten before she swallowed. She ate a second piece. On the third piece, she felt actually *high*. It was one of the most supremely thrilling moments of her life. She could eat anything and everything she wanted and not have to suffer for it.

She thought back to that conversation she'd overheard several weeks ago in the locker room at ballet school. One of the girls her age, Marianne, had been complaining to an older girl, Vicky, about how she was gaining weight and not dancing well,

but that she couldn't seem to stick to a diet. Vicky, who was
admired by most of the younger girls for her fluid dancing, her
thin body and her dedication, had said to Marianne, "Why don't
you just get rid of your food?"

"What do you mean, get rid of it?" Marianne had said.

"You know, throw it up. It's easy—just stick your fingers down
your throat and be sure you have enough liquids in you."

"Is that what you do?" Marianne asked.

"Sure, everybody does. They just don't admit it. I've been
doing it practically as long as I've been dancing. It's the only way
to eat and stay thin enough to dance."

At the time, Jennifer had been shocked that anyone would
vomit on purpose. She was also disdainful of both Vicky and
Marianne for lacking the willpower that she herself had. As
Vicky began to instruct Marianne in the finer points of self-
induced vomiting, Jennifer finished dressing and left, feeling
proud of herself for her supreme control. But now, on her third
piece of garlic bread, she wished she'd stuck around to hear
more of Vicky's tips. At least she knew about the liquids part.
She ordered a glass of milk and more water when the waiter
came with the first course.

The meal passed in an intoxicated blur. Jennifer ate everything even though her stomach began to ache after the antipasto, and she joked and laughed with Caroline and Eve. After
dessert, Jennifer excused herself to go to the bathroom. She had
such stomach cramps she could barely walk straight. She wished
it were the kind of bathroom with a lot of stalls, like at school,
but as she remembered it, there was only one toilet. What if
someone came in and heard her throwing up? What if she
couldn't throw up at all, like the way she could never get up on
water skis at camp when everyone else could? Her excitement
and high spirits turned to agitation, which intensified when she
looked down at her distended stomach.

Fifteen minutes later, Jennifer returned to the table, feeling
calm, controlled and cleansed. It had worked, though not right
away; and no one had knocked at the door. It hadn't been
pleasant, but after it was over and Jennifer's stomach was flat

again, and she had rinsed out her mouth and lit a match in the bathroom to disguise any bad smell, she felt like she'd stumbled onto some kind of magic.

That's how it started. At first, she didn't do it very often. Most of the time she kept to her 500-calorie diet and her rituals and her exercises, and only when she slipped and binged, maybe once a week, would she vomit. For a while she even continued to lose weight—by the beginning of May, she was down to 90. Her mother kept hassling her, which made Jennifer increasingly hostile. Eve kept telling Jennifer that her face was looking thinner (Jennifer never let her see her body). More than once Eve caught Jennifer hiding food in her napkin during dinner instead of eating it. Jennifer had gotten her mother totally confused, because periodically huge amounts of food would completely disappear, but her mother never suspected Jennifer, because she was so thin. Eve would ask Jennifer about it, and Jennifer would say it was the cleaning woman, or that Caroline had been over.

The climax between them came one afternoon when Eve came to pick Jennifer up from ballet class. Usually Jennifer met her outside already dressed, but this time Eve was early—she arrived just as the teacher was leading the girls in some final exercises at the barre. It was the first time in months that Eve had seen Jennifer in her leotard, and she was alarmed. Jennifer's ribs stuck out clearly against the stretchy spandex of her leotard; her thighs were sticklike.

In the car, Eve told Jennifer that she would take her to the doctor if she didn't immediately begin eating like a normal person. Jennifer said nothing. When they arrived home, Jennifer headed straight for the kitchen. Eve followed her. "Want me to eat, mother? Would that make you happy? Okay, watch me. *Watch me!*" Jennifer starting flinging cupboards open, grabbing cereal and crackers and bread and cookies, stuffing them into her mouth. Then she started in on the contents of the refrigerator. From then on, their fights always seemed to escalate to this point of no return.

Now, even with the vomiting, Jennifer was gaining weight.

She would binge and vomit up to five times a week, depending on how she was getting along with her mother. She felt too fat to dance, so she stopped going to ballet school, and no longer bothered with her other exercises. By the end of June she was at 106 and miserable. She'd read somewhere about how the Greeks and Egyptians used a version of laxatives to "purify" themselves, and, hoping that a little extra something would help prevent further weight gain, Jennifer began to make periodic visits to a nearby drugstore.

Needing more money to pursue her habits—the food and the laxatives—than her allowance provided her, Jennifer had begun stealing small amounts of money from her mother's wallet. At first it was just a dollar or two at a time, but then she got bolder and her mother got suspicious. The first time Eve openly accused her, Jennifer got back at her by bingeing in front of her.

Jennifer, still facedown on the quilt, returned her mind to the present. This time her mother had been wrong, but Jennifer had to admit that Eve had every reason to accuse her. Jennifer thought for the millionth time that it was amazing how one innocent little diet could mushroom into a monster and change everything. She felt like she was in one of those fun houses where you kept bumping into yourself no matter where you turned—mirrors that made you think you had all the space in the world, but it was all an illusion.

She was at war with herself, and her bad self seemed to be winning. The bad self was the one who swore and said awful things to her mother. The bad self was born when she entered into a binge; the binge changed her. When it was over, the swearing and bingeing and vomiting, she changed back into her good self, the one who knew how to behave, who cared about people, who felt guilty about hurting them, who worried about driving them away.

Now it was August. In another month she would enter high school for the first time. She wanted to be healthy, happy, normal. She didn't want to feel exhausted all the time from bingeing, vomiting, taking laxatives and fighting with her mother. She had to get herself put back together again.

Teen-age Triggers

> I felt if I could be thinner, my boyfriend would love me more.
>
> Laura, 17

society

Debbie and Jennifer were about the same age when they began their first real diets, based on the idea that thinness was necessary for happiness and social success and that fat was to be avoided. Each girl was highly gratified by her willpower, which bore concrete proof: weight loss. Each developed eating rituals around the loss of weight. Each felt superior to her peers in new ways: Jennifer for her discipline, and Debbie for being able to make herself throw up while her friends couldn't. At some point, each lost control of her dieting and attempted to compensate by self-induced vomiting. As vomiters, each felt an inner split between a good self and a bad one.

The back-to-back ideas that thinness is to be desired and fat to be abhorred are considered to be typical anorexic attitudes. But the extend to which these attitudes were held, and the degree of subsequent anorexic behavior, varied greatly between the two girls. Debbie flirted with anorexia nervosa but never developed its full-blown rituals, nor did her weight plunge to emaciation level. Although she indulged in occasional bingeing and vomiting, she never established a constant pattern.

Jennifer, however, went much further. First, she developed full-blown anorexia nervosa by strict self-starvation. Later, she began to binge and vomit. As her weight rose to her prediet level, Jennifer became a normal-weight bulimic who purged constantly, and she adopted increasingly extreme behavior, adding laxative abuse to the vomiting in a desperate attempt to stave off weight gain. Her bingeing and vomiting were also used as a means of venting hostility toward her mother.

What kept Debbie from hooking into the more chaotic patterns that caught Jennifer? According to Michael Strober, Ph.D., head of the adolescent program in UCLA's Eating Disorders Clinic, the greater a girl's lack of direction as she

example?

Talking about an example

approaches adolescence, the more likely she is to seize upon the idea of dieting as a solution to her emotional stress. A major protective factor for Debbie was that her sense of self and her relationships with others appeared to be more fully developed than Jennifer's before either girl embarked on their diets. Equally important, once the behavior began, Debbie held on to her relationships—even confessing her secret to family and classmates at an early stage—while Jennifer cut herself adrift.

For Jennifer, what began as a way to improve her looks and popularity with boys evolved into a far more complex set of behaviors and attitudes. Her system led her to isolate herself from others, even from her best friend. This self-imposed separation began during Jennifer's diet phase, before she'd lost a large amount of weight. According to widely recognized authority Hilde Bruch, M.D., loss of interest in friendships is an early warning signal of anorexia nervosa.[1] Ironically, as University of Toronto researchers David M. Garner, Ph.D., and Paul E. Garfinkel, M.D., expressed it, "Dieting which was begun to enable the person to feel better about herself and to be more involved with others does not lead to improved relationships but to withdrawal and isolation. This isolation results in loneliness and a sense of social inadequacy. These, in turn, accentuate the worries about self-control and further the preoccupation with weight loss as time passes."[2]

Increasingly, Jennifer's system substitutes for a multiplicity of neglected or avoided relationships and challenges of adolescence that she would otherwise have had to face in the normal course of things. This avoidance is in part an expression of the fear of growing up—specifically, fear of sexual maturation and the assumption of adult responsibilities—that is so often considered to underlie anorexia nervosa, especially in girls of Debbie's and Jennifer's age. The year from 14 to 15 represents the first of two statistically high-risk times for onset of anorexia nervosa; the second is at age 18. Both ages present particular challenges of separation from family, childhood, old connections. At 14, the key bridge to be negotiated is between childhood and adolescence, from junior high to high school, from girlfriends to boyfriends; at 18, the bridge usually involves actual physical separation from home and all the new challenges of living that implies.

If you have a migraine headache, you'll probably do anything to get rid of the pain. If your pain is emotional—say, you're depressed or filled with anxiety—you're not likely to want to go on feeling that way. But weight loss, the key symptom of anorexia nervosa, is experienced as positive by the patient. It's the last thing she wants to cure, because the anorexic's ability to lose weight is what sets her apart from others and provides her major source of self-esteem. Her major fear, of losing control and gaining weight, is kept high, because it helps to guard her against its realization. The budding anorexic is gratified by every lost pound, and that gratification is underlined by the approval and compliments she receives. The ability to lose weight gives her something to hang her identity on, something all her own at which she can excel. It's the one arena of her life in which she is in charge, in control.

The issue of *control* is a major one in anorexia nervosa, for patients are characteristically plagued with what Dr. Bruch first identified as an overwhelming sense of personal ineffectiveness. Weight loss counters this feeling of powerlessness and is supplemented by rigidly prescribed rituals affecting every area of the anorexic's life: her exercise, her schoolwork and, of course, her eating. The rituals must be followed to the letter for the anorexic to continue to feel in control, and they come to form an entire system of living. The development and maintenance of this system, with weight loss at its center, represents what Dr. Bruch termed "the classic anorexic struggle for a self-respecting identity."[3] The more deeply the anorexic comes to rely on her system as her source of identity and achievement, the more bereft she will feel at its loss.

Because the anorexic girl stops menstruating (if she has begun at all), she literally turns back her physiological clock to prepuberty. (Inexplicably, about a third of girls with anorexia stop menstruating before any significant loss of weight.) With her emaciation, she also produces a body without mature female curves or body fat. Thus, her regression isn't just psychological but biological. "In a biological sense," wrote British psychiatrist A. H. Crisp, M.D., "food means weight increase and growth which mean fatness and sexuality, which then demands of her a capacity to cope with the challenges and other experiences of adolescence."[4]

Research conducted by Rose E. Frisch, at the Harvard Center for Population Studies, has shown that there is a threshold weight, relative to the amount of body fat, below which menstruation cannot begin.[5] Dr. Crisp believes that the earlier a girl reaches puberty, the less equipped she is to handle the stress of adolescence. He also suggests that the fact that anorexia is overwhelmingly a female disease (approximately 90 percent of anorexics are women) might be due to the greater biological protection males have—because puberty hits them at a later age, when they are presumably better able emotionally to deal with its challenges.[6]

It's certainly no secret that adolescents as a group are the most self-critical and self-conscious of all, particularly where physical appearance is concerned. They are also highly sensitive to criticism from others. And if you have the psychological makings of anorexia nervosa, you are even more susceptible to the opinions of outsiders. In fact, one of the most common triggers of the disease is a casual comment from someone, usually male, that the girl could stand to lose a few pounds—the sort of innocent comment that pushed Debbie into her diet. Other triggers mentioned by researchers include illness or injury to the patient, death of a loved one, divorce of parents, moving or leaving home—all stressful events.

Once the diet is begun, what Dr. Crisp called a "sexual misadventure,"[7] whether real or imagined, may force matters further, as Jennifer's seemingly mild encounter with Brian may have done. In a study of thirty-one anorexic patients conducted by University of Sydney researcher P. J. V. Beumont and colleagues, more than a third of the subjects felt that anxiety and guilt feelings about sexual activity, demands by boyfriends that they have sexual intercourse, and parental disapproval of a boyfriend with whom they were having a sexual relationship had touched off their illness.[8]

Distorted body image, particularly in the younger high-risk age group, is another major symptom of anorexia nervosa that intensifies as emaciation progresses. To avoid comments by others, the anorexic often hides her body in loose-fitting clothes, as Jennifer did. Denial of illness goes hand in hand with the inability to recognize her own emaciation; if anything, the anorexic would like to get just a little bit thinner.

Though the restrictor anorexic rigidly starves without break-throughs of bingeing, she thinks about food constantly, collects and reads cookbooks, and prepares complicated dishes for other people to consume. This paradoxical preoccupation is not only typical of anorexia nervosa (and, to some degree, of anyone on a strict diet) but is also a classic symptom of starvation, whether forced or self-imposed, as Ancel Keys and colleagues pointed out in 1950 in their classic study of the effects of semistarvation on a group of male volunteers.[9]

When the anorexic's greatest fear materializes and her physiological urge to eat, so long forcibly denied, triumphs over her willpower, she often turns to vomiting. But she has lost that precious discipline that had set her off from others and given her a source, however shaky, of self-esteem. "The frightening fantasy a young girl may have had about herself as an out-of-control eater has been realized," noted psychotherapist Steven Levenkron. "She carries around a sense of shame that replaces the secret sense of pride she had in her ability to resist food."[10]

In addition to the bingeing and vomiting that follow on the heels of constant food restriction for up to 50 percent of anorexics, other impulsive behaviors are sometimes adopted. Stealing is one of them. It usually begins, as it did for Jennifer, with the practical purpose of purchasing food, laxatives, diet pills or other supplements of the bulimic system. According to Dr. Crisp and colleagues, "Stealing occurs in at least 14 percent of patients with anorexia nervosa. It arises in those whose current eating pattern is one of intermittent or sustained bingeing coupled with vomiting. It does not commonly occur at very low body weight."[11] Alcohol and drug abuse, promiscuity and self-mutilation have also been noted by researchers in conjunction with bulimic vomiters.

Family background has a great deal to do with a girl's propensity to develop anorexia, and with her potential for becoming bulimic as well. Psychiatrists have described a number of patterns thought to be typical in certain anorexia nervosa families.[12] Recently, two characteristic styles of anorexia nervosa families were defined by Janice E. Hedblom, M.S.W., and colleagues at The Johns Hopkins Hospital.

In the *emotionally unresponsive* family, the patient was emotionally orphaned, left to struggle alone with her problems when she wasn't equipped to do so. Parents in this group tended to be overwhelmed by their own conflicts and sometimes denied their daughter's problem, reporting to the therapist that their daughter was perfectly happy as a child while the daughter reported the exact opposite. In the *highly emotionally reactive* family, members are overly sensitive to each other's moods and actions, and respond immediately to them with excessive emotion. Such parents often have trouble setting limits or saying no to children, yet tend to react with too much intensity to everything their offspring does. In both groups, marital problems are common, along with separation and divorce.[13]

New research suggests that anorexic daughters from emotionally reactive families appear to be more likely to develop bulimia at some point. There is more dissent and open arguing in bulimic families, says Elaine Stevens, A.C.S.W., of the Cleveland Clinic's Department of Adolescent Psychiatry. According to Stevens, conflict is hidden in restrictor families, but in neither family are conflicts resolved. The bulimic anorexic's family environment is characterized by emotional turmoil and anxiety, says UCLA's Dr. Strober, one of the first researchers to study the differences between bulimic and restrictor anorexics. Dr. Strober notes that, in contrast to parents of restrictors, the fathers of bulimics tend to moodiness and self-deprecation, while the mothers are more anxious and depressed.

In a comparative study of the parents of young bulimic

anorexics versus restrictors, Dr. Strober found that alcoholism affected 36 percent of fathers of bulimics as opposed to 5 percent of fathers of restrictors, and psychiatric illness in general occurred in 50 percent of mothers of bulimics as opposed to 18 percent of mothers of restrictors. Restrictor families were more cohesive than bulimic families, with rules and responsibilities more clearly defined. Dr. Strober found greater tension and distance between the bulimic and her parents, and significantly more alienation from the father than from the mother. Also, there was a greater amount of life stress—for example, illness or injury in a parent or the patient herself—preceding the onset of anorexia in those girls who later developed bulimia.[14] A history of overweight in family members or in the girl herself before she begins to diet is also a common feature of the bulimic form of anorexia.

Sociological studies have shown that in latter-twentieth-century America, the higher your social class, the more you value thinness, specifically in women. For certain socially and financially prominent men—the type of men who frequently turn up as the fathers of anorexic or bulimic daughters—it can be critically important to his own self-image that his women, whether daughter or wife, look the part.

Many experts have noted the subtle but powerful influence that fathers can have on a daughter's eating behavior. In her now classic book *Eating Disorders,* Dr. Bruch identified three groups of fathers who seemed "to consider fatness in a child, particularly in a daughter, as a personal insult: dress manufacturers, movie producers, and specialists in metabolic diseases. The daughters seem to be intensely influenced in a negative way by the father's anxiety." However, Dr. Bruch added, fathers in other professions are not exempt from being highly critical of overweight in their daughters. "Among the well-to-do and educated," she wrote, "the concern is much more frantic."[15] Many achievement-oriented, upper-middle-class fathers often felt second-best despite considerable professional success, according to Dr. Bruch, and therefore tended to be preoccupied with outward appearances.[16] An anorexic daughter may duplicate within herself her father's own lack of self-acceptance, assuming for herself the parental fixation on physical appearance as the only way to be better than second-best. A parent who stresses physical appearance to such a degree may also trigger the opposite response: The daughter may rebel against the pressure by overeating and gaining weight.

Either way, too much parental emphasis on food and weight, which are already universally sensitive issues for most teen-age girls with maturing bodies, may set the stage for the inevitable teen/parent conflict to be acted out in a food-related arena. In anorexia nervosa, "conflict around these issues compounds the helplessness felt as parents watch their child lose weight," concluded Johns Hopkins's Janice Hedblom and colleagues. "The quality of the parent-child relationship deteriorates as the patient feels misunderstood and parents become more frightened. Soon the conflict itself becomes a reason for the patient to rebel, to rationalize her starvation or refuse to comply with treatment." If a child is actively anorexic or bulimic, competent professional help should be sought, which should encompass family therapy. A description of treatment programs currently available across the country is included in chapter 12.

Anorexia nervosa is a dramatic illness that is said to have been increasing in recent years. According to the most liberal estimate, at most one in every 100 teen-age girls in the upper-middle socioeconomic classes will actually develop it.[18] But many millions more will simply continue to diet and fear fat throughout adolescence and on into young adulthood without ever becoming anorexic.

One thousand teen-agers in Berkeley, California—one entire grade of the public-school system—were studied for three years, from the ninth to the twelfth grade, by Ruth L. Huenemann and colleagues. The results of the study revealed that 63 percent of ninth-grade girls wanted to lose weight and 53 percent of the boys wanted to gain weight. In the later grades, the figures had risen in both groups: 70 percent of girls wanted to lose and 58 percent of boys wanted to gain.[19] In a later study of high-school girls, Scandinavian researcher Ingvar Nylander,

M.D., reported that 50 percent of them had begun dieting at age 14; by age 18, the figure was above 70 percent. When Dr. Nylander asked his subjects why they dieted, the most frequent answers were "felt fat" or "couldn't get into clothes." When those who said they "felt fat" but had *not* dieted were asked why they hadn't, they replied "weak character." As with the Berkeley study, feeling fat had little to do with *being* fat.[20]

Obviously, the vast majority of teen-age girls diet regardless of whether they need to. The dream and the promise of a thin body, openly advertised wherever you turn, along with gourmet menus and recipes, is just too seductive. And there is every evidence that such cultural pressure continues to escalate. Coupled with this pressure, and entirely antagonistic to it, is evidence that the American woman, presumably due to better nutrition, is actually heavier today than she was in the past.

David M. Garner, Ph.D., and colleagues point out in their comparative study of twenty years of *Playboy* centerfold models and Miss America contestants, all of whom were under 30, that both the centerfold models and the contestants have been getting thinner over the years (and the pageant *winners* were thinner yet than the average contestant). However, the average American woman under 30 has increased in weight by about 5 or 6 pounds over the same twenty-year period. Meanwhile, as pointed out in the same report, a study of the number of diet articles published from 1959 to 1978 in six popular women's magazines (*Harper's Bazaar, Vogue, McCall's, Good Housekeeping, Ladies' Home Journal* and *Woman's Day*) showed a definite increase over time: from 17.1 articles in the first decade to 29.6 in the second.[21] Such a heavily promoted, society-wide contradiction—that modern aesthetics demand that women be ever thinner, while female biology demands that women be heavier—sets up an abrasive tension that may kick a vulnerable young woman over the line into desperate measures of weight control, and contributes to the apparent increase in anorexia nervosa, bulimia, and other extreme dieting problems today.

In the past, simple, garden-variety dieting appeared to be the most basic weapon against the "fat feeling." Though vomiting and other instant weight-loss methods were certainly indulged in, they weren't written about. Today, however, the subject has emerged boldly out of the kitchen and bathroom and into the living room and den. Even if a girl doesn't have a sister, friend or teammate to tip her off to such drastic measures of weight control, there's always Jane Fonda.

How many young girls were inspired, as Debbie was, by the activities of *The Best Little Girl in the World?* Stacey, now 17, read the Steven Levenkron novel on which the TV movie was based when she was 14. "I learned about vomiting from friends who were always bragging about it, and then I read about it in the book. I looked up to the main character, Francesca, so much, because of her willpower." Stacey succeeded where Debbie failed—she lost enough weight to be hospitalized. The panic over the weight she gained in treatment led her into chronic self-induced vomiting and laxative abuse in an effort to keep her weight under 100. Stacey is currently in group and family therapy to try to work out some of the emotional problems that underlie her disordered eating.

Meanwhile, other girls skating toward chaos wonder if things could get serious. Joni is 15: "Ever since I was twelve," she says, "I've been very concerned with what people think of me. Therefore I started to worry a lot about my weight. About four months ago I came up with the idea that I could eat as much as I wanted to, then throw it all up and hardly gain a calorie, but I would still feel full. Well, it's been working, but I do still gain a little weight. I'm five-foot-six-and-a-half and weigh a hundred and eighteen. I hate to think of all that junk going into my body, then vomiting it all up again, but I can't stick to a diet! I am fully aware of what I'm doing and I really don't think it's serious yet. I'm wondering, though, if it can get serious."

Joni's use of the word "therefore" points up what she perceives as the quite natural and obvious connection she makes between her weight and the degree to which she is accepted by others. Because she can't stick to a diet, she turns to vomiting. If she is not thin, Joni assumes, people will think less of her. This assumption flows as much from cultural messages as it does from Joni's own lack of self-confidence.

With talk of anorexia nervosa and bulimia, not to mention the ever-present topic of dieting, so thickly lacing the teen-age female experience, the word "epidemic" may not be an exaggeration when it comes to eating disorders. Today, "12-, 13-, and 14-year-olds regard bingeing and vomiting as reasonable within their peer culture," says UCLA's Dr. Strober, "and so they resist the idea that it's any kind of psychological problem."

Though the idea of bingeing and vomiting as a peer-approved activity seems to contradict the commonly held assumption that secrecy is a cardinal rule of the behavior, in many teen-age circles—particularly where a low weight is necessary for optimum performance, as in ballet schools, gymnastics teams, or cheerleading squads—the behavior is openly discussed and sometimes even practiced en masse. In such circles, the element of secrecy comes into play not with the behavior itself but with the feelings behind the behavior.

Laura, a cheerleader at a public high school in Michigan, explains matter-of-factly that "everyone on the squad binges and vomits. That's how I learned. But I don't think anybody else feels as scared as I do about everything. I don't ask, though, because I don't want them to know I'm scared, in case they're not." Laura considers her bulimic behavior frightening and awful, except in one context: before cheerleading a game. "Everybody does it then," she says, "so it doesn't seem like the same thing."

If you are a teen-ager studying dance, as Jennifer was, or hoping to become a model, your exposure to the possibilities of extreme weight-control methods is greatly increased. When Richard G. Druss, M.D., and Joseph A. Silverman, M.D., studied the eating behaviors of young ballerinas-in-training, aged 15 to 21, at the Joffrey School of Ballet, they reported the following: "Weight and diet were of paramount concern to the students. They did *whatever was necessary* to keep their weight down. The average daily intake was 1,000 calories. Food faddism approaching the bizarre was not uncommon. Some were on 'lettuce diets,' some on 'yogurt diets,' and one girl ate only carrots. Some students had to be hospitalized." (emphasis added) But as Jennifer had felt, the greatest compliment a student could receive from an instructor was, "Oh, have you lost weight!"[22]

In his book about the dancer's search for the perfect body form, *Competing with the Sylph*, L. M. Vincent, M.D., was even more specific. Out of twenty-four ballet-scholarship students in New York City, one-third used laxatives for weight reduction or maintenance. Laxatives, Dr. Vincent concluded, were almost a fad with the younger ballet dancers, more commonly used to control weight than other methods, including self-induced vomiting.[23] Clearly, if a girl already has a personality vulnerable to the development of chaotic eating patterns, a high-risk environment like a ballet school could put her over the edge.

Many teen-age girls from affluent and achieving families grow up with the message that they must also achieve. As the girl complies with this expectation and the list of her youthful achievements lengthens, feelings of inadequacy may, ironically, develop and deepen. The achievements never seem to be enough; only failure—because it's unexpected—seems to have an impact, on both her parents and her own sense of self. This can be confusing and threatening to a teen-age girl already struggling with a fragile self-identity and who, despite her achievements, feels continually that she doesn't measure up to her peers. These inner conflicts and doubts are streamlined through food abuse.

Laura, the 17-year-old cheerleader who learned about vomiting from girls on the squad, is a senior, a member of the National Honor Society, a star of the swim team and the editor of the school newspaper. She has been accepted at the topflight college of her choice with a full scholarship. But Laura, sadly, considers her only strong times to be when she is successfully dieting. Otherwise, she sees no reason to be pleased with herself.

Last year, Laura, who is 5'7", lost weight following a tonsillectomy. "I thought that was great," she says. "During the summer, I began making myself vomit whenever I had overeaten. When school started, I became real depressed because I was so involved and overboggled with things. I felt if I could leave and go to a different school where nobody knew me, maybe I would feel I didn't have to prove anything to anyone. But I couldn't let my mother know I was so depressed. I stopped eating for about five days and was exercising a lot. I had weighed about a hundred and ten or a hundred and twelve all last year, and was now at ninety-seven.

"I have had so many problems with my boyfriend. He broke up with me. He told me if I would gain weight, he would be back. Well, I wanted him back, but didn't want to gain weight. I was bingeing and vomiting whenever I could. Somehow I gained back up to a hundred and twelve, but things were still shaky. He's now dating someone else and I've been starving myself to lose weight again, but can't seem to stop bingeing.

"I almost considered suicide, something I never thought I would do, but realized I can't do this to my mother. I can't tell her, because she will feel it is her fault, and she has too much to worry about. I'm so scared. I don't know what to do."

As long as there's not a lot of pressure (which is rare, considering the extent of her activities), Laura is able to starve herself. But if there's a big exam to take or an issue of the paper to put out, she finds herself bingeing and vomiting. The more "overboggled" she gets over the pressures of living, the more chaotic her eating behavior.

Many overboggled teen-agers hide behind a cloak of alcohol or drugs or delinquency for the same reasons that drive a girl like Laura to bingeing and vomiting. A well-brought up, eager-to-please, achieving young girl would be intensely fearful of winding up pregnant, in jail or in a methadone center, so she tries to unboggle herself by devising a food system. Food is controllable, understandable; its effects are known. While teen-age males are more likely to deny their feelings, become delinquent or abuse drugs in the face of adolescent trauma, noted Dr. Crisp, females may seek safety in food—its denial, its indulgence or both. "Food," Dr. Crisp wrote, "provides a predictable experience."[24]

   To counteract the teen-age potential for turning to food or other impulsive behaviors as a way to escape the inherent conflicts and threats of growing up, a teen-ager should be encouraged to make decisions for herself, stresses Felicity A. Hubbard, R.N., B.S., coordinator of the Eating and Weight Disorders Clinic at The Johns Hopkins Hospital. It's also important, Hubbard says, not to assume that you know what others are thinking of you before clarifying it for yourself, a common mistake that young anorexics make. Hubbard advises them, for example, to ask for a ride to a party and see what happens rather than simply assume that no one will want to give them one.

   Hubbard works closely with teen-agers in the community, speaking to junior-high, high-school and college audiences, as well as with hospitalized anorexic and bulimic teen-agers. She tells her young listeners not to avoid direct expression of feelings, because avoidance will only intensify their problems. The more you cloak your emotions, she warns them, the more you'll be dependent on and angry with adults, because the adults will take over where you won't. Then you may turn to the control of food instead.

   In the end, learning to adapt to change instead of trying to avoid it is the only means of real control. As Hubbard counsels high-school students, "Change is inevitable, and if you try to deal with the crises of change—such as having to make a decision or say no to a boyfriend or leave home for the first time—by holding back your body weight or by bingeing and vomiting, you will never give yourself the chance to feel truly in control of your life."

ENTERING ADULTHOOD

Sarah

Ever since she was 6 years old, Sarah had felt fat. There was a picture of her at that age in her family's scrapbook, one that she kept meaning to burn. She saw in it a big fat face and pudgy arms oozing out of a sleeveless shirt that was buttoned over a pregnant-looking belly.

When she was 8, an obnoxious boy in her third-grade class nicknamed her "Squish" because, on the day everyone was supposed to bring in a live caterpillar to study, she dropped hers on the classroom floor and accidentally stepped on it, causing most of the kids to giggle. Sarah knew that if a thin kid had done exactly the same thing as she had, there would have been no nickname.

When she was 9, her grammar school instituted the terrifying practice of weighing and measuring students in the classroom in front of everyone; the teacher would shout out the height and weight to a student volunteer, who would record the figures on an attendance sheet. Sarah feared this twice-yearly ordeal more than anything in her world, and hated her teachers and her classmates for it.

Sarah entered junior high school weighing 99 pounds, maybe 10 pounds more than most of her friends. That year she ate just what they did for lunch in the cafeteria—a peanut butter and jelly sandwich, milk, Twinkies and an apple or orange—but it was only Sarah who finished out the year 20 pounds heavier. By then she'd taken to wearing her father's baggy Shetland sweaters and dirty sneakers with her friends' names written all over them. The fatter she felt, the sloppier she looked.

Despite being overweight, Sarah had lots of friends, was getting excellent grades in honors classes and held various class offices. By the ninth grade, her weight stabilized at a plump but acceptable level, maybe 15 or 20 pounds more than her cheer-leader-caliber friends. She cleaned up her attire a bit, acquired a boyfriend, and liked herself well enough.

Through high school, Sarah was conscious of her weight, though not excessively. She was 5′3″ and weighed about 122—not the best, but not the worst either. She wasn't thin or pretty enough to be rushed by the cutest boys, and during summer vacations she'd never be on the beach in a bathing suit without a big T-shirt covering it up. Still, she did okay. She was busy, popular, and had other things to think about.

With a near straight-A average, numerous academic honors, several elected positions in student government and well-writ-ten applications, Sarah was accepted into every liberal-arts college she applied to. She selected a small, highly regarded coed school in the West, agreeing with her forward-looking father that it would be a good experience for her to sample life on the other side of the country. And so, after a summer of working as a waitress and, thanks to an obliging old boyfriend, finally meeting her precollege goal of getting rid of her virginity, Sarah said goodbye to her younger sister and brother, her tearful mother and her beaming father and flew west.

It was the first she'd heard of the "Freshman 10" and, naturally, she was a victim. Freshman year at college was infamous for causing weight fluctuation, and by first-semester exam time she'd gained nearly 10 pounds. One hundred and thirty! It was as heavy as she'd ever been, and Sarah was disgusted with herself. Her diary entries began to contain two recurrent phrases: "Felt and looked ugly" alternated simply with "fat." She knew there was no point in trying to diet with all the pressure of exams, so she set February 10 as Diet Day, the first day back on campus after semester break. By spring vacation in April, she would weigh 110.

Sarah began the diet on schedule, and she knew from the start that this diet was different from any of the others she'd been on throughout her life. A part of her had never really taken them seriously; she'd cheat a bit here and there, and pretty soon she'd give up. This time she didn't have to fight herself; she had no desire to cheat. Her willpower was rock hard. She lost the first 5 pounds in ten days, and she knew she would be thin. During the second week of the diet, she happened to sit next to Kate in her Eastern Philosophy class, and somehow (probably because it was the most important subject on both of their minds), they began talking diets.

Kate had gained weight first semester, too, and had also gotten disgusted enough to begin a diet after break. Soon, Kate and Sarah were eating as many meals as possible together; and as they both began to lose weight, they had the pleasure of gloating about it to each other. Unlike Sarah, Kate had never been overweight until she entered college, a year before Sarah, but had put on 10 pounds freshman year and another 6 last semester. Though they moved in entirely different social circles, Sarah and Kate became tight friends as their diets wore on. Their talk came to include men and sex and philosophy as well as food.

By the middle of March, Sarah's weight was down to her original goal of 110, but she and Kate agreed that perhaps she should shoot for 105. After all, Kate was an inch taller than Sarah, and she had fixed on 100 as *her* ideal weight. Neither of them had any problem sticking to their diets. They routinely declined dinner invitations from men; together they had determined that no dates would be held over food, to avoid both temptation and unwanted questions like "Why are you only eating salad?" Everything was going quite well except for the nightmares. Several nights a week, Sarah would dream that she went off her diet in the worst way—coffee cakes, hamburgers, ice cream, pizza, bagels, huge bags of potato chips and M & M's and doughnuts. During the dream, she would feel terrific; but when she woke up she would be in a panic until she realized it was only a dream.

As Sarah's weight dropped, she began to fantasize about herself. She was no longer pleasingly-plump-but-still-popular

Sarah. Now she was wonderfully exotic, romantic, even noble. The new Sarah never, ever appeared fat to men; she was totally desirable just because she was thin. The new Sarah never sat by the phone praying, "Please, God, let him call." The new Sarah would say and do exactly what she pleased around attractive men without worrying what they thought of her. If they didn't like her, that was their problem. Of course, because she'd look so good, so thin, they'd like her no matter what she did. The fantasy of being so confident with men, of coolly evaluating them to see if they were worthy of her, rather than the reverse, was wonderfully satisfying. If only it were real.

Getting down to 105 was turning out to be tough. Five days of near-starvation, living on grapefruit and lettuce, and Sarah had only dropped a half-pound. "God, I don't know what else to cut out," she wailed to Kate, who was already at 100 and on her way to 97.

"Don't worry, it'll come off," Kate assured her. "Maybe if you cut out the grapefruit at lunch, just have an iced tea. That's what I've been doing. In fact, let's go shopping today instead of having lunch. We ought to treat ourselves to some new clothes for our new figures. I've had enough of these baggy jeans."

That afternoon at the shopping center, Sarah was thrilled. She actually could get into size 5 pants, and, depending on the style, sometimes size 3! Everything looked terrific on her, but the best part was the salesgirl, who kept saying, "My God, you're so small! How do you do it?" and "I'm too fat to wear something like this"—holding up a miniskirt and camisole—"but it would look great on you." Sarah, whose memories of salesgirls went back to the fifth grade when she and her mother would try to buy her clothes and the salesgirl would say, "Here, these vertical stripes will help minimize her figure," kept having to remind herself that the salesgirl was referring to her and not someone else. She began to feel panic. I must hold my weight. Please, God, I must hold my weight. She looked over at Kate, trying on a bikini with her hipbones sticking out, and wondered if she was experiencing the same feelings. Probably not. After all, Kate used to be thin until she hit college; she hadn't gone through her whole life thinking of herself as fat and having salesgirls feel sorry for her.

"You know," said Kate on the way back to campus, "Paul was asking about you after class the other day—seemed really interested. He said you were looking great, and wanted to know if you're hooked up with anybody right now."

"What did you say?" Sarah asked. Paul was sexy, powerful, the kind of guy who always had gorgeous, thin girlfriends. Even though there were only twelve students in her Kierkegaard seminar, he'd never seemed to notice her before.

"I told him to ask *you,*" Kate grinned.

Later, in her room, smoking and starving, with a volume of Renaissance history in front of her upon which she could not concentrate, Sarah thought about Paul. Would he really ask her out? She knew he would never have been interested before she'd gotten thin, but that was typical. Guys always wanted girls to be thin, and they wanted them thin without any visible effort. They couldn't stand girls on diets, and they couldn't stand them fat.

The next day was Sarah's Kierkegaard seminar, the class she shared with Paul, and she wanted to look good. She put on her tight new jeans and the sexy white gauze blouse and bare, flat sandals. In the mirror she searched for her familiar fat thighs that looked terrible in pants, especially tight jeans, but they weren't there. Instead, she looked like all the slender girls in high school who could eat four Nestlé Crunch bars after school and not gain an ounce. She was thin. She was thin. Please, please, let me stay thin, she prayed to the god of weight. She grabbed her copy of Kierkegaard's *Fear and Trembling* and raced off to class.

When she entered the room, the first person she saw was Paul, who smiled at her and patted the empty seat next to him. As she sat down in her tight jeans, trying to act blasé, he leaned over and whispered, "Sarah, you've got the greatest little body." At first she thought he was making fun of her. She'd always had trouble accepting compliments. If someone told her they liked her blouse, she'd counter by pointing out a stain on it; if someone told her she'd written a good paper, she'd reply that it was boring. And she'd had no practice at all handling compliments about her figure. So it was impossible for Sarah to come back with anything witty, flirtatious or sexy, let alone thank Paul for the compliment.

Fortunately, the professor had begun the discussion and all she had to do was smile in response. So much for her big fantasy about being confident. What was her problem, anyway? She reminded herself that Paul was the kind of guy who always went for the prettiest and skinniest girls because that was necessary for his own self-image. The kind who always got away with it because he was so pretty himself. Why was she even interested in a guy like that? They invariably turned out to be self-centered, critical, demanding, and mistakenly considered themselves the best in bed. Yet here she was, literally sweating over what to say to Paul when class was over that would be "good" enough to get him to ask her out. As if *that* would truly establish her worth. And for all she knew, he was a complete idiot.

When class was over, before Sarah had to come up with anything, Paul said, cool as could be, "You know, it's time we went out together," and looked at her expectantly.

"Uh, yeah," Sarah mumbled moronically.

Again, Paul saved her. "What about tonight?"

Sarah had a big exam the day after tomorrow and had planned to spend the evening studying. Tonight was definitely not a good night. "Sure, tonight's fine," she said. Fool, she told herself. Now you'll have to stay up all night tomorrow cramming. The guy gives you two minutes' notice and you jump. Because of course you figure you won't get another chance.

"Great," said Paul. "I'll pick you up at the dorm at eight."

After they said goodbye, Sarah went to the gym to weigh herself. One hundred and four. Another half-pound. She'd revised her goal weight to 100—she needed a safety margin. Mainly because she had no idea how to eat once she ended the diet, which would be soon, and in case she ate too much . . .

Back in her dorm room, Sarah inspected her body in the full-length mirror. Quite the little narcissist, she thought sarcastically. She wore bikini panties and stood sideways to see if her stomach was flat enough to form a straight plane with the elastic of the bikini or if it bulged over the elastic. To her great pleasure, there was no visible bulge, and she wasn't holding her breath, either. She pulled on black corduroy pants, one of her recent purchases, and an angora sweater that always got her compliments whenever she wore it. Then she studied herself again in the mirror. Maybe she didn't look so hot in the pants after all.

Sarah's roommate, Liz, had entered through the open door without Sarah's even noticing her. Immediately, Sarah asked, "Do I look fat?"

Liz stared at her. "You're nuts. You're sick! Of course you don't look fat. You look totally bony. Are you still on that ridiculous diet?" Liz was one of the very few women Sarah knew who never worried about her weight and seemed to be neither fat nor thin, a state of mind and body that Sarah had often envied.

"Yeah, I'm just going to lose a couple more pounds," Sarah said. "And it's not ridiculous, because it works."

"Well, whatever. But despite what you and Kate think, you *can* be too thin. Besides,"—Liz launched into her favorite line—"there are more important things in life."

The dorm switchboard operator phoned to say that Paul had arrived. "See you later," Sarah called to Liz.

Paul was leaning against the counter in the lobby, flirting with the switchboard operator. Sarah liked the way he looked: tall, snug Levi's, dark plaid shirt. Talk about great bodies.

The party was typical: someone's off-campus apartment; dips and chips, beer, wine and tequila; too few bathrooms for too many people; marijuana smoke in the air for those few confirmed pot smokers in the age of 'ludes. Sarah knew a few people. As always, there was someone she hadn't seen for a while who came up and said, "Wow, you lost a lot of weight!" Sarah hated it when people said that. For one thing, it made her think that she must have been really fat before; and for another, she was afraid it made other people, like Paul, aware that she used to be fat. She liked it to seem as if she'd always been thin. Somehow that might help her *stay* thin.

Later, they went to Paul's apartment and had sex. Sarah wasn't sure she wanted to, but she didn't *not* want to enough to say anything when he began. She often found it easier just to go along instead of going through the hassle of saying no. Afterward, she was just drifting off to sleep in Paul's bed when he got up. "I've got an early class tomorrow," he said. "I'll take you back to the dorm."

Sarah thought that was rude of him; she'd assumed they'd spend the night together. She felt hurt that he didn't want her to. She felt angry. "Yeah, it must be getting late," she said, pretending she hadn't planned to sleep there anyway. She didn't want him to think she was the clinging type. Selfish bastard, she thought as she dressed. Why am I always looking for love from guys like this and dumping on the ones who really like me, the ones who were interested in more than just my hipbones? This had been a pattern of hers that she would have liked to break, but so far she hadn't succeeded.

They walked back to the dorm in silence. Paul kissed her briefly. "See you," he said.

"Sure," Sarah's tone was equally casual. "Take it easy."

Lying sleepless in bed, Sarah played her personal version of counting sheep. She called it "Food Fantasy." It went like this: If I could eat anything I wanted and not gain weight, I'd have . . . a huge piece of sour-cream coffee cake with tons of cinnamon. A bacon, cheese and onion omelet. A club sandwich on rye. Coffee Häagen-Dazs ice cream. A huge chunk of Roquefort cheese and fresh French bread. No wonder she had nightmares.

The next morning, Sarah woke up feeling depressed. She hated herself for being so wimpy, so eager to please, last night with Paul. Instead of acting for herself, she'd tried to gauge what he wanted from her and then be sure to give it to him. She'd wanted him to think she was into sex, so she faked climaxes. She'd wanted him to think she wasn't at all hung up about intimacy, so she pretended that when it was over, it was over; why drag it out when they both needed to sleep in their own beds? Meanwhile, he had done exactly what he wanted. He was as self-centered as she had suspected. And still, in the back of her mind, she was wondering if he'd call her!

Liz came in from breakfast. "How was last night?"

"Oh, fine." Sarah didn't care to go into details, and Liz didn't press her. "I went to the store and got some stuff to bake Tollhouse cookies tomorrow night for Steve," Liz said. Steve was her boyfriend. "Want to help?"

"Sure," Sarah said. Maybe she'd make some for Tim. She'd been avoiding him lately, though she'd seen him constantly through first semester. He'd been in love with her, had told her so. But she just couldn't get that passionate about him—he was almost too nice. Now she felt a bit guilty about how she'd handled the situation and thought she might want to see him again. At least with Tim she didn't have to worry about every little thing she did or said. He accepted her no matter what. He hadn't even noticed when she lost weight—she'd had to mention it to him herself. And all he said was, "Why bother? You looked great the way you were."

Sarah spent the day and night studying for her exam, her concentration repeatedly challenged by alternating thoughts of food and Paul. But the exam didn't turn out to be too bad, and afterward, when Sarah stopped at the gym to weigh herself, she was thrilled: 102. She felt wonderful all the way back to the dorm.

Liz was in their room, looking frazzled. "How's your work going?" Sarah asked her.

"Not so great." Liz flopped down on her bed. "My zoology exam's tomorrow and I don't feel confident about it, even though I've been studying for eight hours straight and even skipped lunch so I wouldn't lose time." That was definitely unusual for Liz, who never skipped a meal. She was the most regular person Sarah knew. "Which means I'm totally starving. It's already five-thirty—the dining hall will be open in a half-hour and I plan to be first in line. How are things going with you?"

"Terrific. I'm just about done with the first draft of my Shakespeare paper and I'm in a great mood."

"That's nice for a change," Liz said dryly. She was always

telling Sarah to relax and stop being so compulsive about everything and so critical of herself. "Why can't you just be happy instead of analyzing everything?" Liz would say. Sarah appreciated Liz's perspective, but happiness had never been a big goal of hers. Sarah preferred less mellowness and more passion, even if it meant pain.

"Do you want to have dinner with me," Liz was saying, "or is this one of your fasting nights?"

"No, I'll go down with you." Sarah was in such a good mood that she wanted to give some of it to Liz. All it took was losing 2 pounds to make her into Pollyanna or something.

Sarah stood behind Liz in the cafeteria line. As they moved their trays along the aluminum counter, she studied Liz's selections. She kept hoping that by observing someone she considered to be a normal eater, she would somehow learn how to be one herself. But each time she felt discouraged, because she knew if she ate what Liz ate, she'd be back to 128. On Liz's tray was a salad with Italian dressing, a piece of French bread, a piece of baked chicken with string beans and rice, a glass of regular milk and two oatmeal cookies. Sarah had her usual half-grapefruit and a huge plate of lettuce with cucumbers and shredded carrots. Instead of salad dressing, she sprinkled the plate with vinegar.

At the table, Sarah began telling Liz about her night with Paul, finishing up with a tiny lie: "I made him take me home—I needed a decent sleep."

"Are you going to see him again?" Liz asked.

"I sort of doubt it." Sarah shrugged. "It was really just a sexual thing. In some ways he's almost too smooth, if you know what I mean. Which made it perfect for one night, but over time I bet he would seem pretty calculated, like he'd figured out all the right moves and had it memorized." This, of course, was a less than honest recap of their evening together. Sarah guessed that her interpretation of Paul was probably exactly right, but her presentation of herself as the one who was really in control all along was absurd.

"I know what you mean," said Liz, "but it's great that you got what you wanted out of it and didn't consider it any big deal." Liz drained her glass of milk. "Let's go make those cookies—I've still got studying to do later."

Sarah had forgotten about the cookie project. For a moment she felt fear—what if she ate one? But that was silly. No one was going to force her to eat a cookie. She was in control. She wondered what a Tollhouse cookie tasted like; it had been so long. But she certainly wasn't going to find out now—not this close to weighing 100 and having this nice new body to show off to friends and family at home during spring break.

In the dorm kitchen, Sarah sifted the dry ingredients while Liz creamed the butter and sugar. Sarah was staring at the open bag of Nestlé semisweet chocolate chips lying on the counter, ready to be mixed into the batter. They were making three different batches with three different kinds of chips: chocolate, butterscotch and mint chocolate. One-half of her brain was telling her that a chocolate chip had only three calories, and the other half was telling her to stop thinking about it. The war was going on so intensely that Liz had to repeat it twice: "Are you ready to combine the ingredients?"

When the first batter, containing plain chocolate chips, was fully blended and ready to be spooned onto the baking sheets, Liz sampled it. "Mmmm, perfect. Want a taste?"

Sarah, who felt increasing terror and hoped Liz couldn't read it in her eyes, shook her head. She stuck a piece of gum in her mouth so she wouldn't be tempted to taste anything and began spooning out the batter.

Fifteen minutes later, the first batch was done. Liz took one off the cookie sheet with a spatula and ate it. "God, they taste great when they're fresh and hot. Don't you want to sample your artistry?"

"Uh—not right now. I've got gum in my mouth."

Liz, who was used to what she considered Sarah's weird logic, didn't suggest she remove the gum. "I'm going to get a Coke from the machine," Liz said, leaving the kitchen.

Sarah told herself she could try one cookie. She discarded her gum and had the cookie. Instantly, it was as if a maniac had been released: She went wild, out of control. She was stuffing cookies and raw batter into her mouth so fast that she didn't have time to swallow. Any second now Liz would be back, and she'd notice all the missing batter and cookies. Sarah took all the cookies off the baking sheets—there were so many blank spaces now—and piled them on a paper plate so that it would look like there was more. She took another batch out of the oven. She should try one hot—Liz had said they were so good. She ate two, burning her tongue, and would have continued, but Liz returned. "Smells good in here," she said. She didn't seem to notice the missing cookies.

With Liz there, Sarah didn't eat any more, but she'd already blown it. She might as well play out her Food Fantasy game for real. She wanted to get out of the kitchen and away from Liz. She didn't want to be around anyone if she was going to eat. As Liz took the last batch out of the oven, Sarah washed up and plotted. She wanted a hamburger. And french fries. Ice cream. Cinnamon rolls. A tuna sandwich on rye with potato chips in the sandwich. A bowl of shredded wheat with half-and-half and sugar. She felt panic and excitement and a terrible inevitability. She knew she would do this and *she knew she didn't want to.* Why, then, was she going to do it?

The question plagued Sarah for the next two years. No matter where she was—at school, at home for vacation—she was stuck in a pattern that she couldn't seem to break or even understand. The first year, she managed to keep her weight down by countering her once- or twice-weekly binges with four to five days of semifasting, eating only lettuce with diet dressing or sometimes taking only liquids.

Desperate, she told her mother about it, but her mother said, "You're exaggerating." She sought help at the college counseling center, but the psychologist told her that she was under a lot of stress and it would soon go away. She told her family doctor, when she was home for vacation, that she had gained 5 pounds in two days of bingeing and needed help in learning how to eat. He said, "That's impossible. You can't eat five pounds of food in two days," and gave her a printed 1,400-calorie-a-day diet to follow, "though you don't need to lose weight." She even saw a psychoanalyst, who listened in silence as she described her binges and her panic over them, and then said only, to her amazement, "Enjoy the cycles." But because she managed to cancel out each binge by several days of fasting, she still wore a size 5 or 3 and still got compliments from men for having a nice body.

The bingeing caught up with her during the second year of her panic. In an effort to escape her environment, she chose to spend a semester in an exchange program at another college in a different part of the country. The plan backfired. She was lonely on the strange campus. She didn't know anyone when she arrived, and she seemed to have lost her old ability to be extroverted and strike up conversations with people. Though she lived in a dorm, she had her own room and kept to herself. This made her binge more often. As her bingeing increased to maybe every two days, her fasting decreased, and she began to gain weight.

When the exchange program was over and she returned to her old campus, she weighed 120 and had to put up with more than one insensitive person (usually men) saying, "Have you put on weight?" But she was glad to be back with her friends. She had a new boyfriend who was superintelligent and stimulating. And maybe she no longer weighed 105, but she wasn't bingeing anymore, either. Sarah was sick of the whole thing, sick of asking herself why she had to "punish" herself with food. She decided, at the beginning of junior year, that 120 was better than 130, and she would have to accept it. It seemed that she just wasn't the thin type.

She gave away her size 5s and bought some size 9s, and tried not to fantasize too much about how wonderful it had been to be thin. The real truth was that, in the end, it hadn't been worth it.

Epidemic on the Campus

> If a date takes me out to dinner and he pays, I won't throw up
> the food, because he's spent so much money.
>
> Lisa, a college sophomore

Sarah wasn't obese. She wasn't emaciated. She wasn't vomiting or using laxatives. Her eating behavior wasn't extreme enough for her family doctor, the college counseling center, or the psychoanalyst to take it seriously. Yet Sarah fulfilled all of the diagnostic criteria for bulimia. On the arc, Sarah's place is with the bulimic dieters.

The fact that she never moved beyond dieting into more severe compensatory methods for her bulimia reflects the interactive connection between behavior and psychology: The more troubled you are in your head, the more likely it is to be reflected in your eating behavior; and the more disruptive your behavior, the more it feeds back into psychological difficulties. Bulimics "who do not regurgitate, but go on to abstain from food for a week, have a firmer sense of self and consequently are emotionally better able to tolerate the discomfort and distress caused by overeating," wrote Regina C. Casper, M.D.[1]

Before she ever began her diet, Sarah knew she was someone, knew she had something inside. She had experienced a good deal of success socially and academically since childhood, and she *recognized* her success. She was able to acknowledge the fact that she was popular and had a good personality. When she set out to diet, her determination came from within herself. Though Sarah lacked confidence and had trouble standing up for her feelings, especially when it came to men who attracted her, she was able to form and maintain strong social connections throughout her two-year bulimic episode.

Sarah's perception of her body size was basically realistic; she could tell when she was thin enough. This was partially due to the fact that her thinking wasn't distorted by a starvation weight. And her age was also a factor. Body-image studies have shown that the younger the girl (regardless of whether or not she has an

eating or weight problem), the more likely she is to overestimate her body size. Thus, women who develop anorexia nervosa
in the later age group (at 18 rather than 14) tend to experience
less distortion of body image. However, as Katherine A. Halmi,
M.D., and colleagues reported, body *disparagement*, the feeling that your body is unattractive, is more common in the older
age group.[2]

Sarah's insight into herself and others, and—not to be under-
estimated—her sense of humor, may have further protected her
from full-blown food chaos. She was able to keep a rational eye
on things and a sense of perspective about herself and her
behavior, troubled as she was by it. Eventually, she was able to
move on in her life; her struggles with food and weight didn't
seep and stick into every corner.

Though it's the binge-vomiter who seems to have gotten
much of the attention lately, especially on campus, Sarah's type
of eating behavior may be far more common. "Most of the
bingers I see," notes Raymond C. Hawkins II, Ph.D., psychological consultant at the Austin Stress Clinic, who saw plenty
during his tenure as assistant professor of psychology at the
University of Texas, "are not vomiters. They are rigid dieters."
Dr. Hawkins and colleague Pamelia F. Clement, Ph.D., developed a "Binge Scale" questionnaire to test the frequency of
binge-eating behavior among undergraduates at the University
of Texas. They found that 79 percent of female undergraduate
subjects, of varying weights, admitted to binge-eating episodes.
Binges were reported as frequently among normal-weight
women as among overweight women. But only 5 percent of the
female bingers, regardless of weight, were also vomiters.[3]

The college campus is surely the most fertile land of all for
sowing the seeds of all types of chaotic eating behavior. First of
all, college represents another challenge of separation—for
many, it means leaving home for the first time, with all that
implies, from doing your own laundry to establishing your own
curfew to selecting your own meals. In fact, the emotional stress
of leaving home causes an estimated 20 percent of college
women to stop menstruating or become highly irregular.[4]

Second, campus life usually involves an increase in social and academic pressures and a new anxiety about the future. The future no longer means college, as it did in high school, but The Adult World.

The residential environment itself, a community of peers with no parents around, provides endless opportunities for pass-along behaviors to soften classical collegiate depression. Drugs. Alcohol. Smoking. Dieting. Bingeing and vomiting. As the *Dartmouth Alumni* magazine reported: "Inside a stall in a women's bathroom on campus, a woman wrote: 'I starve myself, then I gorge myself on garbage and make myself throw up afterwards. I am getting out of control and am really disgusted with myself. Does anyone else have this problem?' In response, several others scrawled, 'YES! YES! YES!' "[5]

In an academically competitive environment, the daily pressure and accompanying risk of developing a stress-related eating behavior mounts. "I think I started bingeing and vomiting because I didn't realize how tough it would be to train in a man's world, and I needed a release from all the tension," says a Purdue University woman studying to be an engineer. She sought psychological counseling when her bingeing and vomiting became a daily activity. Adds a bingeing-and-dieting premed student at the Massachusetts Institute of Technology, where maybe 23 percent of the students are females: "You can't come here and not know what you want to do. I know I can do the work required, but there are always those nagging doubts: Am I asking too much? Is this out of my range? At a place like this, with so many more men than women, the pressure to look good in order to get your share of men may not be as intense, but the academic pressure causes lots of women I know to turn to food for alleviation. I'm certainly one of them."

David M. Garner, Ph.D., and Paul E. Garfinkel, M.D., designed the Eating Attitudes Test (EAT) as a way to determine the degree of anorexic behaviors and attitudes held by subjects. They published it in 1979.[6] With the EAT as a tool, they've surveyed thousands of women. Dr. Garner calculates that a significant percentage—about 12 percent—of college-age women have *serious* difficulties (determined by a score of at least 30 on the EAT) with their eating behavior. By "serious," Dr. Garner means that worries about food occupy an extreme proportion of their time and they all use drastic weight-control techniques, including laxatives and diuretics, as well as vomiting.

Since developing the EAT, Dr. Garner and his colleagues have come up with an even more detailed testing tool: the Eating Disorders Inventory (EDI).[7] The EDI goes a step further than the EAT in measuring subjects' general psychological attitudes in addition to their feelings about food and weight. The most current results of EDI testing indicate two significant differences between weight-preoccupied women who are neither anorexic nor bulimic, and anorexic and bulimic women: The weight-preoccupied women don't feel as personally ineffective, nor do they share the same lack of awareness of their own emotions, in comparison to the anorexics and bulimics.[8] However, Dr. Garner notes, "The weight-preoccupied women are less psychologically stable than women who aren't preoccupied with the issue."

Michael G. Thompson, Ph.D., and Donald M. Schwartz, Ph.D., used the EAT to identify "problem-free" and "anorexic-like" groups of normal-weight college women. The first group scored 5.6 on the average; the second, a 36 average. The researchers then compared the two groups with a third: women with anorexia nervosa. "The most dramatic finding," Thompson and Schwartz reported, "was the prevalence of anorexic-like behaviors among normally functioning college women. These women were not impaired in their work, though they often felt that they were struggling. The frequently intense feelings of inadequacy they reported appeared to arise from violation of high internal standards." As far as dieting goes, it was so widespread that the researchers found its frequency impossible to measure. Almost all of the anorexic-like women and many of the problem-free women said simply that they were always dieting.

Even the problem-free women, who did not share anorexic

attitudes with the other two groups, generally reported a constant preoccupation with the desire to eat and the need for willpower. "The overall impression," the researchers wrote, "is of women—anorexic and anorexic-like and problem-free—experiencing their hunger as exaggerated and obscene, secretly wishing to gratify their impulse to eat, and constantly fighting this impulse." Drs. Thompson and Schwartz concluded that "a high percentage of normal, college-age women, under no specific vocational pressure to remain thin, engage in high levels of anorexic-like behavior. Counseling staffs should be alerted to the widespread nature of eating-disordered behavior on campuses."[9]

Dr. Hawkins reports that from 11 to 15 percent of his normal-weight female college subjects regularly scored over 30 on the EAT. When he administered various personality tests to two groups of normal-weight women—one of which scored over 30 and the other under 30 on the EAT—he found that the high-scoring group showed more negative self-image, more neuroticism, more depression and more dieting than the under-30 scorers.[10]

What does the EAT ask? There are forty questions, and they range from "Like eating with other people" to "Find myself preoccupied with food" to "Feel extremely guilty after eating" to "Am terrified about being overweight" to "Engage in dieting behavior" to "Like my stomach to be empty" to "Avoid foods with sugar in them." The test also looks for more extreme behaviors, including whether the subject vomits, uses laxatives, drinks alcohol or exercises strenuously to burn calories.

There are six response choices: always, very often, often, sometimes, rarely and never. To score over 30 and fall into the "serious" category, you'd have to answer "often," "very often" or "always" to many of the extreme questions (such as "Have gone on eating binges where I feel I may not be able to stop" or "Vomit after I have eaten" or "Feel that food controls my life") as well as the more universal ones ("Eat diet foods," "Give too much time and thought to food").

The development of the EAT was significant because it allowed researchers to uncover a formerly hidden population of women who had never had anorexia, who appeared normal in weight and thus couldn't be identified as eating-disturbed by the naked eye of the psychologist, but who nonetheless were burdened with anorexic attitudes. The college campus provided a captive group of subjects to study. Soon, researchers such as Katherine Halmi, M.D., of Cornell University Medical College; Craig Johnson, Ph.D., of the Michael Reese Medical Center in Chicago; and Judith Cusin, M.S.W., and Dale Svendsen, M.D., of the Ohio State University Student Health Center followed Drs. Garner and Garfinkel's lead and administered the EAT to college students. One after another, they came back with alarming statistics that got worse depending upon what group they were looking at.

In the OSU study, for example, Cusin and Dr. Svendsen divided their female subjects into three groups: sorority women, dance majors, and regular coeds. They found that 9 percent of the regulars, 16 percent of the sorority members and 23 percent of the dance majors scored over 30 on the EAT, which is where Drs. Garner and Garfinkel drew the line for serious eating problems that indicate the symptoms of anorexia nervosa.

When the OSU researchers further broke down the responses, they found that 44.8 percent of the regular coeds, 53.5 percent of the sorority women and 64.8 percent of the dancers answered "often," "very often" or "always" to a question asking if they were "preoccupied with a desire to be thinner"; 29.3 percent, 53 percent and 52.8 percent respectively to "Terrified of being overweight"; 37.1, 44.1 and 62.1 percent to "Preoccupied with the thought of fat on my body"; 31.8, 40.4 and 54 percent to "Engage in dieting behavior." Obviously, anorexic attitudes, if not the actual illness, were not just common but rampant at OSU, and studies on other campuses suggest OSU is no exception.

"What college student really feels confident and competent?" asks OSU's Judy Cusin, who also treats bulimic women in individual and group psychotherapy. "An eating disorder is just one method of coping with those common feelings. Alcohol, drugs and depression are others. Women in college feel a pressure to be beautiful; they feel it is a time when they must shine and tend to be rigid in terms of their own performance demands. Often they were precocious kids who stood out in school until they hit college. There the competition and self-measurement intensify, because everyone around you used to shine back in high school, too."

It figures that sorority women, who have chosen a more socially oriented campus life and therefore tend to be even more appearance-conscious than non-Greek women, would score higher on the EAT than the latter. Sororities indeed are almost as notorious as ballet schools for the spawning and maintaining of anorexic attitudes and behavior, according to people who should know. "I am an officer of a sorority with approximately a hundred members, forty-five of whom live in the sorority house," says a woman at a midwestern university. "Many of our members are affected by eating disorders and evidence of self-induced vomiting has been found repeatedly in the bathrooms."

Holly, a member of a UC Berkeley sorority for three years, says that people often joke, "Oh, she's throwing up" when a member starts to lose weight. "I've walked into the bathroom at the sorority house and immediately had to leave because it smelled so bad from vomit." Though everyone in Holly's sorority worries about gaining weight, methods other than self-induced vomiting are frequently used to prevent the terror of fat. "A lot of girls count calories, most everyone goes on fad diets, and people say things like, 'I wish I could have anorexia for just a week or two.' When you're living with sixty-five girls, you're always comparing yourself to the skinny ones, wanting to be able to wear the clothes they do or look like them."

Holly considers herself about 10 pounds overweight, but prefers the Scarsdale Diet as a way to lose weight because "it helps me to discipline myself." She has either avoided or merely dabbled in some of the more extreme weight-control behaviors that her sorority sisters regularly engage in. "Over-the-counter diet pills are really popular in the sorority," she says, "because you can lose weight and stay up all night studying at the same time. Except every so often someone will carry it too far, especially if you drink. Drinking is big on campus, and lots of girls save all their calories for drinking by taking the diet pills so they don't eat. One girl passed out at a party because she'd taken so many diet pills and was drinking so much."

Among the sorority women she knows, Holly observes that fathers have an incredible influence, and usually a negative one. "They always want you to be thin. One girl I know had a father like that; she became anorexic and had to be hospitalized. In the hospital she gained weight and her father actually got mad at her. Another girl had a father who was in the movie business; she'd been heavy all her life, and her father didn't think having a fat daughter was good for his image. He kept sending her away to weight-loss clinics, and she'd lose weight, then come home and binge until she gained it all back. He even paid for her cocaine, because it helped her to lose weight. And these are the same kinds of fathers that like their daughters to be in a sorority so she can have the right kind of social life."

Holly points out that her particular sorority is less socially and more academically oriented than some; appearance pressure is even more intense in the more social houses. If you can bring glory to the house only by snaring the best men, then the methods you use to achieve the right look, which is always a thin look, can veer toward the extreme.

Renee, now a senior at the University of Arizona, belonged to such a social sorority. She'd never had a weight problem until freshman year—at 5'6", her weight in high school was about 110—but the simultaneous pressures of leaving home, trying to meet people at a big school, going through rush and having to look good every second lest she fail to get into the best sororities conspired together to make Renee eat to get rid of the pressure and thus worry even more—about her weight.

"All the people I was in contact with were throwing up," she says, "so I started to do it, too. At first it was physically uncomfortable, but then it got better. In the sorority, you eat and you throw up after meals. Period. Everyone is thin, pretty and outgoing, and you have to compete with everyone in the

house and with all the other sororities, too." Renee and her
friends practice their behavior openly, especially if they're
bored. "We go out together and spend thirty dollars on food,
knowing all the time that we'll throw it up. If we're somewhere
with only one bathroom, we take turns throwing up, but if there
are stalls, we'll do it at the same time."

Like most bulimic vomiters, Renee tries to diet between
binges. On diet days, she avoids social eating whenever possible. Unlike others who engage in the behavior, Renee is not
ashamed of it; she is, in fact, completely open about it—with her
boyfriends and family as well as with her sorority sisters. Once,
her brother wanted her to join him and several other friends for
dinner at a French restaurant. "I told him I was dieting and I
couldn't go, but he insisted. I said okay, after I explained to him
that I'd have to throw up the food. At the restaurant after the
meal, I got up and announced to the table that I was going off to
vomit, and everyone applauded."

Renee doesn't binge and vomit every day; the longest she's
gone without has been three weeks. But once she starts, often in
response to being upset with her boyfriend and not being able to
open up and show her feelings, she usually repeats it three or
four times, until she's so exhausted that she goes to sleep.
Despite her efforts to control her weight, Renee now weighs
130, and she hates it. "I'm bothered more by being heavy than
by bingeing and vomiting. My weight is my life, and when I'm
fat, I'm completely miserable."

What does Renee plan to do about her problems? "Maybe
once I graduate and get out of the sorority life, the bingeing and
vomiting will go away. But I doubt it. The only real reason I
want to stop is I'm afraid all the vomiting might affect my unborn
children. Otherwise, I just want to be thin, whatever it takes."

Another high-risk area of college life where bingeing and
vomiting is peer-approved is competitive athletics. Karen Lee-
Benner, R.N., M.S.N., clinical coordinator of UCLA's Eating
Disorders Clinic, treated two world-class gymnasts for bulimia.
She says that at least one of those patients told her that the

entire gymnastics team would binge and vomit together following a meet—a purely social thing.

One star gymnast on a major university's female team developed anorexia nervosa in conjunction with bingeing and vomiting up to ten times a day and had to be hospitalized. She'd been in training since the age of 10. For all those years, keeping slim wasn't just desirable; her future as an athlete literally depended upon it. The day-in, day-out pressure to maintain control, starting at such a young age and combined with a certain personality and family background, ultimately took a permanent toll on her future. But for a very long while, vomiting seemed the perfect solution to this athlete.[11]

Teammates aren't the only sources of weight-maintenance tips in a competitive college environment. Zealous coaches intent on a winning team—particularly in gymnastics, where the physical appearance of the athlete has a great deal to do with his or her performance in the eyes of a judge—have been known to suggest self-induced vomiting as a means of weight control to team members. Once the athlete realizes the magic of getting to eat whatever she wants for the first time in years of training and still being able to perform, the potential for chronic chaos is set up.

Even without the intensified peer pressure that comes with sorority life or the performance pressure of competitive college athletics, there's always the famous Freshman 10 to struggle with. It's the weight gain that so many women experience during their first year in college when they are separated from the family refrigerator and easy access to their mothers' shopping baskets, and confront instead starch- and sugar-laden dorm food. Freshmen men tend to lose weight that first year, which annoys their female peers. "In a coed situation," says one Radcliffe sophomore, "you want to eat what the men eat, but you gain and they lose."

Jan Henderson had never had a weight or eating problem before entering college, but she slowly began to put on weight during her first year at a large midwestern university, where she lived on campus in a dorm. "I wasn't bingeing," she says, "just eating dorm food and having snacks late at night after studying." By sophomore year, she started hearing comments from her family, especially her mother, who would say, "Go stand on the scale and let me see what you weigh." So Jan went on a diet— lots of exercise and skipping meals—and dropped 15 pounds. Then the weight crept back on, the comments started up again from her mother, her sisters and her boyfriend, and Jan began to binge regularly every time she was criticized about her weight. At a family picnic the summer before her junior year, "my cousin, who was anorexic, gave me the idea to vomit. She had learned it from her roommate, who'd heard it from her sister."

Once she'd learned about vomiting, Jan was eager to return to school where she could binge and vomit in peace without her mother nosing around. She knew it was wrong, but thought it was a great way to be able to eat what she wanted. Ultimately, Jan's bingeing and vomiting severely disrupted her life. First she was doing it a few times a week, then every day, then twice a day, and on up to ten times a day. En route, she also developed a drinking problem—begun, Jan insists, to help her stop eating. She finally sought inpatient treatment at a psychiatric hospital.

Again, it was the combination of a stressful environment with a certain vulnerable personality and probably a particular family history *along with* constant indulgence in a potentially addictive behavior that created such danger for Jan. Relatively few college women would be suffering from all of those factors at once; a far greater majority binge and diet, like Sarah, or binge and vomit only on special occasions.

Members of the latter group are "situational" binge-vomiters. They don't suffer from the intense psychological problems that Jan had; they may even like their bodies. They may simply be looking for a quick method of coping with temporary stress. Arnold E. Andersen, M.D., director of the Eating and Weight Disorders Clinic at The Johns Hopkins Hospital, notes that situational bulimia is common among college students, without known serious consequences for most people. For the situational binger or binge-vomiter, the behavior doesn't become habitual; the ongoing psychological need for it is lacking.

Overall, the very nature of the college life-style may create, especially for the female student, an upsetting tension between work orientation and dating concerns, says Dr. Hawkins. Interpersonal problems—such as rejection in love or academic difficulties—may precipitate overeating, with the expectation that "eating will make me feel better and who else cares about me anyway, so I might as well eat."[12]

Dr. Hawkins's on-campus research shows a roller-coaster effect between interpersonal relationships, lack of self-esteem, and confusion over professional goals. Bingeing has a knockout effect against such conflicts. The feelings that follow the binge—guilt and self-deprecation, plus the fear of weight gain—distract the binger from the original problem. At this point, says Dr. Hawkins, the binger makes the logical error of redefining her problem as being the uncontrolled eating itself, or her overweight appearance.

Because he believes that working to clarify professional goals is a firmer ground on which to build self-esteem than romantic relationships, which tend to be much less controllable, Dr. Hawkins emphasizes career planning in treatment of college women with food-control problems. Feeling directed plays a crucial role in getting a college woman past chaotic eating behavior, Dr. Hawkins stresses. When she gets involved with a new idea or project, she relates to her body and herself more positively, he says. The trick is to make that state of mind a permanent one by focusing closely on that idea or project—and channeling it into a viable direction for the future.

4

FEAR OF FAT:
JUST A WOMAN'S PROBLEM?

Jonathan

Jonathan Silverstein was feeling terrific. He was flying home to
Chicago first-class after a resoundingly successful business trip
around the country to New Orleans, Miami, Philadelphia, New
York, and Boston. As a photographers' agent, Jonathan made
these sweeps a few times a year to ad agencies and corporations
specializing in the manufacture, marketing and sale of clothing,
cosmetics, jewelry and accessories. Over breakfast or lunch or
dinner or drinks, he'd schmooze with his old, established accounts and make contact with new ones, all the while lining up
important gigs for his well-regarded stable of commercial photographers.

Jonathan pushed the recline button on his seat and sipped his
Perrier. He'd done pretty well for himself. Just 36, he was
pulling in maybe $70,000 a year and enjoying more of it than if
he were on a salary somewhere and unable to write off all of
those operating expenses. Considering that he'd been on his
own for just three years, he was in great shape.

It wasn't just the flush of financial success he felt at the
moment. He'd met a fabulous woman, Nina, in New Orleans,
the art director for one of the agencies he'd gone to see. She was
very responsive to his clients' work, and after a lengthy meeting
with Jonathan, she'd hired three of his photographers for major
ad campaigns. The meeting had begun at three, and by the time
they were winding down, it was after five. Jonathan had no plans
for the evening, so—taking a chance on the fact that she wore no
wedding band and hoping that he hadn't misread what seemed

to be a mutual sexual attraction underpinning their business talk—he asked her if they could finish things up over a drink.

Drinks led to dinner, and once they had shared a bottle of wine, they felt comfortable enough to drop the convenient shield of business gossip for more personal things. They exchanged life histories (both were divorced and both had come to similar conclusions about life and marriage that each had thought was unique to him/herself). Several Cognacs later, they were in bed together. For his remaining two nights in New Orleans, Jonathan's social life was thus pleasantly assured; and when he left for New York, Nina managed to line up some business there and went with him. After four fine days, they went their separate ways, he to Boston and she back to New Orleans, each promising to meet somewhere sometime soon.

So that was another unexpected pleasure of this trip, Jonathan thought—but even that wasn't the one he was most thrilled with. More than the money he'd made, more than the brief but passionate affair, was the fact that he hadn't lost control of his eating once during the entire seventeen-day trip, even though he was wining and dining in mostly excellent places. Of course, he could attribute his control partially to his fling with Nina. He hadn't experienced his usual feelings of social and sexual inadequacy with her, which after years of self-examination he had isolated as a binge trigger, because he'd encountered her on a business level first instead of a purely social one. He was always confident in a business situation. And being with her meant his other frequent binge trigger, loneliness, wasn't operative, either.

But he'd only been with Nina for a week, leaving another ten binge-free days. It was probably because he was doing heavy business, and when he had to perform in that situation he was always disciplined. On the road, he had to keep clear, sharp; there was no room in his schedule for blitzing out—that's how he thought of bingeing. Also, he would never allow himself to lose control in front of anyone else, and since he did so much business over meals, he was very careful.

He needed to be strong and together when traveling, and

because he needed to be, he was. He always felt more insecure when he was home. He wasn't exactly sure why, but he could feel the transformation. When he checked his bags at the airport, the in-control Jonathan took over immediately; when he picked them up at baggage claim, it was the reverse.

During his reverie, the stewardess had served dinner. Jonathan ate the salad and most of the fish and vegetables, but ignored the bread and rice. His plate had been cleared, and now the stewardess was wheeling the dessert cart through the cabin, serving cheese, crackers, fruit and what appeared to be an ice-cream bombe with chocolate sauce. When the cart got to him, he found himself asking for the bombe. With the sauce. He knew what was happening. He was switching into his on-the-outside-looking-in mode in preparation for the return home. He ate the bombe quickly, accepted the after-dinner chocolates from the stewardess and, with thirty-five minutes to go before landing at O'Hare, planned his evening. First a bag of peanut M & M's on the way to baggage claim, to tide him over during the cab ride home. Then he'd take the car, do a little marketing, stock up on plenty of ice cream. . . .

For the next five days, Jonathan went into his typical homecoming trance. He canceled the few social engagements he'd made before he left, turned down other invitations that came in upon his return, avoided everyone he knew and did only the most necessary business. He holed up in his condo, bingeing mostly on ice cream, with an occasional box of Ritz crackers or bag of pretzels for a salty, crunchy contrast.

"I turned it into a destructive hibernation of unhappiness, loneliness and negative feelings," Jonathan explained a few weeks later. "I've been doing it for years, but I'm more in control now, because as the years go on I accept myself more. Now it's not so serious, even when I'm doing it—I have more compassion for myself. I don't feel quite as lost, as caught up in insecurity. But it still brings me down and holds me back. I close myself down; I don't hear or feel as well.

"I know I'm trying to suffocate my feelings, to take myself out of the scene. I want to avoid facing up to things I don't want to face up to. I want to hide from people, even though being around them would probably help. When I come home from a trip, it usually means a week or two of being self-destructive with food." Jonathan talks fast and looks tired. His dark eyes have deep circles underneath, though he is, as usual, carefully groomed and fashionably dressed.

"Right now I'm not allowing myself to pig out, because I'm leaving for New York on Monday and there's a battle going on in my head to maintain control and not give in to my weaker, self-destructive side. That's why I look so strained. I'm feeling a lot of anxiety right now, because I'm battling my desire to get away from this table, to get home alone and binge. My stronger side knows that I need to be in good shape, physically and mentally, when I leave on Monday. But since the last trip and the last binge, I've been regressing a bit. I always go on a strict diet after one of my binges, and this month I was right in the middle of the diet when my dad went into a coma and died. I knew it was no time to be weak.

"I think that part of my giving up control has to do with holding on to being a kid and not taking total responsibility for my actions. But whatever fluctuation I have between man and boy, I knew I had to assume the man role and be strong for my family when my father went into the coma. It's only been a month since he died, and after it was all over, I guess the boy in me reasserted himself and I started in on the food thing again. Now I'm trying to get the man back."

Jonathan traces his problems with food back to the age of 12, when his family moved to a new city in the Midwest. Before the move, Jonathan was his school's number one athlete and had his own fan club of adoring little girls. "I was a real somebody there, and then we moved and I was nobody. It freaked me out. I became reclusive and stopped feeling proud of myself. I started eating; and from that point on, food was always an issue for me.

"When I was younger, I was more self-destructive. I binged all the time. I thought about food all the time. I fluctuated between bingeing until I felt sick and waiting for the ability to eat again. I didn't feel any enjoyment. I knew it was a self-destructive thing and I was anxiety-ridden about it. The pattern was always this: In the morning I'm strong, strong enough to withhold from bingeing, strong enough to really go on a diet; and as the day wears on, I weaken and give in."

Jonathan is 5'11". Though now he never allows his weight to go over 190 (he fluctuates between 170 and 190, and can go up and down maybe 7 pounds in any given week), he was up to 235 when he was in college. It was the first time he'd ever been away from home, and his feelings of social inadequacy were painfully heightened. The more inadequate he felt, whether with women or men, the more he ate.

"I thought being heavy was a good scapegoat, a shield, something to blame my inadequacy on. And it was an excuse for not doing anything about my problems. People never thought I was fat, because I was big-boned and could carry it pretty well."

After college, Jonathan got a job in a photo lab. He wanted to be a professional photographer, and his plan was to shoot as many pictures as he could in his spare time and try to sell them to newspapers and magazines. He had access to the lab's darkroom and other equipment, which was the main reason he wanted the job. But after a year of trying to get together a portfolio, shlepping it around to various publications and photo agencies and not even getting close to an audience with an art director, he was ready to give up. Failing to reach the goal he had long aspired to motivated more than one binge during this period. He tried one more agency, and though again there was no interest in his work, he managed to get an audience with the photo editor, who just happened to be looking for an assistant. Jonathan got the job.

He did well at the agency, slowly gaining more responsibility and, accordingly, more self-confidence. His weight went down to 210 as his binge episodes lessened. He was feeling much better about himself, better than he had since he was 12. In this positive state of mind, his social life picked up. He was dating more, taking more risks, and when he was 24 he fell in love with Beth, a woman he'd met through one of his colleagues at work. The feeling was mutual: After four months of their affair, Beth and Jonathan moved in together; and four months after that, they were married.

One of the things that secured Jonathan's relationship with Beth was the discovery, shortly after moving in together, that they shared the same problems with food control. Beth had been heavy as a kid, dieted throughout high school and began bingeing in college, but with ever-stricter diets she had managed to keep her weight down to a reasonable level. When they were in the first flushes of love and sex with each other, it was easy for both Jonathan and Beth to forget about food. But after they'd set up house and settled into a routine, Beth confessed to being a binger one night over dinner when she was feeling bad about eating too much ice cream.

Jonathan, who had felt the same thing and was already considering making up an excuse to get out of the house so he could buy and eat another pint in secrecy, never loved Beth more than at that moment: She had the same conflict he had, with all the same feelings of self-hatred, and lack of control, and isolation. He, too, confessed, and she felt the same intimacy and relief. Together, they vowed to help each other control and ultimately eliminate the urge to binge. That night, instead of eating more ice cream, they made intense love.

For the first year of marriage, Beth and Jonathan really did help each other with the eating thing. Though one or the other of them would occasionally slip and binge, they would admit it afterward, and knowing they could do that and not be judged lessened the self-hatred and pretty much prevented one binge from becoming two or three or four. But, imperceptibly, things began to change. For the worse. Sometime during the second year of marriage, Jonathan and Beth began growing apart.

Jonathan had begun to travel for the agency and was usually away from home a few days a month. The traveling set off mutual insecurities. One night Jonathan called Beth from his hotel, and because it was 11:00 P.M. and there was no answer, he began to suspect her of fooling around. He called again the next morning at 7:00; again, no answer. Beth was *always* at home at 7:00; she didn't get to work until 9:30, and her alarm was set for 8:00 every weekday morning. Obviously, she'd spent the night with another man.

Jonathan didn't believe Beth when she told him that she'd spent the night with her friend Tricia; that she'd heard strange noises around the apartment and had gotten scared and driven over to Tricia's to sleep on the couch. Beth, frustrated and upset that Jonathan didn't believe her and continued to make reference to that night, began to think that maybe he was guilty of what he accused her of; why else did he persist? So one night when she came home late from work and he started in on her with sarcasm—"I suppose you've been with Tricia"—she shot back, "You're so obsessed with this fantasy that it's probably your own guilt for cheating on *me* during one of your precious trips!" Jonathan slammed out of the apartment and jumped into the car. He headed directly for the nearest Baskin-Robbins, bought a pint of jamoca almond fudge and ate it with a plastic spoon in the parking lot. He ate it so fast he got a headache.

He's not sure, even now, why this whole thing with Beth started happening. Deep down, he really didn't think she was having an affair, but he wanted to doubt her. "Maybe things had been going too good," he said. "That sounds ridiculous, but often I feel that I don't deserve to be happy.

"Anyway, from this point on, the marriage started to fall apart, and we both used bingeing to help along its downfall. I'm convinced we did it, or at least I did, to get myself from a good frame of mind into a negative one, into feeling bad about myself. Then it could serve as an excuse to start a fight. I put on about twenty pounds.

"We separated when I was twenty-eight and began divorce proceedings. I decided I was sick of being heavy and went to a diet doctor, who gave me pills. I got down to one-eighty-five, about thirty-five pounds less than I'd been, and was feeling great. But after the divorce I can remember going out, getting laid, feeling good—and not even allowing myself to get home with the good feelings, because I'd stop at a doughnut shop on the way. I went through a period of feeling paranoid, unhappy.

"I got caught up in drugs—'ludes, coke, and I was smoking a lot more grass—as a social thing. Just what everyone else was doing. I had a good time with it, but now I see it as being self-destructive, having to have something in my mouth all the time, like the food. Only food was more of a habit for me, and the food issue isn't as cut-and-dried as drugs, because you have to eat. But like the food, the drugs were a way of getting comfortable, not dealing with the feelings I had. I would have been better off without them.

"When I wasn't bingeing or doing drugs, I was still feeling bad. Finally I decided that I didn't want to live my life that way. I began a self-improvement program. I went into therapy, and that's helped me get a clearer picture of myself and why I do things. I pretty much stopped doing drugs, and I made an effort to meet people who were more positive, more together.

"I feel that I've continued to go forward in a lot of ways. I no longer feel that I need to control people and situations to be happy. I'm trying to set things up so that I win whether things go my way or not. My acceptance of myself has increased in all areas. Though I still have a tendency to hide my feelings, I'm more able to be unhappy around people and not care that they know.

"As time goes on, I'm better at really enjoying a big meal and not waking up in the morning and feeling awful about it and then setting myself up by getting into a negative frame of mind so I can do it again and again. I think that's growth.

"I know the food thing is one of the last negative things I'm going to let go of. But I've run out the pattern so many times—the holing up and canceling out my feelings by bingeing and cutting myself off and then taking control—that now I know I can come out of it. I know the pattern is running its course and the time will come when it will no longer happen because I'll no longer need it."

Danny

Danny had never been big on moderation. He liked his highs high and his lows low. If he wanted to do something well, he wanted to do it beyond compare; if he wanted to fail, then the failure must be abysmal. Many times he really preferred to fail; it was more comfortable down there. Besides, he never quite trusted his success. On the one hand, he knew he was a genius; but on the other hand, he suspected he might be a fraud and that all his grandiose visions of his own creativity were just that—visions. To avoid learning the truth, Danny made sure to fail periodically, at this gig or that relationship or whatever was going on. When he allowed himself to succeed, everyone took notice, because he was more than talented; he was special.

That was a given from childhood. Danny had a famous father whose picture was always in the paper, and he and his older sister were the only Jewish kids in the neighborhood. He was considered a prodigy—his IQ was so high that people from the university were forever coming to test him. But it wasn't so great being special then, because it also meant being different, and when you're a kid, you want to be like everyone else. Until he was 16, it never occurred to Danny to get anything but A's; it was simply expected.

Then his father—his moody, quiet, famous father—turned the gas on and killed himself, and Danny got D's and F's for the first time. He'd always kept himself in check before for fear of embarrassing his father, who, after all, had been a public figure. Now Danny figured he could, *would,* get totally messed up.

He certainly didn't mind getting back at his mother once his father was dead. He'd always found her to be mean, sarcastic, verbally abusive to nearly everyone in her path, including his father. Danny and his sister credited their mother with their own massive inferiority complexes; she had a gift for making you feel like dirt. When Danny was a skinny, scrawny little kid, she'd make fun of him, telling him he looked like a "CARE package." At his father's funeral, his mother, in front of everyone, turned to Danny and screamed, "I bet you wish it was me in that coffin!" She was always creating some kind of scene— yelling in public, passing out. She even made a botched suicide attempt not long after Danny's father succeeded in his. Danny was always mortified by his mother's histrionics. In defense, he learned how to steel himself, how to maintain total deadpan cool in public.

Danny maintained the facade into adulthood, though his mother was no longer an issue. Now 29, he augments his act with certain details of dress: punkish dark glasses, boots, lots of black clothing. Put that on his long, lean frame and he looks as tough as anyone walking the streets of Greenwich Village, where he lives, and paints when he's not strung out. It surprises him that others sometimes find him scary, intimidating, impenetrable, for he thinks of himself as "tapioca packed in armor."

Saddled with a good deal of insecurity and a demanding ego (it often amused Danny that the two usually went hand in hand), it was difficult to live life level. He swallowed his first tab of mescaline when he was 14, and quickly added speed, grass, acid and a host of downers to his repertoire. The drugs very neatly took care of keeping his highs high and his lows low. With the help of one or another substance, he could easily lose himself or dull himself at will. What he couldn't stand was being clear. Clarity brought him too close to the anxiety of accomplishment, of productivity, of fulfilling his own potential.

At 21, his paintings hung in a prestigious Manhattan gallery. His art was discussed and debated by the most eminent critics, who used flattering, if inflated, phrases to describe it: "the power and the purity," "scathing symbolism," "awesome prowess and promise." The acclaim gratified his ego and stoked his insecurities. Though Danny knew his work was wholly original, he fantasized that someone would expose him as a plagiarist.

When people actually began to collect his work in earnest and the gallery owner asked for more pieces, Danny proceeded to sabotage himself. He upped his intake of drugs so that he was always either going way up or crashing way down. Both directions freed him of the ability to concentrate, and so he was unable to paint except in crazed spurts motivated by whatever upper happened to be in his blood. When he came down—from the coke, the crystal, the black beauty—he'd see that what he'd produced was junk. He'd rip it up and, to escape his self-hatred, would pop a 'lude or a few Valiums or some codeine, or, if he was flush, he'd shoot smack. The only intoxicant he had no taste for was alcohol, because alcohol neither calmed him nor upped him, just made him depressed.

It didn't take more than six months to accomplish his goal: The word in New York art circles was that Danny had burned out. No more "awesome promise." He'd even managed to drive away the woman he'd lived with for two years, whom he'd almost loved in spite of himself. But at this point, because Danny could never quite give up on himself after all, he knew he had to pull himself out of his custom-designed hole.

He had to stop the spiral of drugs, so he turned to food. Food calmed him, dulled him. Fortunately, he was naturally slim, and the few pounds he gained came off easily with occasional stretches of fasting and sometimes vomiting. But Danny feared he'd lost the ability to regulate his intake. Food became a drug that, like all drugs, he used to excess. He'd go up and down Broadway buying granola bars and oatmeal cookies and dried fruits and nuts (he'd tell himself that health-food-store sweets were better than stuff from the A&P). He'd eat his bagfulls on long, sick walks through Riverside Park.

Slowly he was able to paint again. But his canvas would often be marked by food stains, since he would get up every few minutes and pull something from the fridge—a fingerful of peanut butter, or eight carrots dunked in mustard, or bread smeared with jam. On one occasion, after a frustrating bout in front of the canvas, he actually ran from his apartment to a corner bodega and bought himself a half-dozen apples, which he proceeded to eat, though by the fourth he was already repelled. This done, and his stomach swelled and throbbing, he stumbled into a Spanish takeout restaurant for a plate of rice and beans. He was, by now, almost too bloated to walk. His face felt swollen and his eyes were flushed and glazed.

He thought it was disgusting that he had to stuff himself with such a frenzy, because it meant that his life was never full enough. Oddly, he didn't regard an excess of drugs in quite the same way; they enhanced life. Also unlike drugs, Danny's food abuse made him feel ashamed of himself. He thought it—
unmanly.

Robert

How he deals with the bread is a giveaway: Without looking at the basket, without taking his eyes from his dining companions, he plucks and eats piece after piece, but pays so little attention to his actions that they appear to be unconscious. Other bingers, particularly women, are much more careful when eating with others. They don't want anyone tuning in to their behavior and will go to great lengths to fool their companions by picking at their food, declining dessert, getting people to think that food is just food to them; planning their gratification for later when they will be alone. Not Robert Davino.

Davino's business—not, in retrospect, coincidentally—is food and wine, as it has been for twenty years. "I was drawn to the food area," he says, "as a drug addict is drawn to growing poppies." He began in the field fresh out of college as a writer for restaurant-industry publications, spent ten years in a position of high responsibility for a prestigious food magazine, and was soon widely recognized as a specialist in his field. Five years ago, he acquired enough financial backing to begin his own specialty publishing company. It surprised no one that the venture was a success.

Robert, who is always well-dressed and witty, returned ten days ago from a three-week eating trip through France with one of his more famous authors, a food critic and writer of cookbooks. During those three weeks, Robert and his author ate approximately sixty meals in restaurants of the highest repute. The author, as was his practice, sampled a little of everything and completed the tour at the same weight he began it. But Robert, who secretly had been terrified of the trip from the start, gained 15 pounds. From the very first meal, he just blew it. Immediately upon returning home, he began a rigid diet. Five days after his return, he ended the diet with an all-day binge on forbidden sweets and carbohydrates.

Robert is convinced that he has a biochemical dysfunction; that it is an actual physical need that drives him, not just a psychological need. It's been going on for so long, as long as he can remember. He has never led a normal eating life; it's always been bingeing and dieting. When Robert eats just one forbidden food, one cookie, one spoonful of ice cream, he truly fears that if he tried to stop himself from eating more he wouldn't survive—the compulsion is that strong. The physical discomfort preceding a binge is intense; the headaches remind him of Eve's in *The Three Faces of Eve*. They can come over him anywhere, at any time when he has been dieting. He can eliminate them only by bingeing.

Robert, who is 42, fears that he won't reach his fiftieth birthday unless he can cure what he regards as his food addiction. "I must lick the problem," he says. "I am at the midpoint of my life. I am successful in my business, yet I feel inadequate around men who are slim, who leave food on their plates. They are self-assured, in control. I must get control. I must be able to decide what I'm going to eat and then eat it. Not just be driven. I must rid myself of the compulsion, whatever it takes. But when I 'split' and go on a binge, all of those thoughts fly out of my head."

Split. Robert feels it not just with food. For him, sex is food's Siamese twin, so intertwined are they in compelling Robert's behavior. When one rises, the other falls, in a lifelong rhythm. As far as food goes, Robert can't accept himself out of control, fat; as far as sex goes, he can't accept his need for other men. The slimmer he gets, the more he craves sex, yet he deeply fears the gay life-style, its dangers and diseases. To avoid *that* craving, he turns to food, which means safety. Once he gets fat, he is no longer desirable on the gay circuit.

The protection Robert seeks is not just for himself, but also for his wife of nearly twenty years and their 10-year-old son. He married in part because he badly wanted a heterosexual life-style and a family; he had been actively gay, with a few heterosexual experiences thrown in, since the age of 18. Though his wife knew of his homosexuality before they married, Robert has kept his frequent postmarital homosexual encounters hidden from her. He has tried to confine them to anonymous one-night stands that pose little emotional risk. The few times there was a threat of involvement, Robert immediately gained weight. "It took me out of the running; each time I was dropped. As soon as the men noticed my compulsive need to eat, they thought something was wrong with me. I was both hurt and relieved each time.

"I highly value my marriage. I'm frightened and repelled by the homosexual life-style, but I'm still drawn to it. When I deprive myself of food and get very slim, I feel like a stud and want sex with my wife every night. I also feel the strong compulsion to get approval, sexual approval, from men. When I'm fat, I know I'll be rejected by men, so I stay home and eat. If I had my druthers, I'd prefer to be slim and sexually straight, but I don't think I can eradicate forty-two years of either problem. Nor can I accept myself where I am right now." At a shade under 5'11", his weight ranges from 180 to 240.

It's not easy for Robert to look back at the genesis of his twin conflicts. He knows it all comes from somewhere, but he feels that with things going so well for him now in so many areas, he ought to be able to forget his childhood. Of course, his fear of professional failure never leaves him; even though his projects are consistently applauded by his colleagues, he is always sure that the next one will fail.

Robert's childhood was, by any standard, traumatic. It's easy to see where food and sex and compulsion and fear and safety got all mixed up.

Robert was the product of a middle-class Italian family from Detroit. His father worked for an international construction firm and was constantly traveling; it seems that the family was only together for carbohydrate-laden Sunday dinners of spaghetti and bread. Robert came to associate those carbohydrates with his fleeting and infrequent sense of family.

But his mother was his real trauma. She had very strong insecurities of her own, plus a food-control problem that kept her weight fluctuating by 80 pounds up and down. From the time Robert was 6, he and his mother had a daily routine together: She beat him in the morning and, penitently, fed him all afternoon. At night Robert would wet his bed, fearful of the next day's beating; in the morning, his bed-wetting served as his mother's excuse to punish him. The bed-wetting, the beating and the feeding did not cease until Robert was 13, when he went off to boarding school.

As a protection and solace during those seven years of childhood, Robert developed a rich and vivid fantasy life. He spent his free time at the movies, accompanied by all the popcorn and candy he could carry into the theater. He loved all the pretty, frothy films of the day, especially the Betty Grable musicals, and the ones with strong family stories.

As a teen-ager weighing 220 pounds, he was ridiculed by his peers. He began to fear his homosexual tendencies, though he didn't act on them until he was 18. He didn't want to be gay and fought his feelings from the first. He wanted peer approval, and he knew he'd never get it if he were fat and gay. "I was the jolly stereotype of the fat man, and it felt ridiculous. I felt that if I looked different, I'd act different, *be* different. I wanted to be normal, gung-ho, Joe College."

When Robert was a junior in high school, he went on his first diet—the Rockefeller Diet—but it wasn't until he entered college, when Metrecal wafers were introduced to the public, that he lost a significant amount of weight. The wafers kept him slim throughout college despite regular binges. He felt attractive and was sexually active with both men and women.

Five years out of college, he was working in the food business and pursuing an exclusively gay life-style. Though his body was trim, he wasn't happy with the life-style. That's when he met Linda, the woman who would become his wife. They had in common a problem with overweight and compulsive eating; they worked in the same field; and they both wanted a family. Linda was aware of Robert's homosexuality and was willing to help him "overcome" it.

As soon as he and Linda got engaged, Robert began to gain weight. By the time of the marriage six months later, he'd put on 25 pounds. In hindsight, this was a protective measure against the lures of homosexuality. What Linda was protecting wasn't quite as obvious, but she, too, put on a good deal of weight. Together they made periodic visits to a now infamous Dr. Feelgood in Manhattan. Each time Robert and Linda emerged from the doctor's office on Central Park South, they carried a box filled with pills, all in different colors. They were instructed to take five a day.

For three years they took pills and stayed thin, but as soon as Robert, who feared he was becoming addicted, went off them, his weight went back up to 240. Then he discovered Weight Watchers; he remembers the period as "the most successful sixteen weeks of my life." His weight dropped back down to 180, but eventually it went up again.

Since starting his publishing company, he's been on the Stillman, Scarsdale, and Beverly Hills diets and others in between binges, but his weight has continued to rise. The constant anxiety of getting a new business off the ground is surely a factor, but there are others of at least equal significance. For one, at about the same time Robert went into business for himself, his wife lost a good deal of weight and has kept it off for five years.

Robert admits that Linda's success exacerbated his problems. "I resented it, and I know that's my problem to work out; she's entitled to all the compliments she gets. But her weight loss made me feel less adequate, because she'd been successful at something I've been a failure at all my life. Before, I had felt stronger than my wife in so many areas, and I liked being the protector and provider. Now she was stronger than I."

His ex-analyst (dropped because Robert found him "cold, insensitive, not attuned to my problems") had a few theories to explain Robert's desperation. The analyst suggested that Robert's professional success was literally killing him; that he would do better to pursue a less anxious life-style that would not propel him to use food as an escape from the pressures of business. The analyst also felt that if Robert simply stopped his homosexual activity, his problem with food would cease. "I don't want to do any of that," Robert insists. "I want to be able to accept success and learn to treat my body as a healthy organism. And I can't imagine leading my life entirely straight.

"My analyst thinks I am literally committing suicide with food. I don't think I want to do myself in, though it may be a very insidious poison. I console myself when I hear about others with the same problem. Food is a friend. It fortifies my body and wards off cold, attack; it gives me strength. But I also know that right now I'm hiding from my own success behind a wall of fat.

"I want to accept myself. I know I have some fantastic qualities. But men can't be out of control; and when I'm eating, I'm not in control. It's become a big factor in my professional life. Before, I worked for others and wore their banners, but now everything I do reflects my own company. That's why I've got to stop this addiction."

Where the Men Are

> Mention *binge* to a woman and she'll say *food*. Mention it to a man and he'll say *alcohol*.
>
> Ray Hawkins, Ph.D.

For Danny, food abuse was the lesser evil, the alternative to other abuses that he judged to be more self-destructive, and also more pleasurable. He didn't experience the back-to-back drives that women with all levels of food-abuse behavior share: fear of fat and desire to be thin. But he does share with them the self-hatred that comes with loss of self-control.

Ironically, Danny could be out of his mind on drugs and not worry about being out of control. Drugs were pleasurable; drugs were sexy; drugs made him feel good. Food was different. Food filled him, dulled him, but didn't give him the high that he got from drugs, the high that eclipsed the unwelcome thought that told him he needed something with which to fill his life. When Danny was bingeing on food, he was always aware of that need. He much preferred drugs as a way of blitzing out of life, but he knew that drugs were destroying his specialness, and that made him feel guilty.

Jonathan used food as a way of quelling anxiety and avoiding social interaction and adult responsibility. His history of binge eating was a long one, starting in early adolescence, and his experience of himself as a fat person had equal longevity. Accordingly, his fear of fat was at least equal to his fear of losing control. Unlike Danny, Jonathan chose food as his primary substance to abuse. Food was *it*.

Robert's relationship to food was far more intense than Danny's or Jonathan's. Robert experienced himself as a Jekyll-and-Hyde personality on many levels—sexual, social, emotional, physiological—and his myriad connections to food were so entangled with memories of his abusive mother that he often felt his very life was threatened by his behavior. Food was Robert's champion and his enemy; it protected him and left him vulnerable; it was a way out of himself and a way in. Food was promiscuity and celibacy. Food was Robert's life.

Virtually nothing has been written about a hidden population of male food abusers—men of relative accomplishment like Jonathan, Robert and Danny. The assumption has been that men don't turn to food to fulfill emotional needs as women do. However, it's an oft-mentioned fact that men are less likely than women to seek psychological counseling for any problem; and if the problem happens to be something that men aren't supposed to have, it would follow that they'd keep away in droves. If men don't come in for treatment, there's no way for researchers to draw conclusions about them.

The little that has been written about men in the area of eating disorders stems from studies involving obese and anorexic males. A British physician named Richard Morton was the first known writer to describe a case of male anorexia nervosa, in 1689. He was also the first to offer a clear medical analysis of the disease itself. Dr. Morton's report concerned the 16-year-old son of a minister who "fell gradually into a total want of Appetite, occasioned by his studying too hard, and the Passions of his Mind . . . without any Cough, Fever, or any other Symptom . . . And therefore I judg'd this Consumption to be Nervous. . . ."[1]

Researchers estimate that men make up about 10 percent of the anorexia-nervosa population, and they appear to share some of the concerns of female anorexics, including the fear of fat and the need to establish a sense of control. As A. H. Crisp, M.D., and others have noted, both sexes also share a fear of growing up, and use dieting and weight loss as a way to turn back their physiological clocks and escape the emotional and social demands of adolescence.

Dr. Crisp has observed that a sexual conflict, whether real or imagined, has often triggered the onset of anorexia nervosa in both male and female patients. However, for females this conflict is most typically heterosexual; for males, it is frequently homosexual. Dr. Crisp wrote that in four out of six cases of male anorexia nervosa he'd seen, homosexual conflict preceded onset of the illness.[2] From a sociological standpoint, it would indeed seem that homosexual, but not heterosexual, activity or fantasy in teen-age boys might trigger the same feelings of guilt and confusion that heterosexual activity or fantasy might in teen-age girls.

According to British researchers Peter Dally and Joan Gomez, male anorexics don't seem to develop the same obsession with cooking that females do; and though both sexes tend to be intelligent and of the upper social classes, males are more often underachievers, working hard but often in a chaotic and haphazard way, unlike the obsessively ordered work rituals that female anorexics typically develop.[3] Males are also considered more difficult to treat, come from more emotionally disturbed families and, overall, have a more dismal prognosis than females, says John Sours, M.D.[4]

There are male restrictor anorexics and bulimic anorexics, as with females, but excessive exercise is said to be more commonly practiced among men than is self-induced vomiting, and laxative or diuretic abuse is rarely if ever mentioned among men. In reference to male bulimics, Richard Pyle, M.D., of the University of Minnesota Hospitals, says that "there's no pattern, no typical age of onset, no consistent similarities in eating behavior. The only consistency I've observed is that overexercising is more often used to compensate for bingeing than vomiting is."

Hilde Bruch, M.D., and others have noted that anorexia most typically occurs in preadolescent boys, with the age of onset somewhere between 10 and 13, as opposed to girls, who have generally entered puberty and are between the ages of 14 and 18. Dr. Bruch speculated that the psychobiological impact of the male sex hormones may in part explain why anorexia nervosa affects so few males: "Male pubescence will flood a boy with such powerful new sensations of a more aggressive self-awareness that the event of puberty makes a new self-assertion possible, something he was not capable of in prepuberty."[5] Such sensations of power and aggressiveness, then, would give the adolescent male a feeling of adequacy that he may have lacked before, thus protecting him from "needing" anorexia nervosa.

According to Dr. Sours, a trio of fears often underlies the development of anorexia nervosa in males: fear of fatness, fear of femininity and fear of sexuality.[6] Dr. Crisp and colleagues noted that only very obese males or those with major sexual-identity problems are likely to diet and possibly go on to develop anorexia nervosa, as opposed to the quite common female-adolescent desire to be slim.[7] It's more typical of the adolescent male to wish to be bigger and stronger.

Physical exercise has traditionally been to males what dieting has been to females: a peer-approved, media-promoted means of attaining bodily perfection. And though many studies have shown that males have a more accurate picture of the dimensions of their own bodies than females do, certain young boys may develop a distorted body image, with or without anorexia nervosa, while trying to be bigger and stronger. According to Karen Lee-Benner, R.N., M.S.N., clinical coordinator of UCLA's Eating Disorders Clinic, one young man hospitalized for anorexia nervosa had been bicycling compulsively 50 miles a day in his attempt to emulate Arnold Schwarzenegger. He stressed his body so extremely that his hip joints degenerated and he had to undergo bilateral hip surgery.

Often, male runners are said to get hooked into a spiral of

anorexic behaviors and attitudes in which the merest fantasized suspicion of fat will produce an orgy of purge behaviors. "Many long-distance runners, mostly men, astoundingly resemble adolescents with typical anorexia nervosa," wrote Dr. Sours. "They are hyperactive, full of energy, and hardly ever tire. They restrict their food intake, go on food fasts to attain the ideal weight, and follow repetitive and routinized daily exercise programs with intense dedication. The fear of fat is constantly with them. They can only freely eat if they first run long distances, the reverse of the bulimic vomiter who eats first and then rids herself of food. Body-image distortions are common. Many runners cannot believe that they are thin, for they tend to overestimate their body size. They distrust their body percep-tions, unless they are photographed along the course."[8] When psychotherapist Steven Levenkron asked a 15-year-old boy hospitalized with anorexia nervosa who his role models were, Levenkron got this reply: "Of course, I'm a runner. Everything I read tells me to lose weight. All the books on running describe how you're supposed to be thinner than other men. I read one book that said, 'We runners are loners, different and separate from other men. . . .' "[9]

Gretchen Goff, M.P.H., coordinator for bulimia treatment in outpatient psychiatry at the University of Minnesota Hospitals, mentions a male patient in one of the bulimia groups who binges and runs. Meir Gross, M.D., head of child and adolescent psychiatry at the Cleveland Clinic, had a male bulimic patient who compensated for bingeing by exercising four to five hours a day. Because of the time involved, the man was unable to hold down a job. Dr. Pyle had a middle-aged male bulimic anorexic patient who compensated for his binges by overexercising, fasting and taking saunas. The patient couldn't lose enough weight merely by dieting and exercising, says Dr. Pyle, so he'd stay in the sauna for as long as an hour at a time.

There are a handful of case histories to describe and much speculation, but there are still few known facts about male anorexia nervosa. However, at least it can be *seen*—although it's often misdiagnosed because so many doctors simply don't expect to see anorexia in a male patient. But sniffing out normal-looking young men with food-control problems is near impossible.

Once you get away from the extremes of anorexia and obesity, the combination of internal and external pressures that drive men into chaotic eating patterns may be quite different in nature than they are for women. It's hard to argue the conclusion reached by University of Cincinnati researchers Orland W. Wooley, Susan C. Wooley and Sue R. Dyrenforth, after examining countless studies, that "fat is a woman's problem more than a man's because less deviation from 'ideal' is allowed women."[10] Yet the average woman has twice as much fat on her body as the average man—and in far more conspicuous places. The tension resulting from the clash of cultural ideal against physiological reality creates a sort of trampoline effect: Women can push off, but inevitably bounce back to the source of tension.

This damned-if-you-do, damned-if-you-don't pressure, from which men on the whole are pretty much exempt, helps to explain a fascinating observation made in 1963 by researchers K. Krumbacher and J. E. Meyer. In studying the fluctuations of appetite in normal people under stress, Krumbacher and Meyer found that women were four times as likely as men to react by either undereating or overeating; the *absence* of any change in appetite under stress was observed three times more frequently in men than in women. The conclusion? Women may be predisposed to react orally to stress.[11]

The more pronounced the emphasis on your physical appearance as the key to success, the more likely it is that you will come to entangle self-image with body image, for already you are being judged by the people you want to please primarily on how you look. If that is how you are measured and evaluated by your peers, that's how you'll come to measure and evaluate yourself. Once you've tied your self-image up tightly enough with your body image, you're in danger of defining yourself as a worthwhile or worthless person based on whether you're thin or fat. Thus, a gain in weight that may be merely annoying to someone who keeps self-image and body image in their proper places is experienced as a direct blow to self-esteem by someone who doesn't. Women are widely familiar with this feeling; so, apparently, are gay men.

In fact, one place in American society in which the pressures on men to maintain perfect bodies in order to achieve social and sexual success may equal the pressures on women is in the gay community. The fact that homosexual men tend to police their bodies more rigidly than heterosexual men in response to their particular peer culture suggests that dieting, bingeing and related behaviors may be relatively common in that culture. Gay men, like women, are more likely to feel the self-deprecating side of the behavior, because the stakes are so much greater and the peer judgment of overweight so much harsher than for heterosexual men. "Most men who tell me they binge," notes Dr. Hawkins, "don't experience it as depressing, the way women do, but as a good time; the emotional tone is different. The men I've seen who do experience a binge as a highly negative act have frequently been homosexual."

In the gay world, sexual opportunities are ever-present and ever-changing. The constant opportunities for new partners and brief encounters make physical appearance more important than ever. As in a heterosexual singles' bar, where contact must be made and often consummated in the brief space of one evening, there's little time to discover the nonvisual attributes of a potential partner.

"Sexually speaking, it's a pretty competitive world," admits Tony, a gay male from Washington, D.C., in his mid-twenties. "Unless you're really, really tops in your field, and your field is a creative one like photography or design, your professional stature isn't nearly as important as your clothes, your body—how *GQ [Gentleman's Quarterly,* the fashion magazine] you look. If you're paunchy, forget it. The community is practically pathological when it comes to fat. No one's going to pick up on you if you're fat, unless you're *both* fat, and I don't see that too often around here."

Fred, 30 and gay, lives in San Francisco and says he is bulimic. "There's so much pressure to look good. You're always in the gym working out in tight Dolfins [nylon briefs]. They look terrible if you're flabby. You have to do all kinds of things to keep the devil away. I do fifty push-ups every day and lift weights. I run at least two miles or swim a half-mile every other day. I never let myself eat sweets or stuff like that except when I pig out, a few times a month.

"After a pig-out, I don't show up at the gym for a day or two or three 'cause my stomach is real bloated-looking. Instead, I work out like mad at home where no one can see me and I run at least five miles a day for the next few days. If I have some coke or speed, I'll do it so I don't get hungry; but even without it, I try not to eat anything for two days."

Like most men, gay or straight, and unlike most women, Fred doesn't pay attention to his weight per se—he doesn't own a scale and has no "magic number" beyond which he must not climb. Instead, he focuses on the way his clothes fit and look on his body and on the "fat feeling." Fred relies on exercise, food restriction and, occasionally, drugs to counteract his "pig-outs," rather than purging.

At present, the view in many professional circles is that most nonanorexic men who indulge in self-induced vomiting are likely to have a practical rather than psychological need for the behavior. "The men we see get into it because of their professions," explains Dr. Gross, who has treated many male wrestlers, dancers and actors for bingeing and vomiting. In such fields, which demand a low body weight for maximum performance and success, the pressure to remain svelte is not just a cosmetic matter; one's very livelihood depends on it. But as we've seen, the price of any constantly applied self-deprivation of food is an eventual cutting of the cords of control.

So the athlete or actor binges, but must immediately evacuate the food or his performance will be at risk. A jockey cannot show up for a race 10 or even 5 pounds heavier; a wrestler is weighed before his fight; actors and models must not appear bloated before the camera, which is well known to add 10 pounds as it is. If the binger's next job isn't scheduled for a week or two, rigid dieting or fasting and intensive exercise can compensate for the excess, but if the job is the next day or even that very evening following the binge, more immediate measures are necessary. "The behavior starts out as a necessary evil," explains Dr. Gross, "but as it continues, the patient can develop self-hatred and low self-esteem and he'll often get into depression."

At least as often, though, the behavior remains just that—a behavior—without sinking the practitioner into psychological quicksand. Dr. Gross sees those patients who are disturbed enough about their eating to seek treatment, but many other male and female athletes, models and actors never develop the psychological symptoms of guilt, pathological fear of fat and self-loathing that accompany true bulimia. These "situationals" will indulge in bingeing, vomiting or related behaviors only at certain times, and never develop a consistent pattern. According to Eugene L. Lowenkopf, M.D., chief of the Mental Hygiene Clinic of City Hospital Center at Elmhurst, New York, people whose professions require them to be slim use self-induced vomiting and other extreme methods to keep their weights low. "Even prizefighters and wrestlers," says Dr. Lowenkopf, "can force themselves into lower weight categories while retaining the muscle bulk of a higher category, giving them a relative advantage."[12]

Some observers maintain that the various degrees of weight-control behaviors are spread widely across society, regardless of sex or status. As L. M. Vincent, M.D., put it: "Self-induced vomiting exists throughout all strata of our society. Whether it be the 'flipping' of jockeys or the 'dieting' of models, actresses or housewives, this practice pervades, and is bred by, a culture that equates thinness with beauty and success."[13]

5

ON THEIR OWN

Pamela

Pamela was on her own without ceremony at 23, when she divorced her husband of four years and her parents ended their role as the financiers of Pamela's education. If she could leave her husband, her parents reasoned, she could damn well support herself. Luckily, Pamela had just six months to go before she earned her M.S.W., and she'd been assured of a position in the community's mental-health-services department. She was able to arrange for a stipend to take care of the rest of her tuition, and took a prestigious part-time job as research assistant to one of the graduate school's star social scientists, winning out over most of the master's degree candidates.

But Pamela was scared. Never in her life had she been responsible for her own financial support. She'd never had a trust fund or anything like that, but her basic needs—tuition, books, clothes, food, housing—had been taken care of by her parents. When she'd married Stan in her sophomore year, her parents had continued to pay her tuition and related school expenses. Stan, who was five years older than Pamela and already a C.P.A., paid their basic living expenses, so it was easy for Pamela to tend to her personal needs with the money she earned working three afternoons a week in the campus bookstore. As a student, she didn't need much in the way of clothes.

At first she was relieved to be married. She needed a rest from men, because she got too emotionally involved. Since her teens, it seemed she was always falling in love, hard and fast, and always getting dropped after the first few dates. Friends would warn her to stop acting so desperate, but she couldn't help it; she was so happy when a new man wanted to be with her. She never seemed to have a problem attracting them. It was keeping them that eluded her. And she'd get so down when she was dumped that it would take weeks to recover.

It was after a particularly painful rejection by someone she'd really thought was *him* that Stan came along. He seemed safe enough; he was the earnest, plodding type, and clearly he was in love with her. But it wasn't long before she was utterly bored with him and yearning for passion. So she ended the marriage.

With no Stan and no parents, the outside world seemed suddenly confusing and unpredictable. She needed control; she needed structure. It was precisely at this point that Pamela— 5'4½", 113 pounds, all her life a normal eater with a minor sweet tooth and no weight problem except for being too thin as a child—decided she was too fat. She wanted to see bones.

She cut out carbohydrates entirely, because one spoonful of cake would trigger an enormous desire to eat. She felt a tremendous rush of physical energy, the kind of energy that isolates you because it doesn't get focused on other people. She used it for endless sessions of running and swimming before and after work. Her weight dropped to 95.

People she knew told her that she'd stopped eating just to get attention. Pamela wondered about that. She also noticed that she was having trouble maintaining normal relationships with others, because in the back of her mind there was always the weight thing—it was her alter ego, her identity. She was never without dates, but now she felt she was just going through the motions without much real contact. In some ways, that was a welcome switch.

Around men, it seemed there were two people coexisting inside her: the fat one, who stood for everything that had ever hurt her; and the thin one, someone she'd created, who'd entered the world as a full-blown adult and had never been miserable as a child, never picked on by other kids, never rejected by her father. The fat personality was the dependent, helpless one, and she would do everything possible not to click into it. The fact that she had no memory of being fat because she had never *been* fat was irrelevant.

Other weird attitudes asserted themselves. She began to consider certain foods, especially meat, to be contaminating; she felt that if she ate these foods, it would be like an invasion and she'd be destroyed. She developed a taste for what she called "antisocial" foods: margarine, gelatin, hard-boiled eggs. Weirdest of all was that these strange new thoughts and behaviors had a positive effect; they seemed to be getting her somewhere. She had succeeded in taking care of herself. She hadn't been forced to crawl back to her parents for a handout. She was really doing it: supporting herself, operating on a very tight schedule, just the way she wanted it. Structured. And for the first time she wasn't getting emotional over men. Over much of anything, for that matter.

For five years following her divorce, through the earning of her graduate degree, through many fleeting relationships that Pamela didn't care much about, she kept her weight at 95 by overexercising and rigidly controlling her food intake. In all that time, she didn't touch sweets or carbohydrates, except for an occasional tiny helping of brown rice.

But at some inexplicable point during the summer of her twenty-eighth year, toward the end of one more relationship that didn't seem to go anywhere after all, she bought a bag of peanut-butter cookies at the bakery and ate them all. That episode was followed by others, interspersed with strict dieting. By September, she had gained about 10 pounds.

The worst was that she couldn't seem to get her control back the way it used to be. She was no longer able to avoid sugar and flour entirely; now she could only go so long without them and then she'd have to binge. She didn't dare incorporate them into her daily diet, because she knew she'd weigh 200 pounds before long. One taste of the forbidden foods and she'd have to get away from everyone and eat until she was sick. Sometimes she'd go as long as three or four months between binges; sometimes it was every ten days. Since the bingeing began, she'd also lost that ability to remain detached from men. She was back to getting hurt all the time.

Then her next-door neighbor in the apartment building, Ellen, tipped her off to vomiting. Ellen couldn't believe that Pamela had starved herself for five years without ever bingeing, and that once she'd started bingeing, she hadn't known about vomiting. Thanks to Ellen, Pamela's binge episodes increased to maybe once a week, because now there was no threat of weight gain.

After a year or so, Pamela found that she liked barfing better than bingeing; the act was hypnotic, soothing. And she knew that when she closed the bathroom door, she was untouchable, unreachable, until she opened it again. Sometimes she'd binge just so she could barf. It became a very effective way of handling the outside world, especially now that she was under increasing pressure to carry a bigger case load—the clinic was badly understaffed. As it was, she found it difficult to avoid emotional involvement with many of her patients. In a county-run clinic like hers, she might see in any given day an abused child, a family torn apart by alcoholism, a manic-depressive adult, a suicidal teen-ager.

The stress and anxiety she felt would build during the day, and finally, when her shift was over, she could release the feelings only one way: by eating until she was stoned, and then barfing. The process took about four hours, and at the end Pamela was very relaxed. She didn't feel guilty about doing it, because she didn't think she was harming herself; nor did she think it was disgusting, just expensive and impractical. She didn't feel out of control, either; she felt she was making a clear choice each time. And she continued to reinforce the behavior because it worked—it released the tension of her day. She could have been addicted to drugs just as easily. She considered the process of bingeing and barfing like a drug, but more benign.

At 30, Pamela was aware that her strange eating behavior was now serving a different function. It had begun back when she was 23 as a way of controlling the world and organizing herself, and it had to do mostly with denial and discipline. Once she introduced vomiting, it became a way of getting rid of the world; it meant release and relaxation rather than structure. It was comforting. By "it" she meant the vomiting. To get to the vomiting, she had to binge. As far as her weight was concerned, that was less of an issue than it had been. She kept it at about 107, which was fine.

Depending on the state of her social life, Pamela would operate a bit differently on her days off. Usually she wasn't feeling the stress that built up in her head and made her want to explode by the end of the day. But if she was between boyfriends and feeling lonely, or if she had a boyfriend whose interest in her seemed to be waning, or if she was in a social situation that made her ill at ease or insecure, she used her "process" to alleviate those feelings, too.

The process intensified around her thirty-first birthday, when she decided to take a rest from men—from everyone, really. She began to turn down friends' invitations, because she'd feel obligated to be charming and sociable and she just wasn't into it. Another reason was that she always expected too much of every party, every date, even every conversation. So rather than be disappointed, she would just beg off. She had her vomiting to look forward to. It was so soothing, and demanded nothing other than a binge.

One night there was a going-away party at a nearby restaurant for a member of the clinic staff who was moving out of town. Pamela thought it would be unkind of her not to show up for a few minutes. She had a glass of champagne, spoke to a few people and left. Once she got outside, she had a bit of trouble identifying her car, because there were two identical dark blue Datsuns, same model, same year, same everything, parked next to each other in the restaurant lot.

"Great minds and all that," said someone over her shoulder. "Is one of them yours?" A good-looking man, keys in hand, had come to claim his car—or was it hers? Pamela was instantly attracted. They joked about the cars for a minute, then realized they'd been at the same party and hadn't noticed each other. His name was Bobby, and he was a family friend of the staff member who was leaving. Pamela, satisfied that they had enough mutual connections and he wouldn't turn out to be a Mr. Goodbar, dispensed with her plan to have a binge-and-vomit session when he suggested they have a drink together. The whole thing was so spontaneous that she felt more relaxed and natural than usual when meeting a new man. When Bobby dropped her back at her car, they exchanged phone numbers and agreed to see each other soon. Then Pamela went through the same old thoughts: Would he call? Did she act all right? Could this be *the* man?

He did call, and this time they came back to her place and made love all night. In the morning, Pamela lay around passively, wishing she didn't have to go to work, wishing that he'd stay, or at least make a definite date with her before he left so she'd be sure he'd see her again. Finally, Bobby was the one to act. "I've got to get to work—don't you?" When he left, hugging her goodbye but not saying anything about future plans other than "Talk to you soon," she just lay in bed, feeling desperate. She called in sick to the clinic and spent the day crying and listening to the saddest blues albums she had.

After a few days, she got up the nerve to call Bobby and ask him to see a movie with her. He sounded warm but distracted on the phone. He said, "I'm in the middle of something right now, babe, but we'll catch one soon." Pamela hung up and immediately hit the market for binge fixings so that she could vomit. Hours later, when she'd completed the cycle and was feeling relaxed, she concluded that she was acting high-school-ish; she hardly knew the guy anyway—if he called, he called. But that cavalier attitude was only operative postvomit. The more she worried, the more she needed to vomit, because that seemed increasingly to be the only way she could arrive at a fresh perspective.

One night after a particularly tough day at the clinic, Pamela completed her ritual and, feeling calm and cleansed, curled up on her living-room couch. She was thinking about her mother. Pamela often thought about her mother after vomiting, because it was the best time to do so, when she was feeling generally mellow and compassionate. At other times, thoughts of her mother were likely to make her angry—angry at her mother's dependency, her manipulativeness, her quiet alcoholism, her lying, her hostility, her denial.

When Pamela had been growing up in the house with her mother, she had sometimes felt her mother was driving her crazy, playing the passive martyr, saying things like "My life is over, you have everything" whenever Pamela did well at something. Pamela felt most accepted by her mother when she had failed, like not making the tennis team in school. Whenever her mother launched into her long-suffering, how-can-you-leave-me act, which she did even on nights when Pamela was going out for just a few hours, Pamela felt she meant the opposite, that it was her mother who didn't want to be with her.

Pamela always had the sense that she was the mother and her mother was the child. Pamela's mother had resented taking care of her children, because she wanted to be taken care of herself. She hadn't wanted children at all, but in 1949 that was what you did. Pamela, the firstborn of three, was force-fed every two hours as an infant. She had come to see that early feeding as the beginning of a long split between who you are and the body you carry around with you, a split that didn't surface until she was 23.

No doubt the split deepened during her parents' prolonged breakup, because food became part of their struggle: Pamela had been a picky eater as a child, and her parents would displace their anger at each other by taking turns literally shoving food down her throat and then criticizing each other for not getting her to eat enough. When Pamela's father, whose temper was as explosive as her mother's was passive, finally left home, her mother announced, "He wouldn't have left if it weren't for you kids," and spent the next three days moaning and crying in her bathrobe.

In her postbarf clarity of thought, it occurred to Pamela that perhaps she'd been fooling herself. Like her mother with the booze. Telling herself that everything was fine, that she was fine, that there was nothing wrong with bingeing and vomiting daily, that in fact there was everything right with it, because it *helped* her. But no: it did help her. It cleared her head, calmed her down. It was the opposite for her mother—alcohol fogged her up, made her morose. It was different for Pamela. Wasn't it?

Francine

It was only 11:00 A.M., but Francine had already managed to chew off two nails. That's why she had weekly manicures—to try to counteract the weekly destruction. Her manicurist would get so excited at those occasional times when Francine had left her nails alone, but Francine would always warn her that it wouldn't last. Still, without the manicures she would probably have ten shorn fingers instead of the current two, the way it had been back in junior high. It wasn't a big deal to anyone but her father then; but now, in business, she certainly didn't want one of the executives to notice such an obvious sign of anxiety. She prided herself on seeming totally together at all times at the company. She knew they were grooming her.

Francine wasn't just a whiz kid; in her field, it was even more impressive that she was a *female* whiz kid. She had been magna cum laude in math at Cal Tech, went on for her master's in computer science, and was receiving handsome job offers before she'd completed her graduate degree. She allowed herself three weeks between finishing her master's and beginning work at a *Fortune* 500 manufacturing company based in New York City, whose offer she had accepted over the others in part because she felt it would be a good experience to live in New York for a while.

She'd been hired to do systems design work at a starting salary of $26,000 a year and had quickly pleased her direct supervisor. He'd been with the company for years, and was too secure as a man in a man's world to feel that Francine was in any way a threat to him. He continued to delegate more and more responsibility to her. Over his lengthening lunches with other male supervisors, he would frequently comment, or so she'd been informed, "I tell you, hire yourself some sharp young girl like Francine—they work their asses off and you can still pay them half of what you'd pay a guy."

Because she made Steven's life so much easier, he frequently arranged for merit raises for her. Now, just two years with the company and only 25 years old, Francine was already making $33,000. Despite her relative lack of experience, she had an innate understanding of the protocol of power; she assumed that Steven would be careful to take personal credit for any good programs coming out of the department, including ones she'd designed, and for the moment she'd take her payoff in merit raises. Francine was careful not to grandstand for herself and possibly antagonize Steven. At least not yet. She would know when the time was right.

It might have come already, which was why she'd bitten the two nails and would surely bite more before the day was over. An hour ago, one of the corporate VPs had bypassed Steven for the first time and come directly to her with a major assignment: to find a serious flaw in the company's inventory-control program that had prevented them from catching the theft of items at ten outlying branch warehouses, and then to design and implement the appropriate program changes. "I need it done in sixty days," said Gene, the terse vice-president. "Can you do it?"

"Of course," Francine said without hesitation, as she had trained herself to do. "Is Steven aware of the project?" She had to let Gene know, subtly, that she was aware of his dismissal of protocol but was still loyal to her own supervisor. Fortunately, Steven would be in Boston until Monday—it would be too late for him to pull her off the project.

Gene smiled and shrugged. "Not yet, but he should be. I'll take care of it." He got up from his desk; Francine knew it was her cue to leave.

"Thanks for the shot, Gene," she said, and let herself out of his office. She smiled at Gene's secretary on her way out, nodded to a few other people in the hallway, and finally escaped into the ladies' room. She locked herself into a stall and sat down on the toilet to calm herself in private. She was nervous as hell. It was good she had her act down so well: Ms. Assurance and Confidence. The more insecure she felt inside, the better her act. She found the correlation as puzzling as it was consistent.

Suppose she couldn't pull it off? Suppose it would mean her downfall, a quick plunge from whiz kid to has-been? Suppose she couldn't find the flaw, let alone design a properly functioning system? Oh, stop it. This is what you've been wanting, a chance to prove yourself, to leapfrog over Steven, right? So get to it already. Francine shushed her warring inner voices by biting off another nail. She spent the rest of the day engrossed in her new project.

At 7:00 P.M. she removed her boring corporate-looking pumps and replaced them with her old canvas Nikes for the thirty-block walk to her apartment on the Upper West Side. On her way she stopped at Pasta & Cheese and picked up a big round of Italian bread and a hunk of Gorgonzola. She walked quickly as usual, and as she walked she'd dip her hand into her big shoulder bag, tear off a piece of bread or cheese and eat her way uptown. She enjoyed eating while walking. It was like having company.

Francine let herself into her apartment—a five-minute project since there were four different locks to deal with—and headed for the minuscule kitchen. She wanted to put the cheese away, but when she went to retrieve it from her bag, it wasn't there. Could she have dropped it on the street? Fool, she told herself. You ate it. All of it, a whole half-pound. As for the bread, there was only a tiny chunk left from that huge loaf. She stared at the poster taped onto her refrigerator door, which depicted a skeleton in jogging clothes headlined, "Runners never die . . . they just thin out." I can't believe I'm still doing this to myself, she thought. I'm a rational, intelligent human being, an athlete and a scientist, in control of everything in my life—except eating.

She knew better than to blame her little binge on work pressure. Excuses were pointless. There was always some kind of pressure if you were past 10 years old; and from what she had seen so far of life, it was obvious that stress would only increase, not decrease. Why did she persist in using a self-destructive mechanism to release the pressure when there must be other ways? Why couldn't she wean herself from such a hateful means of instant gratification? It had been nearly seven years.

The whole thing had started during her sophomore year at Cal Tech. She had been a long-distance runner and knew she could compete better by getting down to a lower weight. Also, it would help control her asthma, which bothered her more when her weight was high. She was 5'8" and weighed about 130; she thought that 120 would be her optimum running weight. To reach that goal, she stepped up her daily distance to 12 miles and stuck to a lean diet—fruit, vegetables, skim milk, a limited amount of cheese. She had numerous food allergies and she was also a vegetarian, so she didn't eat on the school's meal plan; she had a refrigerator in her room and prepared her own food. Because of her heavy academic schedule and her part-time job serving food in the dining hall, Francine's meal times were erratic.

Within a few months, she'd gotten her weight down to 118 and felt terrific, but she worried about not getting her period. She'd been amenorrheic ever since she stepped up her running, and even before that her periods had been irregular. She'd read enough about the physiological aspects of long-distance running to know that it stripped women of body fat, and if your percentage of body fat was low enough, you would cease menstruating. At 118 she had only 12 percent body fat on her, which was extremely low—the average for women was double that. Then her doctor told her that if she didn't stop running and gain some weight, she'd endanger her health.

Francine didn't know if he was using scare tactics on her or not, but she was afraid to take chances. On the other hand, she was aware of how differently she walked and dressed, how differently she acted toward men, at 118 than at 130. She was much more confident, felt more desirable, and men definitely flocked around. But her fear won out; Francine followed her doctor's advice, stopped running and increased her food intake. Without doing those 12 miles a day, the weight came on rapidly. At 135 she got her period.

Shortly thereafter, a guy she used to run marathons with came up to her and said, "Francine, haven't you put on a lot of weight?" She couldn't very well explain to him that her doctor had told her to, that she needed to get her period, that it wasn't due to her own lack of control. *She* knew all that, and still the comment hurt. Because the fact was simply that she was now fat. The comment triggered Francine's first real binge—on bread and cheese, her favorite foods. She took a loaf of dark, fresh pumpernickel and a large wedge of sharp cheddar back to her dorm room and ate it all in maybe a half-hour.

Afterward, feeling like a two-by-four had wedged itself into her stomach, Francine couldn't believe what she had done. She, the brainy math major, long-distance runner, social organizer and family mediator, who believed in resolving things for herself, by herself in a logical, orderly manner, was indulging in such slovenly and self-indulgent behavior. She couldn't blame it on one innocent little comment. That would be absurd. She could only blame it on something weak inside herself that had apparently been dormant.

Francine thought back to a situation that had interested her last year, when one of her dormmates, Barbara, was caught stealing vast quantities of food from the dining hall. Eventually Barbara left school. Once she was gone, her roommate told everyone that Barbara would binge on stolen food every day and then make herself vomit. At the time, Francine had found it all very curious, like a freak sideshow. Now, she felt empathetic. Fortunately, Francine would never go so far as to make herself vomit—she couldn't stand vomiting, even involuntarily. But she could certainly no longer turn her nose up at people who lost control.

The day after that first binge, Francine ate nothing, and the following day she decided to defy her doctor and go out for a run. With the extra weight on her, she couldn't do more than 3 miles without her asthma acting up. But she refused to weigh 135 and be the object of people's tactlessness. She refused to waste hours every morning trying to get dressed in something that wouldn't make her look fat. She refused to continue to avoid looking at herself in mirrors. Without exercise, she would never get the weight off, so she'd have to keep running. She designed a fitness program: Three days a week she would consume only fruit juice; on the other four days, she would eat moderately and exercise by doing an hour's run, forty-five minutes of jumping rope and an hour of lifting weights.

Things didn't go exactly according to plan. Francine found herself overeating—she didn't call it "bingeing" because, though constant, it was spread out over the course of the day—on the days when she was supposed to be fasting. To compensate, she would eat almost nothing on the exercise days, and she added a half-hour of swimming to her program. Despite the fact that she did engage in full-fledged bingeing to alleviate pressure during exam time, all the exercising enabled her to get her weight down to 128.

By the time she finished college, she was stuck with eating too much or too little, never just the right amount, but her weight stayed around 128 as long as she didn't let up on her exercising and didn't allow more than one real binge a week. (By "real" she meant, say, the solitary consumption of at least 3,000 calories in less than an hour—not the same as simply overeating at meals.) The weekly binge became a sort of reward for her control the rest of the week, and also served as a tension reliever when her work load or her boyfriend got to be too much. Francine wasn't happy about her little system, but she felt that it was at least somewhat manageable.

She sank back into the armchair covered in brown corduroy that she had bought for a song on Ninetieth Street. Seven years, and not only was she still indulging in the same behavior but she had the same puzzles to solve. Why can't I control my impulse to eat? Why, when I am feeling like a beached whale, do I tell myself it doesn't matter anyway so I may as well eat, when that's the time it matters most? Her approach to work presented a similar puzzle: When I know what it is that I want to accomplish, why do I panic and defeat myself?

She wanted to go for a run in the park, but she was too stuffed. She would get up at dawn tomorrow and do at least 5 miles. She had to be feeling good about herself to face the day, the new project and, later, a possibly miffed boss.

Francine had often wished that she were less closed in her personal relationships, though the pattern had proved an advantage in the business world. As a child, she had learned to manage conflict by either sidestepping it entirely or mediating it for others, avoiding direct involvement. Listening to her parents argue, it had been clear to her that it was easier to agree than to take a stand, and it was best to keep her feelings to herself. Placate and leave—that had been her role. Her parents had always sought her opinion on their fights, though Francine would have preferred to ignore them. She used to hate going somewhere with one of them alone, because she'd have to hear the latest horror story about the other. It made her really value her privacy, and also set her up to withdraw from others whenever confrontation seemed inevitable.

This posed a problem with her current boyfriend, Philip, who wanted her to be more direct. He complained that she would often lead up to something and then hedge around it, making it impossible for him to know what she wanted. Typically, she would hedge because direct confrontation, especially over negative aspects of their relationship, might lead to a fight or other unpleasantness. Francine had a problem telling anyone, man or woman, that she was angry with them—unless she was doing so in a professional capacity.

When she was a senior in college and had been made student food-service manager, she had often been in a position of creating confrontation, for she was in charge of setting up work loads for the student employees and monitoring their performance. If someone screwed up, she had to deal with it. But somehow she'd had no problem being direct in that situation; she was expressing the views of management, not her own, and so it was more abstract, more impersonal, and therefore more comfortable. In her present position, hedging was definitely the way to go. She had studied the style of interaction at her company from the beginning, and it was not a place geared to direct expression. The more covert and manipulative you played it, the more you got what you wanted. Men played the covert game to perfection, and seemed to expect that a woman would reveal herself. In a field with few women, Francine knew she should play it their way. Fortunately, their way had always been her way.

She certainly looked like the perfect Young Career Woman: well groomed, minimal but skillful makeup, clear nail polish, attractively but never provocatively (nor, for that matter, mannishly) dressed. She had the right kind of haircut, up-to-date but not overly trendy. She had the kind of boyfriend who looked right and acted appropriately when she needed an escort for a company function, and he had a respectable profession himself—law. She knew how to conduct herself at business lunches, over drinks and on business trips. She knew exactly where to draw the line between flirtation and feminism so that the men to whom she reported were at ease with her.

She was, of course, very good at her work, but that part came naturally. Deep down she had enough raw intelligence and ability to compete with anyone; it was the polish that she felt was always in danger of chipping. If she showed a lack of confidence in herself, then she'd never convince anyone else that she deserved their confidence. No one knew this better than Francine. Years of observing her mother in action had convinced her of it.

Her mother should have been a terrific role model—she was highly regarded as an administrator in her field, accustomed to managing 800 employees and managing them well. On the job, she was competent, efficient, controlled. But at home with her family, Francine's mother was volatile, demanding, insistent on having her own way, and easily hurt. Her mother had rarely been home when Francine was growing up. Her father worked at home; he was a scientist, a gourmet cook, a patient and loving man. Francine had always been her father's daughter, and her mother felt the odd man out. As a result, she was usually either yelling at Francine or crying and making her feel guilty.

Mother and daughter reached the nadir of their relationship when Francine was in her first year of high school and her mother found a series of letters Francine had written her father when he'd been in Europe working on a grant the year before. In the letters, Francine had complained about how awful her mother was and how she couldn't stand to live with her. Foolishly, Francine's father had kept the letters in a drawer at home; he'd wanted them in case the couple divorced and there was a custody fight. Upon reading the letters, Francine's mother became hysterical: "You bitch, you goddamn bitch, how could you be my daughter?" Her father stayed out of it, which Francine judged to be the only rational approach; she didn't expect him to jump to her defense. She understood his behavior perfectly. She would have done the same. His only mistake had been leaving the letters around.

After the crisis, which her mother managed to prolong for several days, was over and Francine had stopped feeling guilty, she decided her mother's hysteria and melodramatics were extremely distasteful—so sloppy, noisy. Francine vowed not to be like that, and until that first binge, she'd stuck to her vow. She rarely lost her temper. Friends often complimented her for being so calm, even under pressure.

She hated the idea of turning to food, hated it. It was too easy, too obvious, too open. But as vices went, food was her only one, unless you wanted to count nail-biting. She never had sex with strangers. When she was seeing someone regularly, she was nearly always monogamous. True, she'd already had affairs with two married men, but she considered those fairly harmless, short-lived as they were, and they'd turned out to be surprisingly satisfying. Married men seemed to appreciate her detachment; she supposed it made them feel safer, more comfortable, because it meant that she probably wouldn't make things messy for them down the road.

She drank on social occasions, but only moderately. She didn't smoke cigarettes. She had smoked grass in her student days, but didn't bother anymore. She liked to be in control far too much to try crazifying drugs, such as psychedelics or hypnotics, and she thought that cocaine was for people in Hollywood.

Francine simply could not accept herself out of control, even if it was restricted to one area that didn't hurt anyone else. Eating an entire loaf of bread and a half-pound of cheese was a big deal, and not just in terms of getting fat and possibly not looking the part of the Perfect Career Woman on the Move. She could be making $50,000 before the age of 30; she could get up at dawn every morning and run 5 miles or more a day; she could even hold her parents' marriage together. *But she couldn't control her eating.* Why? Why lose control over *food* when she hit some kind of snag? Recent snags included pressure from Philip to get her to open up; a crack from her mother over the phone that Francine didn't care about anyone but herself; frustration from an entire day of staying home waiting for the exterminator, who finally showed up at 5:45 P.M.; and, now, the chance to really make her mark in the company, a chance that should thrill and please her and instead seemed threatening and fraught with failure.

But no need to overdramatize the whole thing. That's what her mother would do. The plain fact was that any challenge brought stress with it, and she was using food to take the edge off the stress. She simply had to find a better solution. Again, the problem was that food was so easy—just about the easiest thing she allowed herself to get away with.

Mary

Once she swam out of her shame, Mary made a rule: She would never, ever do it at work again. Here she was, Mary T. Farrell, M.D., accomplished physician with a successful private practice, on the faculty of a major university teaching hospital, caught at 3:00 P.M. today by a colleague in the women's rest room in the act of self-induced vomiting following a lunchtime binge.

Caught not by just any colleague, but by one of the child psychiatrists who'd had plenty of experience with adolescent anorexics on the ward and who could not be fooled into thinking that Mary had a touch of stomach flu. The psychiatrist, whom Mary had worked with for three years, said, "Don't worry, I'll never mention this. But if it would help to talk about it with me, please don't hesitate."

Mary forced herself to say, "Thanks, Pat, it's an old habit left over from medical school. It's been almost a year since I needed to release tension this way, but the week was a tough one. You know how it goes."

Pat nodded. No doubt she knew Mary was lying, but protocol demanded she drop the issue. And the time of day demanded that Mary also drop the issue. She had patient rounds to do at 3:30, and it was 3:25 now.

Mary appreciated Pat's offer, but the last thing she needed was another psychiatrist. She was already in five-day-a-week analysis and, using a pseudonym, had joined a Saturday-morning group for adults with eating disorders. She hoped that none of the members had children destined to be her patients someday.

Despite her problem, Mary was a total professional. She would never have let her bingeing and vomiting interfere with routine commitments at the hospital; she carefully scheduled her episodes for free periods. In an emergency, even if she was in the middle of an episode, she could stop instantly and deal with the crisis. But now she had to declare the hospital off limits. It was just too dangerous. She knew Pat would be entirely discreet, but she simply couldn't take the chance of exposure again. At least that would force her to cut down on the behavior. It had really gotten bad these last few months, to the point of five to eight sessions a day. Now she would be restricted to doing it at home after work. And there were always those awful, empty weekends.

Mary felt a major, hospital-quality depression coming on. Perhaps she should have herself admitted for treatment next month, when the Miller operation was over and little Tommy was out of the woods. She was close to the edge again; she used the current intensity of her bulimic behavior as her gauge. It had been mounting since last year when those three deaths hit her in quick succession—her two uncles and her dear friend Carl.

Carl's death had been the worst blow. She'd last seen him at his wedding, six months before he was shot when violence erupted during a civil-rights demonstration. Right after Carl's wedding, Mary had gone on a 1000-calorie-a-day diet and dropped 50 pounds in a few months. Her goal was to get down to 125, another 30 or so pounds, and then surprise Carl. But he died before she got the chance. Then her uncles died, felled by heart attacks within a month of each other. In a six-week period she'd had to get through three funerals.

Though there was no more Carl to diet for, Mary still wanted to lose the remaining 30 pounds in his memory. But in big Catholic families like hers, the ritual of mourning traditionally took place over vast quantities of food eaten in company, and Mary needed the comfort of tradition. She began to vomit during this period to compensate for the sorrowful feasts.

Mary continued to vomit after she returned to work and dieting. She cut her food intake back to a maximum of 300 calories a day. She became hyperactive—biking, swimming, running, always alone—and she began to dose herself with powerful diuretics. Her psychoanalyst, aware of the onrush of anorexic symptoms, increased her sessions from four to seven days a week. He told Mary that it was up to her and her internist to determine when the medical situation demanded hospitalization. At that time he would recommend another psychiatrist for her, for he could not contaminate the psychoanalytic relationship by seeing her himself as long as she was in the hospital. Mary understood.

When her weight dropped to 104, Mary and her internist determined that hospitalization was necessary; she was suffering from dehydration and electrolyte imbalance. Mary was admitted to a medical ward with a blood pressure of 40/0. She knew she met all of the diagnostic criteria for anorexia nervosa, but since she was hospitalized for purely medical reasons with no psychiatric watch kept on her, she was able to continue vomiting while in hospital. She was on an IV for a few days because she was unable to swallow more than a bite of egg—she was terrified of blowing up.

Mary remained in the hospital for five days, until her blood pressure had risen, and then returned to work and to her analyst. But she resumed her diuretic abuse and intensified her vomiting, for she had begun to binge heavily and was damned if she'd gain all that weight back again. Within a few months she was back in the hospital, again in medical danger from dehydration, low blood pressure and electrolyte imbalance. Often she would check into the emergency room at a community hospital for IV fluids overnight; once her vital signs had stabilized, she would leave.

Admittedly, it was a bit eerie. She was an M.D. in personal consultation with two other M.D.s—her internist and her analyst. All three of them were perfectly aware of what she was doing to herself; all three of them were carefully monitoring her physical and psychological states. In a sense, it was as if they were observing, diagnosing and treating a fourth person. That's why Mary could calmly assess the fact that she would need psychiatric hospitalization soon, and why she could begin to plan the particulars now, being sure to schedule it so as not to conflict with her professional commitments. Emotionally she was detached from herself, as if she were a robot.

Mary was only 38, but she knew she looked a good deal older because of her thinning, graying hair. She tried to cover up the bald spots by brushing over them, as a man would do. Of course, a man's bald spots would probably have been caused by nature, not by his pulling clumps of his hair out as a nervous habit as Mary had done since adolescence. Pulled it out right in class, in front of everyone. It had earned her many lectures from her parents, who told her it was a mortal sin to disturb her body and threatened to tell the priest. Lately she'd been thinking back through the years. Her most recent hospitalization, when she was on the IV, had triggered her memories, because the experience took her back to the very beginning of her eating problems.

She had begun menstruating early, in the fifth grade, and had attained her full adult height, 5'2", by the age of 11. Though she hadn't been thin as a child, she hadn't been heavy, either. But the roundness that came with puberty and forced her into "chubbette" sizes had begun to upset her. Especially with the obese aunts and cousins in her family and her lean, mean mother. Her mother was openly horrified that Mary's first bra was a 36C, and always threatened, "You'll look like your relatives if you eat that cookie." So, between the family pattern of obesity and her mother's threats, the stage had been set for Mary to fulfill her mother's dire prophecy.

When she was 12, Mary caught a stomach flu that had been going around. The symptoms were diarrhea and vomiting, and she was ill for a week or so. But even after she recovered, she continued to feel great anxiety whenever she put something in her mouth. Soon she began to induce vomiting whenever she ate, because of her great discomfort. Over the next few months she lost 25 pounds, going from 137 to 112. She had to be hospitalized for dehydration and was put on an IV. Mary felt terribly guilty because her father had no medical insurance and had to give up his vacation pay to cover her ten-day hospitalization. Perhaps because of the guilt, Mary's symptoms ceased once she left the hospital.

Soon there were new ones, however. In junior high, Mary began eating two or three boxes of cookies each night to get her through her Latin homework—secretly, of course, because her eating made her mother hysterical. Mary's baby-sitting jobs gave her the money to buy food without anyone knowing, and by the time she was 15 her weight had risen to 150. She felt like an outsider everywhere. She was clumsy; she wasn't pretty or good at sports. She had brains—but brains, especially female ones, weren't valued in her blue-collar, Catholic, Irish/Italian/Polish neighborhood. The fact that her father was an alcoholic who occasionally beat his children with his belt after a few drinks was more understandable in Mary's environment than she herself was. The man across the street was the neighborhood mailman; the man next door was an auto mechanic. Mary's father worked in electronics as a skilled professional and was unique in his circle for having actually gone to college.

It was a culture in which working women were looked down upon and an atmosphere in which negative emotions were simply not supposed to exist. Men got drunk and beat their children or their wives; women got fat or depressed or both. Mary's mother was a little different; she had only a high-school diploma but held responsible administrative positions in a state agency as well as a political office. The only other woman in the neighborhood who worked was forced to, for her husband was an incapacitated alcoholic. When Mary was in her early teens, her family moved to a better neighborhood, but it was predominantly Jewish. There, Mary felt no less the outsider.

Mary's mother always had the last word, and her way was the only way to do anything. Mary's father never dared to oppose his wife except for a few times when he was drinking. And because Mary's mother's own upbringing had been rigidly Victorian, her only outlet for frustration was verbal abuse— sarcasm and denigration heaped upon her children. Especially upon Mary, who was smart and achievement-oriented and intellectually assertive, like her mother. By the end of the fourth grade, Mary had read her way through the entire children's branch of the town library, and by the age of 13, she knew she wanted to go into medicine. Her mother was furious with Mary's aspirations; she wanted Mary to be a housewife—unless she was unable to land a man, in which case she should be a secretary.

As a child, Mary didn't realize that her mother's own insecurities were so rampant that she felt compelled to treat everyone the same way, humiliating them, criticizing them, rejecting them. All Mary knew was that her mother's behavior was contagious. When her mother sneered at her for gaining weight or getting an A, Mary would feel so bad that she'd turn right around and heap verbal abuse on her younger sister.

Mary wasn't exactly unpopular in high school—she was on student council and worked on the yearbook—but she felt socially inept. Though she never expected to be a member of the jock/cheerleader clique, she thought she should have been accepted into the superbright-achiever clique. But even there she didn't fit in. Oh, they'd talk to her, sit with her at lunch if she initiated the contact, but they'd never seek her out. And she never dated. Her mother told her it was because she looked too fat and acted too smart. She ought to play dumb and feminine and coy, her mother warned, or she'd never have a date.

At 16, Mary weighed 165 and became a charter member of Weight Watchers because she wanted very badly to go to the junior prom and knew that, at 165, no one would want to go with her. She lost 40 pounds and felt she looked presentable enough to ask her older brother if he would fix her up. But her brother was embarrassed about having such a creepy sister and was afraid his friends would make fun of him or worse for asking such an enormous favor. So Mary didn't get to the prom after all. And there now seemed to be no incentive to keep the weight off.

The weight kept coming when Mary was a senior and agonizing over her future. She wanted to go away to college, to study medicine and get out of the house; her mother wanted her to go to secretarial school. They finally compromised: Mary could go to college as long as she lived at home. A scholarship covered the tuition, and that summer Mary saved enough money working to pay for room and board on campus her freshman year. By the time the year was over, Mary had her first real friend, Theresa. However, Mary's weight was up to 190, the highest ever.

Mary had done a lot of thinking that first year in college. She knew for sure that socializing and dating would never be her forte, and she didn't want to be labeled an old maid as her aunts had been. She also knew that she was terrified of sex and had used her brains and her fat to avoid dealing with it. So she decided to reject a social and sexual life before it rejected her entirely. She entered a convent along with Theresa. She would practice medicine, but as a nun.

Mary really enjoyed her first year as a postulant. She was active and involved in the life. Relieved of social pressure, she lost weight spontaneously. But the next year, everything changed. For some reason, the novice mistress chose Mary as her personal scapegoat. It was like an instant replay of her relationship with her mother. The novice mistress told Mary she didn't belong, that she was worthless and had nothing to offer the convent. Although Mary's anxiety grew so intense that she could eat very little, the novice mistress made Mary sit next to her at meals and would tell her throughout that she was eating too much and abusing God's bounty. By the end of that second year in the convent, Mary's weight was down to 130, but she was desperately unhappy.

If Mary had felt better about herself, she might have been able to handle the novice mistress's constant criticism. It might also have helped if Theresa had been allowed to give her emotional support, but as a novice you must struggle alone with God and not seek out others. The novice mistress's abuse precipitated Mary's first major depression. She gave up her dream of being a nun and left the convent under extreme emotional stress at the end of the second year, knowing she was badly in need of help.

When she told her mother she was seriously depressed, her mother's reply was "You shouldn't feel that way." And when, on her own, she saw a psychiatrist, he told her that she was simply lazy and stubborn and ought to go back to school. That made him the third person in a row to tell her that she was no good. By now, Mary didn't have any trouble believing it. But she knew that she would be unable to concentrate on her studies if she went back to school; her depression was too deep. So she worked as an aide in a nursing home during the day and as a supermarket checker at night. She was able to function because neither of the jobs required her to think. After a semester's absence, she decided she was ready to reenroll, but kept her night job so that she'd avoid her typical evening anxiety and depression. She couldn't avoid her perfectionism and obsession about her studies, however. She graduated magna cum laude, weighing 190 and in the throes of another depression.

At this point, Mary knew she was in no emotional shape to go to medical school and survive; she could handle the material, but not the pressure. She knew she had a problem with low self-esteem, anxiety and depression, and that her weight fluctuation was a symptom of all of that. She also knew that she wanted to be a doctor more than anything in the world, more than losing weight or functioning with men or being accepted by her mother, but first she would have to get her head on straight. She mapped out a plan: She would get a good job, preferably at a lab, and she would get therapy. After she'd saved enough money and had enough therapy, she would enter medical school.

She got the good lab job—three of them. Each one fell through when, after she was hired, she had to go through a routine physical exam and was told repeatedly that she was obese and, if employed, would affect each company's group-health-insurance policy adversely. Mary had to scratch that plan. Instead, she took a job teaching math and science at a local high school.

Mary felt good about her teaching. She was relaxed with the kids and had no discipline problems with them. As she began to acquire some self-confidence, she thought she ought to look as good as she felt—by now, her weight was up to 208. After ten months back at Weight Watchers and regular exercise, Mary's weight had dropped to 132.

And then, weighing 132 and looking almost pretty, Mary met a guy at a family picnic and he asked her out. It was the first time in her life that anyone had ever asked her for a date. Naturally, her mother was delighted. For once, she almost approved of her daughter—finally, her weight was normal and a man was interested in her.

But Mary was more anxious about his interest than pleased by it. Her anxiety increased when he asked her out a second time and then a third. They had done no more than hold hands, but she was deeply afraid of further contact. There was one surefire way out: Mary turned herself into a human garbage disposal. She put on nearly 100 pounds in seven months. At 225, she no longer had to worry about sexual intimacy—and she no longer had the pressure of trying to maintain her mother's approval.

The sexual crisis and subsequent weight gain drove Mary into the community mental-health clinic, where she finally found an insightful social worker and began seeing her three times a week. Mary and her therapist focused their work on the anger that lurked behind Mary's depression and how she turned it in on herself. They talked about how she could turn it out, express it, without fearing rejection. They talked about self-esteem and Mary's need to move out of her mother's house. Mary began feeling good again, and though her weight remained at 215, she moved out of her shell once again and began socializing. Not dating men, of course, but seeing friends, some of whom were male. Finally, she felt ready for medical school.

Mary entered med school on a high, still feeling sociable, and proud that she had pulled herself through everything. But her depression returned within months. She thought it was due to leaving her teaching job, where she'd felt competent and rewarded, and returning to the stress and anxiety of studying, which was so much more of a self-centered activity, with no diversions. She also was far from home for the first time, living in a rented room, away from the social worker who had helped her so much. Mary had learned a few things that helped her, though: She maintained a part-time job, because she knew she could do her schoolwork as efficiently and with less anxiety in two hours than she could in six; and she continued to socialize. But after six months without therapy, she sought help at the student psychiatric clinic.

It was the beginning of a five-year period of intensive, analytically oriented therapy that helped Mary in several areas, particularly with her anger toward her mother and her need to separate her own self-concept from her mother's. The treatment had a positive effect on Mary's relationship with her mother and with her family in general. But when Mary and her young, attractive, male therapist began to deal with some of her sexual anxieties, there in the therapist's tiny, closet-size office, Mary became very self-conscious and felt sexually aroused—felt her body on fire—for the first time in her life.

To please her therapist, Mary lost 90 pounds. But he didn't

say a word about her weight loss, didn't even seem to notice that she'd gone from 220 to 130! He could have been her mother, refusing to recognize her achievements. Mary played her part of that particular scenario by seeking revenge the only way she knew how: gaining weight. It was only after she'd put on 50 pounds that her therapist finally said something: "What are you doing to yourself?"

That wasn't exactly the kind of recognition Mary had been looking for. Besides, she was under a great deal of stress since beginning her internship. She'd recently gone through the death of her first young patient. Also, two members of the university-hospital staff, each of whom was married to someone else, were having a rather flagrant love affair. She felt very uncomfortable witnessing their overt expressions of sexuality toward each other every day. Mary responded to these anxieties in her typical way: Her weight went up to 225. It stayed there throughout the completion of her internship and then her residency.

She had earned a fellowship in her chosen subspecialty, which necessitated a move to a different university for a year. It proved to be the most wonderful year of her life, with the possible exception of her first year at the convent. The experience was rewarding on a personal as well as professional level, for it was the first time she had ever felt she'd met a true kindred spirit: Carl. They shared the same medical orientation, and soon they shared their wishes and dreams and most of their free time.

Mary couldn't believe it: She weighed 225, but Carl didn't care. He accepted her completely, made her feel like a valuable human being. He was so gentle and she felt so comfortable with him that she wasn't even fearful of the sexual feelings she was beginning to have, though he had made no approach of any kind in that direction. Then Carl told her that he'd lived with a woman before coming to the university, and that he would probably marry her when his fellowship was over at the end of the year.

That was okay with Mary. She could shelve those unnerving sexual feelings again. She told herself that now she was safe; she could be Carl's kindred spirit and the other woman could have him for sex. It was true that at Carl's wedding she wished she were the bride, but still she continued to feel relieved that he could be her friend and she didn't have to worry about anything sexual.

But then her delicately constructed world caved in. Carl was murdered; her uncles died one after the other; her emotions exploded into physical chaos. And now she'd allowed herself to be exposed to a colleague in the most degrading way. It was indeed time to seek protection. The hospital could be a refuge.

The Safe World of Work

> I can't believe it when people I work with say they find me intimidating. If they only knew.
>
> Nancy, a 29-year-old marketing director
> and a bulimic vomiter

Their ages range from 25 to 38, their backgrounds from working-class to privileged, the severity of their eating behavior from mild to extreme. The details of their lives vary widely. Yet the similarities between Pamela, Mary and Francine are at least as striking as the differences.

All three have met, matched and often conquered the challenges of career choice, performance and advancement despite such personal problems as low self-esteem, self-doubt, consistent feelings of ineffectiveness, unworthiness, depression. All three are high achievers in the professional arena and under-achievers in the personal. They all feel most confident and competent at work and most insecure outside, in their social, sexual and familial lives. They allow or encounter few real pleasures that don't have to do with productivity and accomplishment. All three lack, to some degree, *balance* in their lives. The greater the discrepancy between their professional and social selves, the greater the degree of imbalance, and the more chaotic their eating behavior.

Mary is, of course, the most extreme. Within her lifetime, she has met the technical criteria for bulimia, obesity *and* anorexia nervosa. She had an alcoholic and physically abusive father. She has inherited the family mantle of major depressive illness in female relatives and has struggled against depression as intensely as she has struggled with weight. She consistently endangers her life by abusing diuretics and by self-inducing vomiting. Her sexuality remains something she cannot face; at the age of 38, she is a virgin. She has been in Freudian analysis and other forms of psychotherapy for many years.

Yet somehow Mary pushed herself past such formidable obstacles to achieve the professional goal she set for herself in adolescence: to become a doctor. She continues to set further professional goals and to accomplish them, but outside of work, her loneliness is intense; she has only bingeing and purging for company. Mary's eating behavior is the most vivid symptom of the underlying depression that has plagued her all her life; it is also the major tool she has for keeping her depression in check. Her analyst has frequently told her to cease the bingeing and vomiting so that her depression could flow out and her feelings could then be dealt with directly in treatment. For that very reason, Mary may hang on to the behavior even more fiercely.

Compared to Mary, Francine's life looks pretty good. Though she has plenty of problems in her personal relationships, with her family and with men, she has a wide circle of friends and is socially and sexually active. Of the three women, her life is most balanced; correspondingly, her eating behavior is the least disordered. She is bulimic, but only occasionally, and her behavior doesn't encompass the physically endangering and habit-forming purge mechanisms. She exercises and restricts her food intake to compensate for her binges. She prides herself on being rational, a scientist, self-contained. Only over food does she allow impulse to take over.

Though Pamela and Francine may share similar feelings of social inadequacy, Francine expresses it by appearing detached and cold, while Pamela slips into passivity and dependency, particularly with men. Sooner or later, men pick up on Pamela's dependency, which turns them off and ultimately makes them reject her. The rejections send Pamela into a depression, which leads to bingeing and purging. The depression continues until Pamela embarks upon another affair. The embarkation is always exciting, providing enough of a high so that her bulimic urges disappear temporarily. She has no trouble attracting men to her on a superficial level; the trouble is in getting them to love her.

Pamela's emotional pattern of intense ups and downs, particularly in connection with the men in her life, appears to fit the description of "hysteroid dysphoria," a psychological state so labeled by Michael R. Liebowitz, M.D., and Donald F. Klein, M.D. People with hysteroid dysphoria, according to Drs. Liebowitz and Klein, are usually female. Characteristically, they spend their time seeking approval and attention, especially romantic attention, to which they respond with a high level of energy and exuberance.

But when the hysteroid dysphoric feels rejected, she has a "crash-like reaction, characterized by loss of self-esteem, and accompanied by one or more of the following: *overeating or craving for sweets;* increased sleep or time spent in bed; a sense of leaden paralysis and inertia." (emphasis added) In contrast to patients with typical clinical depression, hysteroid dysphorics are able to snap out of negative feelings if they get enough attention and applause. Physical appearance is of great concern to such women, and their self-esteem is dependent on constant approval from others. Their romantic relationships tend to be intense but brief; because they demand so much stroking, their partners often can't take it, and leave.[1]

For Pamela, self-induced vomiting has emerged over time as the more important half of her cycle. In fact, she is interested in bingeing primarily as an entry into effortless vomiting. This switchover—the drive to vomit overtaking the drive to binge as the main source of gratification—is not an uncommon pattern, particularly in people who maintain the cycles for many years. "It is difficult for most of us who think of vomiting as an uncomfortable and involuntary reaction to view it as tolerable and desirable, even pleasurable and addictive," wrote psychotherapist Steven Levenkron. "But for those who learn to induce vomiting voluntarily, it begins as a necessary unpleasantness and evolves into a sensual, addictive muscular convulsion."[2]

Francine doesn't vomit, so she can't binge as often as Pamela does or she would gain weight. Francine has developed alternate ways to release tension, primarily physical exercise. Her eating behavior, while certainly not normal, is fairly stable. Though she puts on a flawless act of supercompetence at work, she admits to a constant struggle with self-doubt, with a fear of failure and of being found out, particularly by the men around her who are responsible for future promotions. She knows she can't be just good in her field; she has to be better than her male peers.

This is a fact of life for Francine, as it is for many women trying to get ahead in what is still a man's world. Francine's perspective was expressed perfectly by *New York Times* columnist Betty Rollin: "It seems to me a lot of women don't feel entitled to make a mistake. And I know why. It's because men let us in and we feel we have to be perfect. We're there because they allowed us to be there—sometimes because they *had* to— and we know it and they know it and they know we know it. So we better be good. But it's hard to be good when you're constantly nervous that you're not."[3]

Francine knows that if she's going to do any faltering or lose her grip, it had better be during her private time. The constant at-work pressure of not just performing well but performing brilliantly in order to get ahead is not a distorted, perfectionist idea of Francine's but is actually quite real in the company and profession she has chosen. The continual at-work pressure sets up her need to relinquish control, but it must be done away from her professional environment. Food is the easy release, easier than loosening up with other people. If Francine could allow herself to relax more in her personal life and stop investing so much energy in keeping emotionally level, even with her lover, her constant self-interrogation over her lack of food control might be at least partially resolved.

Judith Gordon, Ph.D., a Seattle psychologist with a special

interest in addictive behaviors, recently completed work with a group of bulimic career women, aged 22 to 54. All of the women vomited or used laxatives; all were of normal to thin weight; none were anorexic or obese. Physical appearance and dress were extremely important to all of them, and equally important was professional achievement. In addition, they were "stereotypical women" in terms of their sex roles—meaning they had to be the perfect wives and mothers as well as the perfect professionals.

"They used bingeing as others use drugs or alcohol—to blank out and to indulge, because these women maintain tremendous control most of the time," Dr. Gordon explains. "The bingeing functioned as any compulsive behavior would. They felt guilty because of the secrecy of it, and they had the sense of being split into a good person and a bad one. The difference is that with the purge, they could immediately undo the bad thing they'd done.

"They all had endless lists of things they had to accomplish every day, but the things usually involved pleasing someone else—boss, husband, children. They rarely did anything purely for themselves. Because their lives were so oriented around meeting the demands of others, they were very out of touch with their inner selves."

As part of therapy, Dr. Gordon asked the women to introduce into their lives, at least two or three days a week, something that they wanted to do purely for themselves *other than bingeing*. The women had great difficulty with this seemingly simple assignment, both in deciding what they wanted to do and then letting themselves do it. "They didn't know how to relax," Dr. Gordon says. Typically, when the pressure of accomplishing all those tasks on their lists built to an intolerable level and their selves cried out for attention, attention was paid—by bingeing and purging.

Though all of Dr. Gordon's bingers were workaholics and perfectionists, the psychologist believes that another group of female food abusers exists—women who are underachieving, underproductive and not using their skills. Instead, says Dr. Gordon, they use excessive behaviors to ward off feelings of emptiness and lack of meaning in their lives. Though the high-achieving bulimic's compulsion to cross off everything on her daily list and to keep as busy as possible (which bears many parallels to the typical anorexic) may be the flip behavior to cope with the same empty feeling, at least the high-achiever *achieves*. Occasionally, she even lets herself feel pride in her accomplishments.

But this pride is usually fleeting. The professional high-achiever more often tends to put herself down with the underlying thought: *before someone else does*. Why such negative anticipation? "Usually, they are involved with very critical men or extremely demanding parents who may have been abusive, either physically or psychologically," says Dr. Gordon.

On the simplest psychological level, if you started out with parents who expected great things from you, and you continually felt short of their expectations (whether or not *they* felt the same) and thus of their approval, you may have learned early on to measure yourself against what other people seemed to want from you and neglected to set up your own standards. In your head—and that's all that counts—you are always at the mercy of someone else's judgment. Perversely, you may continue to perpetuate the problem by seeking out more of the same one-way judgmental relationships in your adult life.

"Without knowing it," says Solomon ("Sandy") Perlo, M.D., clinical director of the Woodview-Calabasas eating disorders program in Calabasas, California, "a bulimic woman will often pick a man who'll reinforce her own negative self-image by downgrading her. She's frequently not interested in men who will accept her, who don't underline her inner feeling of inadequacy and ineffectiveness." She may reject the man who truly accepts her in a strange version of a superiority hang-up: If she knows herself to be nearly worthless, then anyone who considers her worthy of love and attention must himself be a lesser person. Why else would he set his sights as low as her?

Dr. Perlo mentions a very talented and attractive artist in one of his bulimia groups who continues to pick bad men, men who perpetuate and re-create for her all the unsuccessful relation-

ships in her life. Another patient of Dr. Perlo's, a highly
successful attorney, was so passive in her personal life that she
was afraid to answer her phone for fear that a certain man whom
she disliked but who was clearly interested in her might be
calling to ask her out. She was afraid that she'd be unable to say
no. If her fears come true and she is indeed unable to say no,
she'll feel forced into doing something she doesn't want to do,
then angry at herself for getting into the situation in the first
place. Once that chain of emotions materializes, the odds are
that she'll have set herself up for a binge.

Professionals tend to be fascinated by this particular population of bright, articulate, achieving career women in early to
middle adulthood who happen to abuse food. "What interests
me," says Elaine Stevens, A.C.S.W., of the Cleveland Clinic, "is
noncrazy women, the kind of women you'd want to know if you
spotted them across a room. They are highly accomplished, yet
inside they feel defective and are afraid they'll be found out.
They seem on the surface to be functioning just fine, but
underneath there's something missing. So they develop a symptom for this emptiness, this feeling defective, and they are then
able to define themselves as 'having an eating problem' rather
than having a missing part."

Despite feeling defective and despite considerable performance anxiety, it is at work where most bingeing workaholics
feel most comfortable. Craig Johnson, Ph.D., and his colleagues
at Chicago's Michael Reese Medical Center, demonstrated this
when they compared a group of food-abusing women to a group
of normal women by having the subjects carry beepers for a
week. The researchers beeped the women at random times
during the day and had them record their moods and eating
behavior at the time of each beep. The results showed that the
moods of the food abusers were more upbeat and positive than
the moods of the normals—at work.

Dr. Johnson believes that the nature of the workday as a
structured period of time contributes to its having a positive
effect on the bulimics, whose personal time is too often unstructured.[4] In many cases, the most reliable pattern in their per-

sonal lives is the bingeing-and-vomiting cycle itself, which only reinforces their dependency on the behavior, for it offers the security of familiarity.

Work is also an environment in which interaction with others tends to be fairly predictable; there aren't too many unexpected challenges to interpersonal skills. How to act and what to say to co-workers is more clearly defined than in outside social situations, and the subject of work itself is an easy icebreaker in most office conversations or encounters. And each office tends to have a set pattern of interaction, a style—whether stuffy or open, formal or casual. Some companies stress memo-writing and three-piece suits, while others are oriented around verbal exchange and sometimes blue jeans. Whatever the style, it tends to be easy to follow once you've been exposed to it—unlike social situations, which have as many moment-to-moment variations as there are individuals.

"Success at work demands performance, but not necessarily insight or even interaction," says Janice Hedblom, M.S.W., assistant director of social work at The Johns Hopkins Hospital, who works with eating-disordered patients and their families. "For bulimics, it's their arena, so they'll compete there, but it doesn't really help them because in the end they denigrate their successes."

Julia, now 36, is an Ivy League–educated attorney, one of the few female partners in an East Coast Establishment law firm. She has been bingeing and vomiting since she was 19 and preparing for a trip abroad, a venture whose prospect depressed her because she would be traveling alone. Only recently has Julia begun to understand at least a little of what triggers her eating behavior: being alone and being left. Her worst period came at age 30 when her marriage broke up and she began living alone for the first extended period in her life.

"I was bingeing and throwing up three and four times a day. I'd be frantically busy all day and not think about food, and when I'd get home I'd take a sleeping pill so that I'd sleep and not binge. But invariably I'd be just about asleep and then I couldn't resist; I'd throw on my clothes and go out in the car and get food.

One night at around eight, I was lying in bed trying desperately to stave off a binge, and they announced an Overeaters Anonymous meeting on the radio. I raced off to the meeting, but everyone there was obese and I didn't fit in. I didn't want to go home alone that night, so I went to the market for a bag of food for company."

Julia's bingeing and vomiting subsided when she fell in love with a new man and moved in with him, but it would be triggered when he went away on business. "The minute he'd tell me he had to go out of town, I'd be planning my binge. The reverse of that was sometimes I wouldn't eat at all when he was gone, but when he came back I'd start bingeing heavily. If it was me who had to go out of town, there was no problem."

Fortunately, Julia—who for many years has been the envy of all the females in her family for her beauty, brains and slim figure—feels much less self-loathing as she grows older. The behavior isn't as intense as it was: "I can be kinder to myself now, and besides, my body can't function as well as it used to on bingeing and purging. I'm not willing to make myself feel that bad now, and I don't think I could take it anyway. I even gained three or four pounds on vacation and for once I'm not hysterical about it and don't hate myself for it. It used to be that I'd have just one dessert out to dinner and would throw up as soon as I got home because I felt contaminated."

Julia thinks her improved behavior is due to several factors: the increasing rationality that comes with age; the fact that she is finally at ease with herself as an attorney, when before she felt undeserving of her many professional accolades and successes, including the respect of her colleagues; and to the symbiotic and warm relationship she has with her second husband, the man she'd been living with. Yet all is not resolved.

"I still don't fully trust myself and I'm still fearful that if I lived alone, *it* would happen again. I'm just not that secure that it's over. And even though aloneness seems to be a trigger for me, the patterns aren't that consistent. Very recently I went home to visit my mother, with all the warmth and comfort that suggests, and I found myself stuffing continually."

It's been said that daughters, consciously or unconsciously, tend to adopt the coping styles of their mothers—often in spite of themselves. Daughters who have experienced their mothers as helpless and passive, yet manipulative, fear becoming like them and feel especially vulnerable when they catch themselves behaving like their mothers.

Pamela identifies very strongly but very negatively with her mother: The characteristics they share are the ones Pamela loathes in herself. Francine was more successful in shrugging off her emotional heritage: Not wanting to be hysterical and melodramatic as she perceived her mother, Francine adopted a detached, cool style. She's aware of the trade-offs: being closed in her relationships and fearing intimacy. Mary's mother suffered from such low self-esteem that she was driven to torture her children with their own shortcomings; she passed her sense of worthlessness on intact to Mary, who, unable or unwilling to toss the poison onto the world as her mother did, drinks it down herself.

All three women belong to the same generation, sociologically speaking: the first to subscribe officially to the women's career consciousness born in the Sixties. And their mothers belong to the last generation of women for whom society had no greater expectations than that they keep home and hearth and children and husbands in top working order. Because of the shift in societal expectations of women that coincided with the coming of age of Pamela, Mary and Francine, it's not so farfetched to speculate that the collision course along which parents and children—especially those of the same sex—confront each other in *any* generation may have been that much more precarious for this one.

"Nice" women born to an age in which a college education was the entry to snaring a suitable man, and a career was merely a holding pattern to be dispensed with when the time came to start a family—an age in which being assertive and expressing your feelings were not recognized as valuable qualities—could get by with fewer interpersonal skills and ways to handle stress. Not so for their daughters.

Italian psychiatrist and anorexia-nervosa specialist Mara
Selvini Palazzoli wrote, "There is little doubt that the modern
girl is weighed down by a host of cultural and social pressures
that tend to aggravate inner conflicts. The most important of
these conflicts are due to such factors as the admission of women
into traditional male preserves, when previously they were
confined to the home to play the role of good housewife and
mother. At the same time female narcissism has, if anything,
increased rather than diminished.

"Today, in fact, women are expected to be beautiful, smart,
and well-groomed, and to devote a great deal of time to their
personal appearance even while competing in business and the
professions. It is quite obvious that the conflict between so many
irreconcilable demands on her time, in a world where the male
spirit of competition and productivity reigns supreme, exposes
the modern woman to a terrible social ordeal."[5]

The world of this modern woman is a world of more freedom
and therefore more decisions to agonize over, including sexual
and professional ones; more responsibilities to confront and
challenges to meet. But all too often she is still burdened with
her mother's insecurities and armed only with her mother's
interactional tools, which frequently consist of anticipating and
fulfilling the needs of others in only one world, the world of
family.

"My mother always had a nonstop smile on her face; I could
never get a reading from her," says Maggie, 31, a bulimic dieter
who makes over $30,000 a year as a fashion designer. "She loves
to manipulate situations but all the while pretend that she's
doing it all for you. More than anything else, she adores being a
martyr. I love my mother because she's my mother, but I don't
want to be like her. Unfortunately, I'm probably more like her
than unlike her."

Maggie tried to flee from her mother's influence by being a
wild teen-ager, by choosing a college 2,000 miles away from
home, by becoming successful in her field, but still she couldn't
divest herself of that pattern of living through others and making
them feel guilty for it, picked up from her mother. "I find myself

pulling that stuff with men, and I hate myself for it. I don't communicate what I feel when I feel it. I whine instead of yell. I let other people, especially men, dump on me and then I feel sorry for myself and play the victim. I let people take advantage of me because I tell myself I'm being nice."

The more Maggie tries to be nice, the angrier she feels; and like so many others, she settles for a secret binge in lieu of dealing with her anger head on. "My goal for the year is to stop being so damn nice and to try to speak my mind," Maggie insists. "It's frightening, so usually I make believe I don't know my mind, which is like lying to myself. But the few times I've managed to act instead of passively stuffing my face, it's made me feel that I can be strong, that there's a whole side of me in there somewhere that has nothing to do with my mother. I would be less than honest if I pretended not to be aware of the certain benefits you get from acting like you're hopeless and helpless. For one thing, you never have to do anything about it."

Marion Collins, of the Cleveland Clinic, observes that many such mothers of food-abusing daughters tend to be overinvolved with their children until their husbands come home, and then the mothers give up responsibility. Their daughters see their powerlessness and fear being like them. "Many mothers of patients I've seen," says Collins, "have struggled with their own low self-esteem and with their weight—they're usually on a diet to please their husbands, though their husbands may never have suggested it."

Like bingeing and vomiting, low self-esteem is very much a pass-along matter. And, of course, so are cultural ideals. In speculating on the prevalence of bulimia and anorexia today, Susan Wooley, codirector of the University of Cincinnati Medical Center's Clinic for Eating Disorders, told *Harper's Bazaar:* "This young generation of sufferers is the first whose mothers were influenced by the thinness mania and who've inherited it, unquestioned."[6]

One clear similarity between young professional women today and their mothers is their inner view of themselves in relationship to men. This is not supposed to be true, of course.

Women today are supposed to be sexually liberated, financially and emotionally independent, individuals on their own terms, contributing their full 50 percent on all levels in a relationship. But the current fantasy of the bright, attractive, purposeful career woman who holds her own in a man's world, who doesn't cry on the job, who can call a man and ask him to lunch and pay for it with complete confidence, who can gracefully yet directly address her sexual needs with men, is all too often just that—fantasy. As with their mothers' generation, women today spend plenty of time waiting for men to act or react so that the women know what to do next.

Psychologists William C. White, Jr., and Marlene Boskind-White have treated many female binge-vomiters in group therapy since the mid-Seventies. They hold a sociocultural perspective on bulimia: that it is related to the struggle to be the perfect, stereotypical female, in which women give up their right of self-definition to others. Most often, "others" means men: first their fathers; later their boyfriends and husbands and bosses. In one study the Whites conducted of fourteen career women aged 18–45 (all but two had been employed for at least three years), subjects were asked to set goals for themselves. These goals commonly included feeling less anxious and insecure in relationships with men and making close female friends without feeling competitive and mistrustful of them.[7]

Thirty years ago, neither women nor society presumed that men were *not* the ones to please. Although today the ability to please yourself first is increasingly recognized as an important step toward breaking the cycle of food abuse, it's an extremely hard process for women to accept and practice. Young professional women are just better than their mothers were at *appearing* to be independent, to be acting for themselves. The work world is the easiest place of all to maintain this facade if you are successful in that arena, for you have its identity to fall back on if you're short on your own.

How many attractive, upwardly mobile, professionally accomplished, seemingly independent women still sit by the phone waiting for the classic high sign of male approval: a first, second, third date? How many women with plenty to offer—professional skill, intelligence, financial independence, cultural knowledge, experience, interests of their own—still wait for men to lead them? How many of them turn to food as resource, release and punishment? In many ways, successful female workaholics today are no different inside from their mothers. They just hate themselves more for it, because society has decreed them independent, and there must be something wrong with them. Otherwise, wouldn't they *feel* independent?

6

AT HOME

Clare

"Today," wrote Clare in her journal, *"not for the first time,"* she underlined, "I began to look at food as my enemy and the prospect of restaurant dining as pure sabotage. I hate the fact that everything social centers around food. Our lives are filled with social events—more so than most. Am I a victim of the good life? If I refuse to eat the beautiful foods around me, will I be no more fun anymore? Will I still *have* fun, all the while exerting such effort NOT to eat?

"And what about my own cooking? Everything I made this week was *fabulous*. Why did I make the rice with topping (full of butter, dates, white raisins, sautéed almonds)? Because it brings *absolute raves*, and we were entertaining as usual. I am known among my friends as a gourmet cook. They expect the best when they are here, even if they are having a diet dinner. One thing I have never been able to do—never in my life—is push food around my plate the way superthin models do."

It wouldn't have occurred to Clare to start a journal on her own. It was part of the behaviorally oriented treatment specified by the weight-control clinic that she had recently plunked down several hundred dollars to attend, as the latest in her lifelong attempts to lose those same damn 20 pounds. Clare is a Yo-Yo dieter, a nosher, alternately adoring and despising food. As the well-groomed wife of an extremely successful stockbroker, *all* foods, from Russian caviar to raspberries in February, are available to her.

Clare's material needs and desires are basically taken care of. Yet she doesn't throw money away, like some of her friends do;

her occasional high-ticket splurges involve works of art—sculpture and paintings—which are investments anyway. She has a supportive, kind husband, Larry, who also happens to be an attentive and loving father, a man who understood her need to have a little business of her own when her youngest child entered school six years ago—even though, as a wholesale-handbag business, it occasionally involves sales trips and shows away from home. Of course, Clare wouldn't mind a little more attention, a little intimacy, sexually and otherwise, from Larry. They have grown apart in recent years; they always seem to be in different rooms when they are home. But that's what you get with a big house.

You could say that Clare's life is a graceful one. The formal French gardens outlining the pool in back of the spacious home she shares with Larry, their two children and sometimes a maid are graceful. The marvelous parties she produces to further her husband's career, superbly detailed and choreographed by Clare herself, are graceful. Her daughters, aged 10 and 12, are, thank God, slim and graceful. But Clare herself did not feel particularly graceful being just 5'2" and weighing, uh, over 120.

Clare felt terribly guilty that she had complaints about her life—she was so lucky, really. Not long ago, right before she began her new diet through the institute, she made a list of all the things she had:

1. A marriage as good as any—a husband who isn't fooling around.
2. Two gorgeous kids.
3. More money than I can spend and all the freedom that implies.
4. Respect and admiration from my personal and business friends.
5. Brains.
6. A pretty face.

The only thing she didn't have was a decent body, and she felt she was destroying the one she did have every day. The pattern was: She wouldn't eat all day, because she'd be out running errands, chauffeuring children or working on her business; but from 4:00 to 7:00, at home alone in the kitchen while her kids were upstairs doing homework or watching TV, she'd nibble constantly, on ice cream, crackers, potato chips, cookies. She wasn't a binger, really, but she had her rituals. They were the subject of another list she made.

1. If there is a tray of brownies with uneven edges, I have to even them off; and if anyone cuts a brownie for himself, I have to even it again.
2. Rather than have a piece of cake, I will gladly consume the crumbs on the doily, the icing on the lid of the box or on the knife, and of course I have to even off any jagged edges.
3. I will eat only *broken* pieces of cookies, crackers and cashews; or *unpopped* popcorn kernels, or crumbs of potato chips. I leave the unbroken pieces for someone else. This is what I mistakenly regard as "free" food.
4. I eat watermelon seeds.
5. I rarely eat an apple, but I will eat an apple core with seeds and enjoy it.
6. After squeezing the children's orange juice, I will eat the orange rinds and pulp. I believe this has less sugar than the juice.
7. After Larry leaves for work, I often eat his grapefruit rind.
8. I will take one-half portion, then half of the remainder, then half of the remainder of the remainder, etc. I never *decide* to eat the whole thing but I manage to do so anyway and then feel guilty.
9. Sometimes I will take half a loaf of raisin bread, one slice at a time, and eat only the sugar-coated raisins. I stuff the rest down the garbage disposal. My children caught me doing this once.
10. No one has seen me with chocolate-chip cookies: I eat the chips and then throw the cookie down the drain. Same

with chocolate-chip ice cream. Whenever I do this, I refuse to get on the scale for weeks.

11. Sometimes I eat frozen foods, too—candy, cheesecake, coffee cake, corn—all hard as a brick, with practically no taste.

12. I even swallow chewing gum! *Always*.

Clare submitted this list to her new weight-control therapist, the director of the institute (she often thinks of him as her guru), adding at the bottom: "I want desperately to be rational. I want to stop this idiotic behavior *forever!*" Later, she begged: "Dear doctor, is it possible to make me indifferent to food? Oh, what a gift that would be!"

It was a tough request from a woman whose nickname at age 5 was "Cookie"—thanks to her passion for the sweet. By the age of 8, Clare was chubby enough to get teased by her peers, but, compared to her even chubbier girlfriend (nicknamed "Butterball"), Clare felt almost thin. Her slender stepmother (her father had been widowed when Clare was 4, and it was during that year from 4 to 5 that Clare remembers being overindulged with sweets by a sympathetic aunt) signed Clare up for dance classes to slim her down, and Clare loved them. She could never understand why her stepmother canceled the classes after Clare had lost enough weight to no longer seem a problem to her stepmother.

Clare missed the dance classes, but her weight stayed down through junior high. She controlled it carefully; she allowed herself one Good Humor bar each week, usually on Wednesdays after school. She was a very good girl, highly sensitive to criticism, afraid to disobey, and alone a good deal. Her father wasn't around much, and she found communication with her elegant, witty stepmother difficult.

In the tenth grade, Clare had her first real boyfriend, but her parents wouldn't allow her to go steady and forced her to give him back his ring. Clare was devastated. But because she was afraid to rebel openly, she pulled her hair out instead, leaving a 2″ bald spot on the back of her head. To spite her stepmother,

Clare started eating candy bars after school, at least one a day, and potato chips when she got home and her stepmother was upstairs reading. It was the first time Clare ever felt compelled by food, her first memory of being a secret eater. In a few months, her weight had jumped from 103 to 118. The battle had begun.

Clare collected diet books and calorie charts. She'd restrict herself—no butter or mayo, no sweets, no snacking—for four or five days running and then she'd give up. She continued to date (although her parents rigidly enforced a midnight curfew and would ground her for a month if she was more than fifteen minutes late), but she didn't attract the boys she wanted. Her self-esteem was too low, she thought, and her weight too high. She resented the fact that none of her friends seemed to be suffering over food the way she was, and felt alone with the problem. But she had a good face and a good personality and was a high achiever in school, so things weren't all that bad.

Still, Clare wanted so badly to be thin. She wore girdles, corsets, Merry Widows. She was constantly measuring her hips. She'd sit in her bedroom saying to herself, "I know where the box of See's candy is, but I'm not going to eat any. . . ." The more she said that to herself the more inevitable it was that she would go get the box and eat not just one but five or six pieces. And then she'd diet for four days. And so on.

Her weight consistently hovered somewhere between 122 and 125 until she moved out of her parents' house, joining a sorority at the hometown university she attended. For the first time, she felt in control of her life. She got down to about 115, she got a job, and her curfews were her own. Though she continued her vigil over food, she was being normal, not a Yo-Yo. She'd have cereal for breakfast, sandwich and fruit for lunch, a balanced dinner and just an occasional sweet. She was too good a girl to indulge in alcohol or drugs, so those posed no threat. She had a fabulous new boyfriend and felt very much in love.

Then her parents decided to take a trip around the world for six months, and they wanted Clare to move back home to supervise her two younger brothers. Obedient as always, Clare gave up her new independence. In return, she gained 10 pounds. Now her once-fabulous boyfriend was ashamed of her appearance; he made it clear he didn't like her fat. Clare knew it was all her fault and that she deserved to be treated that way, dumpy and ugly as she was, weak-willed. But after he called her collect on her birthday, confirming what her parents kept telling her—that he was after her money—she broke up with him.

And then Claire, now 21, stumbled upon the diet that was all the rage, was in fact considered by many to be the first modern fad diet: Dr. Herman Taller's book *Calories Don't Count*. The diet stressed the consumption of protein and fat and the denial of carbohydrates, so Clare ate gobs of safflower oil, margarine and fried chicken. Her weight dropped to 114 and for once she was not feeling deprived. She was convinced that calories really didn't count and that she could eat whatever she wanted. She added everything but sugar to Dr. Taller's diet plan and ended the school year weighing 133.

This time, Clare's usual feeling of helplessness and despair over her fatness was replaced by anger—anger at herself for putting on all that weight. Enough was enough. She accepted her parents' offer to send her to a "fat farm" and lost 5 pounds there. When she returned home, she saw a diet doctor, who supplied her with diet pills. Her weight dropped to 110. Two weeks after the scale registered that number, she met Larry; and six weeks after that, she married him. She was happy enough to stay thin for years, by taking a few precautions.

Unfortunately, when Clare bore their first child, her weight shot up to 140 before delivery. Afterward, she was stuck at 125. She feared that Larry would find her unattractive and no longer love her, and that she would never be able to lose the weight. Feeling that drastic measures were called for, she went on a near-starvation diet. After four months, her weight was down to 108, but after all that deprivation, she almost immediately began overeating. Her weight rose to 116, but she could still wear a size 8. She decided that the weight was acceptable, if not terrific. But then she had a second child, and again put on excessive weight that wouldn't come off.

Clare tried numerous diets, including Atkins and Stillman, interspersed with fasting, but in between she overate. Her weight went up and down the same 10 or 15 pounds, from 125 to 110 to 115 and back to 125. During this period of more than a decade, from the late Sixties to the present, Clare figures that maybe six new diets made a big national splash, and she tried every one.

Six years ago, with her weight hovering around 124 and her time too unstructured, Clare began her business. It took up some of the slack in her days, but was in essence only a part-time thing except during selling season, so she was usually free to attend to her husband and children. Even on just a part-time basis, she found aspects of the business world to be both enlightening and frightening. For one thing, she was dealing with men a lot, and she began to notice a pattern: When her weight was under 120, she'd frequently be approached on a sexual, or at least flirtatious, basis. This pleased her, because it upped her self-esteem, but it also caused an inner conflict, as it would for any historically good girl faithfully married for nearly two decades. Should she respond to extracurricular sexual attention? And to what degree? When her weight fluctuated back up, above 120, the men would stop coming on to her sexually, which made her feel less attractive but much more comfortable. It soon became fairly obvious that she could resolve this conflict simply by gaining weight.

Somewhere between the tenth and fifteenth year of Clare's marriage, things got a little stale between husband and wife. Clare began to feel sexually rejected by Larry once too often, and it made her angry—angry enough to reject herself, in a sense, by gaining more weight. She'd say to Larry, "Please make me feel loved, desired." He'd say she was going about it wrong: If she wanted him to be affectionate, he advised, she'd have to create the atmosphere. Clare felt that Larry rarely initiated sex nor responded when she came right out and told him that she needed it. On the other hand, she thought she probably deserved his lack of response: Here she had this faithful, kind, brilliant man who put up with her *mishugas*. Besides, most husbands in long-term marriages would probably lose some of their sexual desire after all this time. Still, she was angry, and wanted to punish someone. Why not herself?

So, not coincidentally, Clare's weight for the past six years had tended to stay high. And then higher. After three years, her business was a success, and she had learned how to dress for it: Cover your body, clip your hair, wear your glasses. Don't be provocative. Deciding that bigness meant power, she gained more weight. She began to collect sculpture and paintings that depicted fat women, women with big, powerful thighs.

One such painting, by Francisco Zuniga, hung in Clare's sunny breakfast nook beside the wall phone, whose cord was long enough to allow her to walk into the adjoining kitchen while talking. The painting inspired her to develop a new activity: On the days she wasn't working and her house was empty, she'd talk on the phone to friends and look at the Zuniga painting, which would tell her it was okay to be fat, and this would lead her into the nether reaches of the kitchen cupboards and the large refrigerator/freezer; she'd dip into the ice cream or the cookies or the potato chips, still talking, unaware of how much she was eating. It got so she would actually salivate whenever the phone rang. She got fatter and fatter. In August she weighed 125; by March she was up to 135.

Now she was frantic over her fat. She tried to protect herself from the enemy by padlocking the snack drawer; her kids and husband would know the combination and she would not. Except that the kids would go into the drawer, remove a few Oreos from the bag and forget to replace the padlock. Clare would then finish off the bag. Her kids would scream at her for eating the whole bag, and she would scream at them for not locking the drawer. Repeatedly she'd tell Larry that she hated herself for being fat, and he'd reply: "I don't mind you the way you are. I just wish you could be happy." But one day during the early, fat spring months, Larry opened Clare's closet, filled with expensive clothes that no longer fit, and said, "I have a very big investment here." He also noted that it was strange she'd gained weight, because he never saw her eating much.

In April, Claire and Larry and the kids were invited to a friend's condominium in a resort area that experienced very warm temperatures at that time of year. This posed a major problem for Clare. Her thighs were so enormous that she couldn't wear pants, and she certainly could not wear a bathing suit (something she found traumatic even when she weighed 110). But she couldn't very well loll around a swimming-and-sunning resort in her business clothes. She thought a jogging suit might be the answer, so with her younger daughter for company, she drove to a nearby sporting-goods store.

The experience was humiliating. She was in the store for four hours trying on every sweat suit in every size, including men's large. Horribly, she needed the bottoms in that very size, but the top was too big. The salesperson finally agreed to split up a suit and sold her a men's large bottoms and a women's medium top. On the way home in the car, she was crying. She sobbed to her daughter, "I used to be a size six." When her daughter asked her why she wasn't anymore, Clare couldn't answer.

The family spent a week at the resort. Clare played tennis in her jogging suit despite near-90-degree temperatures. At the pool, she wore a long, elasticized-waist skirt over her bathing suit because she would not let anyone see her thighs. And, miserable with herself, she ate constantly. One night she ate all the raisins and nuts out of an entire loaf of raisin bread and threw the bread part down the garbage disposal; she had to sneak out early the next morning to get another loaf of bread so her hosts wouldn't notice what she'd done.

Toward the end of that week of supposed relaxation, Clare thought she'd try her hosts' Exercycle. Since none of the adults was around and it was difficult to operate the machine with a long skirt on, she thought she was safe in just her bathing suit with only her kids to see her. But when she took off her robe, her younger daughter looked at her thighs and said, "Mom—are those your *legs?*" It was one humiliation too much. She had to do something.

Back at home, Clare read every ad for every weight-loss clinic she could find and called them all for information. She joined a

Nautilus Club and went every day. But she didn't stop eating. She didn't want shots or pills, and most of all she didn't want to go on yet another diet. She went to a Schick seminar and signed up for the course, but canceled within twenty-four hours and got her money back. She told her friends that she'd pay $5,000 if she could be thin, because that was the one thing she desperately wanted but couldn't get for herself. Finally, through her internist, she found her guru, a Ph.D. who was the director of a successful clinic that offered custom-made diets, nutritional counseling and behaviorally oriented weight-loss therapy.

For Clare, the clinic meant assurance and attention and, most significantly, someone to please. Someone, she thought, who cared. The proof was there the moment she first made contact with Eric, the program director, her soon-to-be guru. After making the initial appointment, Clare had second thoughts. She decided to call the clinic's answering service and cancel the appointment. But instead of the service, she got Eric himself. He immediately recognized her distress and asked her to come in the next day at 11:00 A.M. That hour was impossible for Clare—it conflicted with her children's car pool—and so Eric gave up his lunch hour for her.

To Clare, this was the key to everything: She felt she'd found someone who really would take care of her, who was genuinely concerned. Someone who would call her back at midnight or 2:00 A.M. if she needed it. Someone who made her feel she was the most important person in the world.

Part of the treatment required clients to keep daily food diaries of where, when, what, with whom and how much food was consumed and the feelings experienced while eating. Clare wrote copiously. She was able to pour out all her frustration and longing to Eric.

"I suppose you're my mentor and my Pygmalion," she wrote one day, "and if what you ask of me is not unreasonable, I'll do it exactly as prescribed. So I'll run for 30 minutes. Look, I can do anything, especially if you expect it—even pass up this veal dish I made for the first time and didn't even try." When Eric suggested she banish dangerous foods from her house and her kids screamed in protest, she told them what Eric had told her to tell them: "If I were an alcoholic, you wouldn't want alcohol in the house, because you would know I had a problem with it. It's the same with food. I'll drive you to the store if you want ice cream or candy and you can eat it there, but you can't bring it home."

Clare wouldn't weigh herself for the first month of her new program, so it's hard to know where she started, but by the end of June she'd gotten down to 120. On July 8 she weighed 117, and wrote in her diary: "I felt very much in need of attention and love. Today I am *much* happier about the way I look, but I am also experiencing tremendous emotional needs—what do I long for? I am *not* insecure. I do not feel unloved. I just need some demonstration of it!"

The funny thing was this: The closer Clare got to her goal weight of 105, the worse that indefinable longing of hers became. "Strange emotional state," she wrote on July 12. "I am filled with romantic longing—fantasize I'm walking along the Seine or the Thames. I need some kind of special pleasure—something exciting—stimulating. Perhaps I am just bored, yet I'm full of intense passion for everything around me—can't get enough of life—I have a tremendous sense of expectancy, and I'm waiting."

At the end of July, when she was down to 114, one of her suppliers openly came on to her, offering low prices and personal gifts and unsolicited loans in exchange for sexual favors. Clare had to be rude to get him to leave her alone; she would have to do without his merchandise in the future. The episode led her to consume, according to her journal, ten coffee-bean candies and a piece of peanut brittle. On August 11, she recorded her moods as "tired . . . bored . . . exhausted . . . sad"; and an addendum: "Please, God, don't let me self-destruct. Make me want to do without the food. Eric, I'm scared out of my mind. I'm afraid to see you and afraid not to. God, I need *help*. I've lost my euphoria. Where did my discipline go? How can I get it back?"

She got it back somehow, because on a Saturday morning that

September, Clare got on the scale and saw that her weight had dipped under 110 for the first time. Ecstatic, she walked into the bedroom where her husband was still semisleeping and lay down next to him and said, "I weigh one hundred and nine and three-quarters and something wonderful should happen this very minute."

He rolled over in bed. "Oh, shit," he groaned.

Clare was angry. She knew it was up to her to convince Larry that she was a different person now; that he had to respond to her sexuality, which had increased in force as her weight had dropped; that he had to meet her needs—or she would find someone who would.

On October 2, with the scale reading 110¾, Clare poured out her heart in a letter to Eric.

Larry just asked me to have tea with him, and I said, "Sure." But I was halfway down the stairs and I envisioned all that gorgeous fruit, so I came upstairs and said, "I can't go down there. I'm sorry. I'm sorry." And now I'm crying and hitting the wall with my fist. And Larry ignored me and went down silently to have his tea alone.

I guess I'm not a happy person, and I don't know what to do about it. I should grow up—take hold of myself—not need to be taken care of. I have so many blessings. I'm the one who always says, "Don't ask God for happiness. Ask for good health. With good health, we can make our own happiness." I can make my own happiness. What I'm so afraid of is that it's not in this place, with this man. My God! He is the best there is, isn't he? To want more than I have is truly unreasonable. Eric, no one can have more. If anything, my weight loss has damaged my happiness. No one will believe that, but I have lost the pleasures of food and replaced them with nothing. A better body for me and the sexuality that goes with it can destroy a beautiful, almost perfect, "made-in-heaven" marriage. No wonder I've been a yo-yo with my weight.

Of course I'm feeling miserable right now. I cannot doubt this marriage. It's irrational. When I'm thin, I won't need him to love me this much, right? He does love me—he loves me now—but just doesn't display it. He also needs me to be strong, by his side, not requiring attention and affection. God, I hate myself this way. I mustn't think about all this, just push away the hurt—must finish my work and my chores, plan a big party, go out and buy clothes, arrange for some good tennis, and keep my chin up. Even for you.

On November 18, Clare weighed 106¾ and worried that she wasn't spending enough time with her children, for her business had picked up considerably. "I'm not wasting time," she wrote in her journal that day. "I'm proving my existence. Unfortunately, it becomes excessive. There's a tradeoff—You never get to the children. They lose out—I lose out. Money is the proof that I'm doing something—smart enough to do it—proving myself every day—a useless existence would be the bridge, tennis, social lunches thing. Time with children doesn't hold as much magic as the adult world—being stroked and lauded for the big sale— admired by Larry."

On November 21, Clare headlined her 9:30 A.M. journal entry "Milestones." It was a Saturday, and she and Larry "stayed in bed rather late, cuddling and talking. He told me how much he loved me, not by saying 'I love you,' but by telling me how proud he is that I'm his wife, how much he likes the way I act, the way I speak, the way I look, how much I've 'matured' the last few years, how happy I make him feel."

That night, Clare and Larry gave a dinner party for eight. She recorded the menu in her journal at 2:00 A.M., when her guests had gone and Larry was asleep: antipasto; artichoke hearts with Parmesan and pumpernickel; poached sole with tomato; lemon chicken; orzo with mushrooms and pine nuts; pear tart; choco-late truffles. Then she wrote: *"I've got it all.* Where's the tradeoff? I'm frightened, Eric. How long can it last?"

On Monday, Clare is anguished.

I'm so scared this last week. I'm suffering from something I can't name and don't know. What is there to be afraid of? Is it the same euphoria I felt months ago? Why do I ache inside, so much, with a longing that's close to unbearable? If it's eupho-ria, why am I so depressed? Maybe I'm feeling truly rotten because my treatment is over. Maybe I don't want to stop seeing you each week. Because when you take care of me, in your loving, giving way, I feel unconditionally loved—not needed, not wanted, just accepted and whole.

I don't know what I dread—why I've awakened each night for the past week or so after four or five hours' sleep—awakened with an emptiness deep within—and a fear that all I have will disappear. I feel so alone—so separate from those who love me. It's a desperation—God, how I need to be needed!—Can being needed quell this yearning? It's irrational to have these feelings—totally, completely irrational. Look at how much I am loved!

Do I feel guilt or shame because of a suddenly perfect life? What would that feel like? And does it make sense to be miserable from *not* having goals to strive for? I'm so full of passion I could explode any minute. Someone, uncork me—let the pressure out—give me a way to express this energy before it eats me alive.

Okay—I don't have to have these feelings. I can suppress them—go shopping for clothes, plan some parties, read some good books, work obsessively. Is this what life is all about? Tell me, professor, am I not an overeducated anomaly who can do, be, have whatever I want? And I don't know what I want to do, be, or have because it seems I have done, been, and had almost everything already. Where, therefore, lies my happiness? I am happy—the happiest girl in the world with two gorgeous children and a husband I adore. So now I ask you, why does it hurt so much? Why the anxiety? And most important, where am I going now?

Clare ended this entry with an overall rating of her emotions for the day: very little depression and resentment; very intense levels of anxiety, emotional sensitivity and loneliness. She ranked her ability to express emotions and her interpersonal relationships as "very low."

As the new year dawned, Clare was both thrilled and depressed. The former because she had gotten through the holidays and all the partying and eating weighing 105. The latter because she was feeling particularly empty and lonely, and, without being fat, she had nothing to blame her feelings on. She thought about trying to work on nonweight issues with a new therapist. It had begun to bother her that she did everything Eric told her to, and she knew there wasn't much he could do about her emptiness and loneliness. And she still felt so guilty. Now she had *everything,* absolutely everything, including thinness. Why wasn't it enough?

For the next few months, as winter turned to spring, and spring to summer, Clare thought a lot about herself—while driving to buy Norma Kamali minisweats for her older daughter, who insisted that *everyone* had them; in her exercise classes, which Clare had added to supplement her every-other-day, forty-five-minute jog; in bed lying next to her husband late at night.

She felt terribly self-centered at times, but she had to figure it out. She wanted to therapize herself out of needing Eric. She felt that her dependence on him lacked dignity—that was the word, exactly—just as piling food in her mouth lacked dignity. She felt (fearing that it might be trite, but no less valid) that her depression was largely caused by having arrived at her weight goal. She hadn't thought ahead, past that goal and on to the next. She needed a new goal that wasn't weight-related. A goal all her own.

It was difficult to change her way of thinking, of living. Though she worried about being too preoccupied with herself, she also realized that, other than the lifelong weight-loss goal, most of her objectives had to do with goals for other people. Helping Larry land a new client through her superb entertaining. Insuring her daughters' futures by seeing that they were accepted into the right private schools, despite long waiting lists. Insuring their places once they got in by keeping in tenacious contact with the teachers and administrators.

Clare's decision that she needed a goal of her own, and the uneasiness that decision brought with it because of its resonance of selfishness, seemed to connect to another realization: *The only way she could stay thin was to be selfish.* She'd have to make other people compromise for her. If her husband and children wanted to go out for pizza, she'd have to say, "No, I don't want to go out for pizza. I'd rather have Japanese food." If they still insisted, she would stay home. But she had to take care of herself first. She'd noticed that the more she spoke up for herself, the less her general anxiety, which also meant less of a drive for food. In exchange for the anxiety, she felt guilty that she was too selfish, but the guilt was easier to handle because it was a different kind of guilt than she had when she overate—a better kind.

The selfishness connection first came to Clare's attention when she accompanied Larry on a business/pleasure trip to New York and Puerto Vallarta. Utilizing the principles she had learned from Eric, along with a few new ones of her own, she made plans well in advance of departure. She would not be so foolish as to attempt to diet at La Caravelle or the Four Seasons or any of the other culinary havens they would dine in, but she would exert control at all times when it came to things she didn't really care about. If she ate bread, she would never use butter; she would pass on salad dressings; she would keep fruit in the hotel room and have a piece instead of a meal whenever possible. Most important, she would pack her running clothes and her jump rope and she would keep up her exercise as if she were at home. She'd found that exercise was actually easier to maintain than a strict diet, and it made her feel disciplined, which made it easier to resist the pull of food.

In New York, as long as Larry had a morning business meeting, everything went smoothly. Clare would get up with Larry; they'd have breakfast in the room (Larry: cereal, milk, fruit, toast, coffee; Clare: fruit, coffee) and Larry would leave by 9:30. Then Clare would run in the park, shower, dress and be ready to begin her day, feeling fit and disciplined, by 11:30. But some mornings Larry was free, and Clare found it hard on those days to tell him that she would be jogging from 9:45 to 10:45 and then would have to shower, wash her hair and dress. What about *his* morning? she thought guiltily. Because he'd say, "Come on, honey, let's be together," and she'd feel torn.

She'd explained that she would be a much more pleasant

person if she could get her exercise, and Larry hadn't argued or done anything to make her feel bad, but she'd felt bad anyway. The result was that she only ran on one of Larry's free mornings. Though she told herself that he certainly wouldn't alter his commitments for her, it didn't help to overcome her guilt, because of course his commitments were business and thus infinitely more important than her personal vanity. The fact remained that they were in New York in the first place because of Larry and his business—and his business, after all, paid the bills.

For the rest of the trip, Clare confined her exercising to jumping rope and doing exercises in the room while Larry showered, unless he had a morning appointment. Then she would run. In Puerto Vallarta, she used the hotel pool and tried to get in forty-five minutes of swimming, but it was hard with all the kids splashing and playing. When they returned home, Clare felt she had acquitted herself well as a wife, but not so well as an individual. She'd gained 5 pounds.

Clare decided, on her forty-five-minute morning run their second day back home, that she would just have to feel guilty for a while, because she would rather be selfish than fat. From here on in, mornings would be for her. She would take care of her own business first. For once, it would be her family who would have to adjust to her. And she would not feel sorry for herself. She wouldn't have to, for she would speak up for herself instead. It was that simple: Goals equaled happiness. Selfish equaled thin.

The Peculiar Plight of the Cosseted Woman

> Eating has been my only legal escape.
> Ann, a minister's wife

Women like Clare hold a central place on the Eating Arc. They share many attributes with the anorexics and bulimics of varying weights: the Siamese-twinned fear of fat and desire to be thin; using food as a way to avoid facing up to people; the tendency to seek strength and direction from others rather than from within themselves. But their eating behavior hardly seems out of the ordinary for many American women, especially the woman who spends a good deal of her time tending to the needs of others.

This woman takes an occasional exercise class, tries all the new diets and, if she can afford it, visits a spa for a weekend here and there. She serves her husband and kids a full dinner while she nibbles on salad and melon and, later, on the remnants of everyone else's plate. She doesn't vomit, doesn't abuse laxatives, doesn't even binge, according to the official definition (see chapter 11). She eats a whole package of cookies over the course of an entire day, while the bulimic does it in thirty minutes.

The eating behavior of such a woman is much too tame to generate enthusiasm among the ranks of researchers. But the fact is that she represents millions of women who spend their days either dieting or breaking their diet. Back and forth, up and down. Nothing too extreme. Often the diet is broken out of idleness, the kind of idleness that comes automatically when your free time is whatever falls in between your household and family responsibilities. There's not much you can do with that half-hour that separates waiting for the plumber at home and picking up a child at the dentist's—except, perhaps, to nibble at something until it's gone.

It's great when you find a new diet or clinic or nutritionist and stop nibbling, even cut out the wine you drink occasionally, and lose those 10 or 20 pounds, but it doesn't seem to change anything all that much in your life. You're thinner, but nothing magical happens. Maybe a strange man starts paying attention to you now that you're more confident because you feel more attractive, but you don't know what to do with that, especially if you're married. Anyway, somehow the weight comes back, and so do the old complaints, but at least they're familiar ones.

Clare was on the right track when she hit upon the idea of selfishness as the way out of her preoccupation with the food-and-weight seesaw, though some more modern types might substitute the word "assertiveness." Because Clare is a member of a generation of cosseted women—a mother and wife whose material needs are taken care of by her husband—she is caught between the old and the new views of selfishness.

Being a cosseted woman involves, like everything else, a trade-off. In this case, the trade-off for being taken care of is that you must cosset others. To do that, you must place their needs ahead of your own and adjust your schedule to theirs. Naturally, such an others-always-come-first approach to life makes you feel unimportant, but you must swallow these feelings because you are being taken care of so well in exchange. If you don't, you feel guilty and selfish. To make your feelings go down better, you flavor them—sometimes with alcohol, but mostly with food. Not too much, though. You've got your children to think of, your husband's business associates. You can't become obese. And you don't have the capacity or desire for really extreme behavior. You weren't raised that way.

This is not to imply that there aren't homemakers of Clare's generation who were and are still anorexic, or who did and still do practice bingeing and vomiting, right on through the bearing and raising and leave-taking of children. But many, many more are like Clare.

These women were married and frequently mothers well before the so-called sexual revolution opened new pathways to instant gratification, well before an increasingly mottled rainbow of life choices presented itself to young women and forced them to deal, well or ill, with futures that no longer automatically encompassed marriage and family. Sometimes today's young woman is moved to deal badly—or not at all—with her choices, but there is always a new drug or man or extreme eating behavior to compensate. Women of Clare's set had and have their stresses and emptinesses, plenty of them, but their ways of coping or escaping, generally, were and are more limited.

"Years ago," complains Eileen, 50, a chronic dieter, "when my children were babies, all women were given Dexedrine for the daytime and Seconal at night. You took one of each and it was totally acceptable. But the next generation, my children's generation, spoiled everything by abusing the privilege. And now we can't get them anymore."

Food provides a socially acceptable indulgence (as long as you are careful) for Clare's group of educated women destined to marry men who made money and to bear their children. For such women, it is impossible to get away from food no matter what. Even if they have maids, women like Clare do the marketing, make the children's lunches and usually prepare the family meals, especially after gourmet cooking became the vogue in enlightened social circles across the country in the Seventies.

Children and husbands need something sweet once in a while at least, so there is always someone else for whom such things are being purchased, someone other than the one doing the marketing. Add the constant presence of trigger sweets to the constant sense of waiting routinely felt by the cosseted woman— waiting on a child, a husband, an electrician, always waiting for someone else so that you can take care of your business—and you've got the perfect environment for the growth and mainte-nance of a mood eater.

Unstructured time is the enemy of control in many indulgent behaviors, from eating to drinking to drug-taking, for unstruc-tured time is empty time, passive time; it creates anxiety if it is not filled. During Clare's and Eileen's days as young mothers, free time—mainly the few hours during the day when their babies were napping—was not what you'd call really free, and certainly not relaxing. The baby's nap time was their chance to get the laundry folded and the vacuuming done, or, if they had maids to clean house and baby-sit, the wives would go out and run errands. Such activity fosters restlessness and nervousness because it is boring and nonabsorbing, and underneath it, sometimes, is resentment at having to do it for others—and guilt because of the resentment.

To cope with the boredom, to cope with the nagging feeling of time that is both filled and empty at once, to keep the resent-ment buried and to soothe the guilt, to have something to look forward to, the cosseted woman reaches for food. She wants something. And feels she has to take it on the run, because she doesn't deserve to be cosseted if she is going to be selfish. In this sense, a woman like Clare—millions of American women— bears a striking psychological resemblance to an adolescent anorexic. "The anorexic is appreciated for what nurturing she offers other members of the family," wrote anorexia specialist Steven Levenkron. "She sees herself as being loved for *not* having needs of her own."[1]

Diane is a 48-year-old cosseted woman—tall, dark, attractive and emotional. Like Clare, Diane has spent a good deal of time in self-study. "I eat for unmet needs in self-achievement and in my marriage," she says flatly. "Nibbling is comforting, rewarding. But I know that what I want isn't food. I have to remind myself of that every time I open the refrigerator. Getting involved in a project helps take care of one of those needs, but it's not the total answer because if I'm home I can always put down the project and eat."

Unlike Clare, Diane is by nature tall and lean, so she rarely appears heavy even when she has the fat feeling. And she has the feeling more and more frequently. "When I was younger, my body could handle food better, but now I'm less active. Also, my nibble habit gets worse as I get older, because after a while you lose interest in your appearance. You don't care as much. Except when you go to buy clothes. I'm on a diet now because my son is getting married and I have a motivation to lose weight to fit into the dress I bought. But I really don't have a permanent motivation to be thin other than clothes."

She has more of a motivation to nibble. "When I'm tranquil and feel happy about myself, I don't nibble," Diane says. "But that never lasts very long. Something always comes up to make me angry or tense, and then I eat without really being conscious of it. I know I have a problem handling anxiety. I have poor control of my emotions and I'm easily frustrated. I have an inability to make decisions and I overreact to other people— especially if they seem critical of me, or if I think I said the wrong thing."

Diane has been in and out of psychotherapy over the years,

and the therapists have told her repeatedly that she has "a lot of anger, which I turn against myself because I feel guilty for being angry, and then it becomes depression." A minor example of how that works, Diane explains, is that she is about to run an errand for her 23-year-old daughter (who has a car, an apartment and a job and is perfectly self-sufficient) and take her watch in to be repaired. "She asked me to do it, and I know she's busy, but already I have to run errands for my husband. If I do too many of these kinds of errands, I feel frustrated, but I can't say no when they ask. Then I get angry at myself for not saying no. The guilt is because I feel that their busy-ness is better, more important, than my busy-ness, and so the errands should fall to me and not to them.

"Maybe the most important thing is being selfish and thinking about yourself and not everyone else," Diane continues. "But it's hard for me to say no to my family if I'm on a diet and they all want to eat Mexican food, although I am able to lie to friends and tell them my husband doesn't like Mexican food."

It's the unconscious part of Diane's nibbling that bothers her most, even more than the fat feeling. Though she frequently goes to health spas to lose weight, she attends Weight Watchers to become more conscious. She needs "the support of it, the lecture, getting weighed every week and having to write down what I eat and having someone else read it. It helps to make me aware. I constantly have to make myself aware of when I'm eating or it gets out of hand. I didn't used to need a support system to lose weight—I never understood until recently why other women did."

Once, in an effort to stob nibbling, Diane took up wine drinking, but found she didn't like to drink wine by itself, only with crackers. The net result of that effort: She *gained* weight. She always seems to gain and lose the same 10 pounds, over and over again.

"I know what a normal portion looks like—that's not the problem with me like it is with some women I know," says Diane. "But I never learned how to maintain the weight once I lost it. No—that's not true. It's because of lack of control, lack of interest in control. Sometimes I ignore my awareness and replace it with anger over my lack of control, and then I just don't care.

"I know I can improve things by changing my attitude. I need to plan what goes into my mouth and not get so mad at myself if I goof. Not make it so hard on myself. And realize that physically and emotionally my body can't handle certain things. Like peanut butter: Some people can have a teaspoon of peanut butter and stop, but not me. And I can always keep out of the house, because eating if I'm out of the house is too conscious an act and I won't do it."

The daily life described by Clare and Diane, and the feelings that surround it, sound suspiciously like the "problem with no name" that became the basis of Betty Friedan's *Feminine Mystique* in the early Sixties. Friedan asked if the problem with no name could somehow be related to the housewife's domestic routine. Friedan also wrote, "There is no problem, in the logic of the feminine mystique, for a woman who has no wishes of her own, who defines herself only as wife and mother. The problem, if there is one, can only be her children's, or her husband's."[2]

More than twenty years after those words were written, Clare can write in her own journal, "I need something I'm not getting and can't name it. . . . No rational person can feel sorry for me, so how can I feel sorry for myself?" Her problem, as she sees it, is that she has no problem. Again, Clare—by all appearances about as normal as a cosseted American woman of middle age can be, right down to her dieting behavior—resembles no one so much as one of Steven Levenkron's anorexic patients. This time, he writes not of an adolescent but of a 46-year-old anorexic woman, married twenty-six years to a successful oral surgeon, mother of three children. The woman told Levenkron: "I feel I shouldn't need help. I have a good life. I have no reason to have problems. I know that's not true, but part of me still believes it, and that's the part of me that makes me feel guilty and selfish."[3]

The woman quoted above is of Clare's generation, but as an anorexic she is definitely an atypical cosseted woman in terms of eating behavior. While cases of late-onset anorexia have been reported (the woman described above didn't develop the illness until her early forties), it's more common for a middle-aged woman with anorexia to have first experienced the syndrome as an adolescent or in college, though it may never have been diagnosed. Over the years, the illness can evolve into a habitual state that acquires a life of its own.

Though the older anorexic tends to be as hyperactive as her teen-age counterpart and can appear thin to the point of emacia-tion, she usually keeps her weight just above the medical-danger threshold (except, perhaps, at times of extreme stress), so hospitalization isn't necessary. Family and friends often think of her as being naturally skinny. So accustomed is she to hiding behind anorexic behavior as a shield against conflict that her ability to deal with problems directly is nil.

Perhaps typical of this atypical cosseted woman is Joanna Stein, who first became anorexic as a sophomore at Wellesley College in 1950. Throughout her marriage and the birth of her four children (her weight, apparently, just made it to the critical threshold for menstruation), she kept up her food rituals and restrictions. But none of her adult peers, including her husband, David, had known her before she became anorexic (at which time she was just a touch overweight), so her rituals and her skinniness always seemed completely consistent. Often, at din-ner parties, Joanna's husband explained to the hosts, "She always eats like a bird—don't be insulted."

Whenever a crisis occurred in Joanna's adult life—the birth of her first child, the news that her third child was caught smoking marijuana at school, the death of her father, the discovery of David's affair with a neighbor—Joanna "turned on" her an-orexia, stepping up the rituals and losing weight, as her only means of dealing with these painful situations. At David's re-quest around the time of the first crisis, when Joanna's weight sank to 79 from her normal 95 two months after the birth of their child, she saw a medical doctor. He found nothing wrong with her physically to explain the weight loss, and recommended a psychiatrist. Joanna dutifully complied with his advice; for fifteen years she saw the same psychiatrist once a week. But because the psychiatrist was unfamiliar with anorexia nervosa, other than knowing vaguely that it was a disease of adolescence, its central role in the ordering of Joanna's life and mind never came up. This was more than fine with her.

Joanna's situation may be rare, but it occurs enough to draw attention—although only very recently—in the medical literature. In the fall of 1981, Soo Borson, M.D., and Wayne Katon, M.D., both of Seattle, published a paper entitled "Chronic Anorexia Nervosa: Medical Mimic" to alert physicians to the possibility that they might fail to recognize anorexia nervosa in a patient who would be highly unlikely to have it.

"In the atypical patient," they wrote, "who is older, whose loss of weight is no longer the subject of public complaint by family members, complications of chronic starvation may develop, which mimic other diseases, confound the diagnosis, and delay appropriate treatment. Persons with anorexia of all ages respond to the demands and needs of others at the expense of themselves; they feel a pervasive sense of ineffectiveness and are unable to label and discriminate emotions and bodily needs."

The doctors concluded their report by warning their colleagues to "bear in mind that in our affluent culture, where food is relatively cheap and readily available in quantity and variety, disturbances in interpersonal and intrapsychic functions have a ready nutritional vehicle for expression—whether by refusal to eat, refusal to limit eating or adoption of bizarre rituals and patterns of food intake unrelated to nutritional need."[4]

Hilde Bruch, M.D., has said that eating is used by women in general as a sign language of their emotions—emotions about which they may feel either ambivalent or guilty, or else be unaware of. Writing specifically of anorexia nervosa, Dr. Bruch emphasized patients' "paralyzing sense of ineffectiveness. They experience themselves as acting only *in response* to demands coming from other people in situations, and not as doing things because *they want to.*"[5] (emphasis added) Both descriptions of anorexics, the general and the specific, apply to the experience of cosseted women such as Clare and Diane. The difference is one of degree.

"Paralyzing," for example, might be too extreme an adjective to describe Diane's sense of ineffectiveness, but the sense is there nonetheless. To Diane, feeling ineffective isn't some vague psychiatric concept; it describes quite concretely the way she feels around her family. By nature an exuberant, emotional woman, she is married to a quiet, well-manicured man who protects himself against what he might call Diane's "female hysteria" by either ignoring her or responding to her with subtle but unmistakable sarcasm. Their three children have adopted their father's approach. And so Diane, quite literally, feels she has no effect on her family because they don't take her seriously. She also feels that she deserves pretty much what she gets. "I know I'm pretty hard to take," she apologizes. "I make a lot of noise." Diane blames herself, but underneath she is angry at her husband and children. Because her anger is passive—unexpressed—it has to be absorbed within Diane, and so she turns to food.

A woman less psychologically healthy than Diane might select a more extreme degree of edible sign language. Though it is probably safe to say that the majority of bulimic purgers are under 40 (the epidemic hasn't been raging openly long enough to have infected large numbers of Clare's and Diane's generation), just as with atypical anorexia, there are bingers and purgers hidden among the ranks of cosseted women.

Phyllis Schultz was one of them. Now 45 years old, she binged and vomited daily for twenty-six years of her life. Though she was married and bore four children during that period, no one in her family knew about her behavior. When she finally decided to seek help (she was also an alcoholic), she told her husband, but he didn't seem particularly interested. At one point, Phyllis tried family therapy, but "my role then was being responsible for my family and being sure they were fixed up, when what I really needed was to help myself."

She knew something was terribly wrong all those years, but felt alone with the problem until she read *The Golden Cage*, Dr. Bruch's popular book about anorexia nervosa. Then Phyllis heard about Elke Eckert, M.D., who was studying anorexics with chemical-dependency problems, including alcoholism, at the University of Minnesota Hospitals. She checked herself into the hospital to be treated by Dr. Eckert. Today, Phyllis remains abstinent from her former self-destructive behavior.

Considering the intensity of Phyllis's struggle, the thousands of cosseted dieters can consider themselves lucky that that's all their personal sign language entails. "It's the same no matter what your age," Phyllis says. "After a while, it doesn't make any difference whether you're gaining or losing weight. You're locked into the behavior and the attitude, until you turn the key."

7

TAKING CHARGE

So how do you go about unlocking yourself?

First, let's assume that you, like millions of others, have struggled to some degree with your weight, your body image and your general opinion of yourself, but are not in any immediate medical danger. Let's assume you've mixed those things up together, with one result being that you're not clear on how to untangle your thinking—not to mention your eating habits themselves. Let's also assume that you really would like to get on with the rest of your life and stop letting food, weight, eating and diet take up all of your time and energy and give you such a good excuse for not dealing with more abstract problems.

To be honest, you will probably always worry a little about feeling fat and gaining weight and how much you're eating; chances are, the subjects of food and weight will always be important to you. But they don't have to be _priorities_. They don't have to represent the final and most accurate measure of you, the individual, nor do they have to stand in for all the things you should be doing and feeling. The key question is not "Can you change?" You can. Where to start and how to make the change permanent are the questions to be answered.

There are many unsolved chicken-and-egg questions in modern psychology in terms of both causes and cures. Along the arc of eating disorders, the dilemmas multiply, for you must deal with what UCLA's Joel Yager, M.D., calls "a habit on top of a psychology on top of a biology."

Some of the more intriguing chicken-and-egg questions cur-

nothing to do with brain

rently puzzling eating-disorder specialists involve, for example, *neurology:* Is anorexia nervosa the result of hypothalamic dysfunction (the hypothalamus is a structure at the base of the brain presumed to regulate hunger and fullness, along with many other bodily functions) or the cause of it? Or *physiology:* Is the carbohydrate craving reported by so many bingers the direct physiological result of denying the body carbohydrates while dieting or does such a craving begin in the mind? Or *biology:* Could the state of depression felt by many bulimics be biochemical rather than psychological in nature, and could it cause the bingeing rather than result from it?

Because of the many interlocking, overlapping factors involved in developing and maintaining chaotic eating patterns, the experts stress that you can't put causes into neat little categories. In fact, neurobehavioral psychiatrist David M. Rudnick, M.D., of UCLA's Neuropsychiatric Institute, says that eating disorders provide the most complete example of the "biopsychosocial model" of human illness—Dr. Yager's habit-atop-psychology-atop biology, plus the added influence of societal demands.

If doctors do isolate a biochemical and/or neurological basis for an eating disorder, medication is usually called for as part of the treatment program. Accordingly, some patients can benefit from antidepressants; some even from antiseizure drugs. But for the majority of bulimics, chronic dieters and anorexics, habit and attitude—the way you act and the way you think—are the key targets of change. And they need to be attacked in unison.

Changing your attitude (psychologists call this *"cognitive restructuring"*) without changing your behavior will probably mean your attitude change is only a temporary one, for it will get no active reinforcement. By the same token, changing your behavior without an underlying change in the way you think about that behavior won't do any permanent good either. If you try, say, to stop bingeing—to change your behavior—without understanding its psychological function in your life and without finding replacements for it, you will find yourself returning to it. And if you or your doctors fail to rule out the possibility, however small, of an underlying physiological, neurological or biochemical basis for your food problems—meaning anything from metabolism to, in the extreme, epilepsy—you may miss the whole picture.

Most accomplished clinicians and researchers now believe that a cognitive-behavioral approach, a combined modification of thought and action, is the most promising permanent cure for a host of addictive behavioral and psychological disorders, including food addiction. Indeed, the idea that you could be addicted to food in the same ways that an alcoholic is addicted to alcohol, a smoker to nicotine, a cocaine user to cocaine or a gambler to gambling is a relatively new one. But all of those activities are based on a cycle of short-term gratification and long-term punishment, and might more appropriately be termed "indulgent behaviors," according to G. Alan Marlatt, Ph.D., professor of psychology and director of the Addictive Behaviors Research Center at the University of Washington in Seattle. The recent research of Dr. Marlatt and others implies that successful treatment methods for one indulgent behavior could work for all.

The first order of business in changing any indulgent behavior is obvious: *You have to want to change.* That means forgetting about the short-term benefits you're getting from your behavior, and for once focusing on the long term: the rest of your life. Assuming you have the desire to get off your personal seesaw, whether yours is bingeing and vomiting or noshing and dieting, you'll need to revamp three key areas: your attitude, your behavior, and the general way you live your life. All three are equally crucial if you want your efforts to produce permanent change. And since we've already seen that how you think about and act around food has a great deal to do with how you think about yourself and act around others, because chaotic eating has as much to do with psychology and sociology as it does with physiology and behavior, positive change will also involve the way you interact with other people.

It sounds like a big deal, but taken in small steps it is manageable. What you're trying to do is to set up a positive sequence of thought and action instead of your old negative one. And you'll want to strengthen and supplement it as you go, so that maintaining the new sequence is pleasurable and preferable to the old one on all levels. It can't be done all at once, and if you insist that it must, you already have set yourself up for failure. What you want is to create a reverse domino effect, one piece at a time. You're the one who built your own domino effect to begin with; you're the one to turn it around.

By their very nature, habits—good ones and bad ones—are safe because you're so used to them. Even when they make you miserable, it seems easier to keep them around than to risk dealing with something unfamiliar in their place. Unfortunately, most self-help books don't tell you that change of any kind, particularly change that involves giving up an indulgent habit, is extremely difficult unless you are totally committed to it. You must make it the key priority in your life until you feel confident that real change—change in your head as well as in your behavior—has taken place.

But once you've found your way out of a bad habit, you realize there's a whole other side to life that you'd forgotten or possibly never knew at all. Getting off the food/weight/diet seesaw is like getting out of a bad relationship or a bad job: The longer you're there, the more pointless it seems to try to get out—until, whether by your action or someone else's, *you get out*. And then you shake your head and say, "My God, it's so much better out here; why did I stay *there* so long?"

Let's start with your attitude.

CHANGING YOUR ATTITUDE

If you've ever asked an ex-smoker how she quit, and felt annoyed when she said, "I didn't do anything special—I just quit," because you thought there must have been *something*, some trick, think again. The ex-smoker must have finally reached a point where not smoking was more important to her than smoking. Suddenly, all the excuses that might have prevented her from quitting in the past—a family fight, tension at work, nervousness in social situations—disappeared. She knew deep inside of herself that she wanted out of the habit and was willing to trade off for it, to chew gum or her fingernails, to cope with the stress and anxiety and insecurity at home, on the job, in social situations as best she could, though it might mean being miserable or irritable or dull or withdrawn or depressed for a while. If necessary, she would even have to gain a few pounds until she learned how to stop eating without a cigarette to define the end of a meal.

What happened was that her head changed. She stopped being ambivalent about smoking. She stopped saying, "I wish I could quit, if only I weren't under so much stress right now [or wasn't afraid to gain weight or didn't need it to help me through a party]." There were no more "if onlys."

More of us reach this stage of habit-breaking determination than would seem from the dour statistics. Repeatedly it is said that 90 to 95 percent of dieters gain back the weight, and that perhaps 80 percent of smokers, alcoholics and heroin addicts who seemingly quit their behaviors are back to them within a year.[1] What we don't hear about are the people who succeed permanently. The reason is simple: The studies from which the statistics come are based on people who seek help from clinics or psychologists because they can't do it themselves, and generally such studies measure only a single attempt to quit the addictive behavior.

Research psychologist Stanley Schacter, of Columbia University, suspected a gap between clinical statistics and real-life fact when it came to cigarette smoking and weight control, and decided to investigate. As subjects, he chose people from the general population (one group from Columbia, one from the permanent residents of a Long Island resort community), not people who had sought professional treatment for their problems. Schacter's results confirmed his suspicions: The rates of successful self-cure of smoking and excessive weight were significantly higher than any reported so far through various therapy programs.

How much higher? Of the ex-smokers, 63.6 percent were considered successes: On the average, they'd been nonsmokers for 7.4 years. Of the dieters (who currently or in the past had been 15 percent or more overweight according to life-insurance charts), 62.5 percent were considered successful cures: They'd lost an average of 34.7 pounds and maintained the loss for an average 11.2 years.

Schacter speculated that studies which investigate *single* attempts at quitting don't take into account the possible positive effects of repeated attempts to quit. "The proportion of successful quitters," he wrote, "cumulatively increases with successive attempts." Finally, Schacter concluded, "It appears that the generally accepted professional and public impression that nicotine addiction and obesity are almost hopelessly difficult conditions to correct is flatly wrong. People can and do cure themselves. They do so in large numbers and for long periods of time, and in many cases, apparently, they're able to do so permanently.[2]

How do they do it? When William Gerin of *Psychology Today* analyzed Schacter's interviews, he found no magic solution. The people who stopped smoking or lost weight over the long term used the same techniques as those who failed. "Though it sounds too easy to be true," wrote Gerin, "it seems that these people lost weight *when they made up their minds to do so.*"[3] (emphasis added)

Such evidence shows that you can indeed break the chain of addiction—whether your "fix" is food, alcohol, nicotine or drugs—if your head is in order. "There's a shift that goes on in your mind, and then it becomes easy to cross the threshold when before you couldn't," says Dr. Marlatt of the University of Washington. "But if you really look at it, each time you tried to quit the indulgent behavior, whether it was bingeing or drinking or smoking, you weren't failing; you were actually learning how to make a success of it."

To get your head in order, you must first learn to identify the irrational thoughts about food and weight that are standing in your way and replace them with rational ones. It's your *perception* of reality that dictates your behavior; altering those perceptions that block change is the first place to start.

One of the most common irrational perceptions shared by anorexics, bulimics, and Yo-Yo dieters alike is the "Either/Or" syndrome. *Either I'm all-perfection or all-failure. Either I'm on my diet or I've blown my diet. Either I'm good or I'm bad. Either I'm fat or I'm thin.* This kind of thinking leaves no room for maneuvering, no room to take chances, no way to learn. It also sets up a clear escape route that leads straight into the open arms of the behavior you want to avoid, for the only options you allow yourself are extremes. It gives you zero flexibility with your self-image; it doesn't allow you to take a balanced view of yourself as a normal human being with good, not-so-good and neutral attributes shifting back and forth depending on the particular situation you're in. If you maintain an either/or attitude, your behavior will follow suit—there will be no possibility of moderation.

Let's say you've been dieting and you're out with friends, and someone stops for ice cream. You take what is in reality a moderate, 250-calorie action: You eat a scoop of ice cream. But you wind up with an extreme reaction: You go on a full binge because your head tells you, "Now that I've had that ice cream, I may as well eat five more, and other stuff, too, because I've blown my diet." There is nothing rational about that at all, but once you think it enough, it becomes truth. Reality is only what you perceive it to be.

Dr. Marlatt used the term "think-drink effect" to explain the results of a study he and his colleagues conducted using male drinkers as subjects. Half the men were told that they'd be comparing three brands of vodka (mixed with tonic water) in a taste test; the other half were told they'd be comparing tonic waters. In reality, half of those expecting alcohol would be getting tonic water only; half of those expecting no alcohol would be getting vodka and tonic.

The results showed that the subjects' expectations dictated their behavior: The alcoholics and social drinkers who thought they were drinking vodka drank significantly more than those who thought they had tonic water only—regardless of the actual presence or absence of alcohol in their drinks. One of the men who expected alcohol but received only tonic nevertheless acted as if he were intoxicated, "stumbling around the room and trying to make a date with our female research assistant."[4]

Is there a comparable "think-eat effect"? Several recent experiments, including one conducted in the mid-1970s by Janet Polivy, then of Loyola University in Illinois, demonstrated that there is. In Polivy's study, dieters who were *told* they had consumed a high-calorie pudding and were then asked to taste an assortment of sandwiches consumed significantly more sandwiches than when told they'd had a low-calorie pudding. What they were told wasn't necessarily true; the point was that what they perceived about the pudding provoked their ensuing behavior. According to Polivy, the dieter's mere belief that he had overeaten was enough to trigger an eating binge.[5]

Take the issue of control that's so central to any discussion of bulimia, anorexia or dieting/overeating cycles. Since being totally in control is a rare state for any individual, most of us range from being pretty much in control to being a little out of control in everyday life. But if only flawless control will do, if anything less than perfection is failure, then you probably experience yourself, irrationally, as being out of control most of the time. Which also means that you see yourself as helpless. And hopeless.

If that's the way you think, you are subscribing to the disease theory of addictive behaviors espoused by such organizations as Alcoholics Anonymous, Overeaters Anonymous and Gamblers Anonymous. The theory first came to prominence in the mid-1950s in relation to alcohol abuse, when the American Medical Association officially labeled alcoholism a form of physical dependency, a disease over which the victim had no control; he had only two options: to abstain or be damned. Though Dr. Marlatt and others dispute the disease view because it assumes the individual has no hope of self-control and thus absolves him from taking responsibility for his actions, it's still considered an improvement over the highly judgmental moral model that preceded the disease model. The moral approach held that the addict simply lacked the moral fiber to resist temptation. Period. Since it's hard for people to admit that they're made of such flawed stuff, the emergence of the disease model is credited with encouraging people to seek help for their problems, for at least they could now blame them on something other than a hopelessly immoral character.

Fast replacing the disease model today is the self-control approach represented by cognitive-behavioral therapists such as Dr. Marlatt. This approach holds that all immediate-gratification or indulgent behaviors, including abuse of food, alcohol, drugs, nicotine and gambling, are learned habits that can be brought under lifetime control by developing and following methods to prevent relapse. The self-control school suggests that there are common factors operating across the board of indulgent behaviors, regardless of the particular substance or activity involved, and that the disease school's requirement of abstinence is a pessimistic approach that may itself ensure failure by suggesting that any lapse is a full-blown relapse. In effect, the disease approach reinforces dangerous either/or thinking and leads the victim straight back to the unwanted behavior. "Unless the person is freed from the dichotomous view that one is either in control (abstinent) or out of control (relapsed)," wrote Dr. Marlatt, "the pendulum may continue to swing back and forth from one extreme to the other."[6]

One of the keys to the self-control approach is the development of what psychologist A. Bandura called "self-efficacy," or confidence in your ability to handle situations as they arise in life. If you have a strong sense of self-efficacy, you trust yourself to get through a stressful situation without having to resort to an indulgent behavior, such as a food binge. Each time you succeed in handling a problem without your crutch, you've increased your sense of self-efficacy. This gets back, again, to how you perceive things: According to the latest in stress research, how well you cope is directly related to how well you *think* you'll cope.[7]

The reverse of that is obvious: If you expect you'll be unable to cope with a given situation, your sense of self-efficacy decreases and your sense of helplessness increases. The more helpless you feel, the more likely you'll be to give in to the situation when it arises, according to Dr. Marlatt. Giving in means turning to the indulgent behavior; and once you do that, you've reinforced your sense of helplessness.

To develop self-efficacy, it's important to stop identifying yourself in the old negative way. For example, if you've been bulimic for some time, you've probably assumed bulimia as your identity; you can't imagine not being that way and don't know how you'd handle stress and anxiety without your personal five-martini solution. Try imagining yourself as a healthy eater. Fantasize about it once a day. The more you practice "seeing" yourself that way, the more accepting you will be of the possibility of a new you rather than the old, helpless-and-hopeless, out-of-control you.

This ability to alter your self-concept through imagining a new one has been shown to be highly effective in predicting long-term maintenance of weight loss. When Richard B. Stuart and K. Guire studied dieters, they found that those who thought of themselves as thin rather than as formerly fat were more likely to maintain their weight loss.[8] The flip side of Stuart and Guire's finding is suggested by a study of the eating behavior of 355 college students, conducted by Katherine A. Halmi, M.D., James R. Falk and Estelle Schwartz. They found that the number of days between eating binges decreased if the individual considered himself or herself to be a binge eater.[9]

It became obvious to the experts that simply removing an indulgent behavior wasn't enough. As anyone who's ever lost weight on a diet knows, the hardest part is maintaining the loss, not just getting there. So people like Dr. Marlatt began to focus on long-term maintenance of behavior change—what happens after you get there.

Suppose you've vowed never to binge again. You're doing fine until you learn that you've been passed over for promotion at work, or your husband is having an affair, or you flunked your astronomy exam, or any number of high-risk situations that might threaten your control over yourself because you feel angry, hurt, rejected or guilty. Despite your vow, you panic under the yoke of stress and relapse into the old behavior, so that you can have *it* first for solace and later to blame for feeling bad, instead of focusing on the initial event that upset you. That's your old trick, but now it makes you feel even worse because you've broken your vow—you've failed. Again. And you've attributed your failure, as usual, to your weakness as a person.

By hopping onto that particular train of thought, says the self-control school, you're missing a golden opportunity to learn from the situation. This is what cognitive-behavioral psychologists call "relabeling": You can turn a failure experience into a learning experience by changing the way you think about it. Now you've redefined your problem—what led you to break your vow. It was *not* personal weakness, but simply a lack of proper coping tools. You don't need to hate yourself; what you need is to learn and practice new responses to stressful or threatening situations, some of which are described in chapters 9 and 10, so that you will be prepared the next time the situation arises. Remember Dr. Marlatt's golden rule: Your behavior is something that you *do,* not something that you *are.*

Think of your slip as a single incidence. Just because it happened once does not necessarily mean it will have to happen again, nor that you will respond the same way if it does. Also, realize that your initial reaction to the slip, which involved self-hatred, guilt and self-blame, was a predictable one given your ingrained either/or attitude. Get past those feelings so that you can study the circumstances of the slip and be alert for them in the future.

You also need to wake up to yourself. Often, people will try to avoid feeling guilty and assuming responsibility for their behavior by taking a series of small actions that somehow accumulate into a major temptation that they just can't resist. Decision-making specialist Lee Beach, Ph.D., one of Dr. Marlatt's colleagues at the University of Washington, calls these actions "Apparently Irrelevant Decisions" (AIDs). "It is as though the person begins to slowly set the stage for a possible relapse by making a series of AIDs," writes Dr. Marlatt, "each of which moves the individual one step closer to relapse. By putting oneself in an impossibly tempting high-risk situation, one can claim that one was overwhelmed by external circumstances which made it impossible to resist a relapse."[10]

Dr. Marlatt calls the culmination of such AIDs the "downtown-Reno effect," in honor of one client who'd abstained from his particular indulgent behavior—gambling—for six months and then relapsed. Here's how the client's AIDs set him up.

The client, a member of Gamblers Anonymous, and his wife had taken a driving trip from their home in Seattle down the West Coast to San Francisco. On their return to Seattle, they had planned a route through the Sierra Nevada and up through Oregon. Everything was fine until they approached the California-Nevada border northeast of San Francisco. At this point, the client got restless. He began to argue with his wife about the route. He wanted to alter their plans so they could see the "amazingly blue waters" of Lake Tahoe. He insisted it was worth the detour. His wife wanted to stick to the original route. Still arguing, they reached a junction in the highway. One direction would take them home the way they'd planned, and the other would take them to the Nevada border and on to Tahoe and Reno. Since the husband was driving, he resolved the argument by taking the Nevada turn.

They saw the lake and drove on to Reno, where they stopped. He just happened to park the car directly in front of a casino and found that he had no change for the parking meter. It was, of course, necessary to get change in the casino. Since he changed a quarter and only needed a dime for the meter, he thought he'd just try his luck in the slot machine with the remaining fifteen cents. It took his wife three days to get him out of Reno, and by then he had gambled all of their vacation money away.[11] That binge triggered many others, until he finally sought help from Dr. Marlatt at the Addictive Behaviors Research Center in Seattle. By tracing the AIDs that led to the Reno relapse, the gambler came to see how, little by little, he'd planned the whole thing.

If your indulgent behavior happens to involve food, no doubt you can recognize plenty of AIDs in your behavior. And you can probably isolate other pockets of faulty thinking in your head that are ripe for picking. For example, many compulsive dieters and bingers, whatever their weight, assume that others are noticing, monitoring and disapproving of what they eat and how fat they look, and then use this irrational assumption as a trigger to rebel by bingeing, or to comply by ever more stringent dieting. Researchers David M. Garner, Ph.D., Paul E. Garfinkel, M.D., and Kelly M. Bemis, B.A., call this thought process "personalization and self-reference."[12] Paradoxically, it combines low self-esteem with high egocentricity: You see yourself as the focus of negative attention in situations that others might see as being totally impersonal.

It would help if you stopped thinking about yourself so much. It only contributes to your eating problems. Just because your thoughts are negative, ranging somewhere between self-hatred and self-pity, doesn't mean they're any less self-centered. At least once every day, try to catch a debilitating self-centered thought and replace it with an outer-directed one. Anything will do—the world political situation, your brother's birthday, the Second Coming—anything but food and weight and what everybody else is thinking about you. One thing that Melanie, a former binge-vomiter from Ohio, learned in her bulimia-group therapy is that "I need to remember I'm not the center of the whole world. That contributed to my bingeing, because sometimes I'd binge in front of my husband to see if he was concerned enough to respond. Basically, it was a form of pouting—I had to have all the attention."

Dr. Garner and colleagues identified other types of irrational anorexic thinking that apply to many other positions on the arc.

—*Superstitious thinking:* believing in a cause-and-effect relationship between unconnected events. ("If I eat a sweet, it will be converted instantly into stomach fat.")

—*Magnification:* overestimating the future effect of a certain action. ("I've gained two pounds, so I can't wear shorts anymore.")

—*Selective abstraction:* basing a conclusion on isolated details while ignoring more relevant, contradictory evidence. ("I am special if I am thin.")

—*Overgeneralization:* making a rule on the basis of one situation and applying it to unlike situations. ("When I used to eat carbohydrates, I was fat; therefore, I must avoid them now so I won't become obese.")[13]

Examples of "bulimic thinking," as outlined by Katharine Dixon, M.D., assistant professor of psychiatry at Ohio State University, are equally pertinent to people with all degrees of food-and-weight preoccupation. Such thinking includes:

—*Denial:* ("I won't be a binge-vomiter long enough to sustain any damage.")

—*Personal weakness:* ("I know I'll keep thinking about food, so I may as well binge and get it over with so I can concentrate on other things. . . .")

—*Displacement of feelings onto food:* ("If I binge, I won't feel so lonely, angry or depressed.")
—*Excuses:* ("I wouldn't have to do this if it weren't for . . .")
—*Repentance and renewal:* ("I'll never do this again. It's my last binge.")

Spotting your own patterns of erroneous thinking is the first step toward change.

Stop thinking in black and white when it comes to food—good food is diet food; bad food is nondiet food. If you instruct yourself to eat only good food, you will soon be bingeing on the bad. But if you slowly introduce "bad" foods into your everyday eating (see chapter 9), eventually they will no longer be bad but only normal, and you won't feel you have to overindulge in them to have them at all. Again, you need to change the way you perceive food just as you need to change the way you perceive yourself and your behavior.

Remember:

—Be honest with yourself. Determine that you would like to get rid of your food-and-weight preoccupation and not try to hold on to it for security's sake.
—You are not helpless or hopeless. Work on giving that identity up.
—Stop thinking in only two dimensions. You will never be perfect, but in a black-and-white world, the only other option is to be a failure.
—If you slip back into old behavior, rethink the experience as an opportunity for learning and growth rather than an opportunity for suffering and self-abuse.
—Don't dwell unnecessarily on yourself. A sense of humor is an excellent antidote to negative self-centeredness. Laugh whenever you can.

Now that you've reoriented the way you think about your eating behavior—no longer as proof of your failings as a person, but as an indirect and inappropriate way of dealing with events and people in your life—you need to design a plan for translating your new thoughts into new behavior. The plan must involve both day-to-day change in your eating behavior itself and a more general life-style change. For the plan to be successful in freeing you of your food-and-weight shackles, you must learn how to anticipate certain trigger situations and how to cope with them differently, and you must also introduce new pleasures into your life that are not related to food.

First: how to put your eating in order.

LEARNING HOW TO EAT

The line between dieting and having an eating disorder is practically nonexistent.

25-year-old ex-bulimic

The Case Against Dieting

Imagine, for a moment, being able to eat normally without purging or skipping meals or eating only lettuce—without dieting—and not feeling fat. Ever. Imagine not thinking about food except when you're hungry, and then just eating it. Imagine giving up the whole battle once and for all and finding that, if anything, you're thinner for giving it up.

Imagination can become reality if you want it to. But first *you must give up the idea of rigid dieting*, or you will always be stuck on your personal weight seesaw. The scientific evidence is formidable and growing that the more restricted your weight-loss diet, the more likely you are to also become bulimic, though you may have started out a simple nosher. The less your diet has to do with real-life eating—with restaurants and parties and Thanksgiving and everyday family suppers—the more confused you'll be about how and what to eat when you're no longer on the diet.

Richard Pyle, M.D., of the University of Minnesota Hospitals, says that a strict diet, especially if you don't get enough to eat or if special diet food is provided, tends to lead to bingeing behavior later on. All you have to do is pick a certain diet and you've set up a high-risk situation for yourself. For example, take Judy Mazel's Beverly Hills Diet. In the *International*

Journal of Eating Disorders, writers O. Wayne Wooley and Susan Wooley published an editorial entitled "The Beverly Hills Eating Disorder: The Mass Marketing of Anorexia Nervosa." They noted that the diet is a form of direct training in anorexic behaviors and attitudes.[1]

The reality is that no matter how much weight you can lose eating only lettuce and grapes, or fasting on liquids, eventually you will encounter a pizza, a carton of ice cream or even just a piece of bread. And you will panic, because you have made such items forbidden and thus minimized your ability to deal with them rationally. Irrationality takes over: You become afraid of them. You think they will "make" you eat them.

Clearly, the flip side of dieting is bingeing. As British researchers Jane Wardle and Helen Beinart concluded: "Binge eating seems to occur in many people, whatever their weight, who are attempting to exercise dietary restraint. This includes normal men and women who would like to weigh a little less than they do, obese patients who aim for a socially and medically acceptable weight, and thin or normal-weight patients who relentlessly seek emaciation." What do they propose as treatment for this problem? *A reduction in dieting.*[2]

It's only recently that researchers have begun to compare dieters versus nondieters, regardless of their weights. And they've come up with some provocative findings. For example, it now appears that eating in response to anxiety, long presumed to be true of fat people but not normal-weight people, is more a function of whether the person is dieting than how much he or she weighs.

In the early 1970s, psychologists C. Peter Herman and Janet Polivy, then of Northwestern University, conducted a study of anxiety, dieting and eating behavior. They chose forty-two female subjects and told them they would taste some ice cream, then be given an electric shock (the anxiety trigger) and, finally, taste some more ice cream. After the experiment, the subjects filled out questionnaires to determine their diet and weight histories and their degree of concern with food and eating.

The results? The nondieters ate less in response to anxiety

and the dieters ate more. The researchers concluded that anxiety seemed to shake the control that the dieters were trying to maintain over their eating. Overeating when anxious, then, may be more a reflection of the chronic hunger that is usually denied by dieting than a way to try to lessen anxiety.[3] It's hard enough to diet stringently when the rest of your life is proceeding smoothly, for dieting in itself is stressful. But if you're confronted with some unexpected trauma, large or small, the likelihood that you'll overeat is greater than if you hadn't been dieting in the first place.

Worse yet, on a physiological level, a continual weight seesaw may make you fatter in the long run. Recent research conducted by Susan C. Wooley, Ph.D., and Orland W. Wooley, Ph.D., of the University of Cincinnati College of Medicine suggests that the longer your history of dieting, the easier it will be for you to *gain* weight each time you try to return to normal eating after losing weight. The reason? Your body reacts to a dramatic cutback in calories as if it were defending against real starvation by slowing down its metabolic rate, and thus its expenditure of calories. The rate appears to remain low when you try to resume normal eating after dieting—meaning that you won't be able to consume as many calories as before the diet without gaining weight, according to the Wooleys. Among other things, this helps to explain the plateau period experienced by dieters, when weight loss slows down or stops without an increase in calories.

"It seems possible," write the Wooleys, "that the loss of five pounds may virtually insure the later gain of six, so that dieting—the major *treatment* for obesity—may also be a major *cause*."[4] In other words, rigid dieting may have the exact opposite effect on your weight from the one you'd intended.

It also appears that *regained* weight brings with it a higher level of fat tissue than before the weight was lost, even if the gain is back to the starting weight. Fat tissue requires less energy (calories) to exist than lean muscle tissue does (one reason why men, with a far greater proportion of lean muscle tissue to fat tissue than women, can consume many more calories per day than women can). The more fat tissue you have, the lower your basal metabolic rate, or BMR (the amount of calories you need to maintain your bodily functions without expending energy).

If regained weight brings with it more fat, the amount of calories you can consume and not gain weight decreases, which in turn will make it harder to lose weight the next time, because you'll have to cut back even further on calories. Susan Wooley cites the case of an airline stewardess treated at the Clinic for Eating Disorders at the University of Cincinnati. The stewardess had been fasting regularly for years to pass the airline's monthly weigh-in. Apparently, her metabolism gradually adapted to these periods of fasting, so that eventually she'd gain weight even on an 800-calorie-a-day diet, and in time could no longer meet the airline's weight standard.[5]

The provocative "setpoint theory" of weight regulation is intertwined with such findings. In 1972, R. E. Nisbett proposed that each individual is biologically programmed to maintain a certain weight (the setpoint), which in some cases may be well above what society and/or medicine decrees to be normal for their height and body build. Thus, someone who appears to be fat may in fact be at his or her setpoint—or even below it.[6]

The setpoint doesn't just regulate weight, but also the amount of body fat. Fat is contained in specific cells in the body, and the number of these cells that each individual carries is presumably set early in life. Fat cells increase in number at particular periods of childhood development; by the beginning of adolescence, their number has basically become fixed. Once your fat cells have been set, you can never get rid of them—one reason why overweight children usually continue to be overweight throughout life.

However, your fat cells will shrink when you lose weight, and expand when you gain. According to setpoint theory, if you force your fat cells to shrink by dieting, they will fight back by demanding to be filled up again. This demand may be experienced as the drive to binge, or it may be expressed by slowing your metabolism so that remaining fat is conserved. If you start out with a lot of fat cells, your struggle to become and remain slender will be that much more difficult.

How do you know what your setpoint is? According to William Bennett, M.D., and Joel Gurin, who together have presented some of the most current work on the subject in *The Dieter's Dilemma*, setpoint is the weight you normally maintain, give or take a few pounds, when you are not thinking about it.[7] But that definition doesn't help much if, like most dieters, you are *never* not thinking about it while you go up and down on the scale.

Medical professionals, most of whom subscribe at least in part to setpoint theory, have had to devise methods of determining goal weights for anorexic and bulimic patients. Most specify that a weight *range* of 5 to 7 pounds, rather than a single magic number, should be chosen, to allow for fluctuation in body fluid without triggering a bout of starvation or bingeing if the magic number does not appear on the scale. For example, Meir Gross, M.D., of the Cleveland Clinic, determines a ball-park setpoint by taking an extensive family history. If the patient's father is tall and heavyset and she is built similarly, her goal of being skinny is unrealistic. In that situation, Dr. Gross urges the patient to make a choice: She can either be precariously skinny at the price of ruining her life and health by bingeing and vomiting, or she can revise her priorities.

Most of us can probably isolate a period of time, postpuberty, in which we were neither losing nor gaining weight; the number on the scale during such a period would have been fairly consistent over a period of months or even years. That number marked your probable setpoint—although, especially if you're female, you no doubt thought it wasn't thin enough. Just another 5 pounds or 10 pounds less. But it's precisely those few pounds, if you believe in setpoint theory, that may make the difference between chaotic and normal eating.

Setpoint theory helped to explain a number of things that had puzzled researchers—for example, the fact that one person may be able to eat only 1,000 calories a day to keep his or her weight at 110, while another person of the same age, height, build, sex and activity level may be able to eat 2,000 calories to maintain the same weight: The discrepancy could be due to the latter person's having a lower setpoint. The theory also helped to explain the emotional trauma and occasional psychosis that a dieting regimen precipitates in some obese people, which has often been shrugged off by physicians as signs of weakness and poor motivation instead of being seen as signals of biological distress, as Hilde Bruch, M.D., has noted.[8]

In addition, the concept of setpoint is relevant to the fact that up to 50 percent of restrictor anorexics turn to bingeing, for they may have forced their weights well below setpoint, and their bodies must fight back. In a study of thirty bulimic-anorexic patients, British researcher Gerald Russell, M.D., stated flatly that the bouts of overeating are a response of the hypothalamus to a too low body weight.[9] (As explained earlier, the hypothalamus, located at the base of the brain, is believed to regulate hunger and fullness, among other things.)

Setpoint theory also provides an alternative way of looking at the issue of control. A dieter who loses weight and then gains it back may be engaged in a struggle with an opponent far more formidable than her willpower—a struggle with her own biology. If so, the nearly universal American contempt for fatness that begins in childhood and continues throughout life may be cruelly misdirected. For if you believe in setpoint theory, our societal presumption that overweight is due to laziness and lack of discipline, and that it is within everyone's ability to reduce if we really want to, is quite wrong.

That's reassuring to our self-image; it means that our difficulties in losing weight are caused not by a weakness of character but rather by a fact of individual biology. But any discussion of setpoint leads inevitably to an uncomfortable thought as well: that some of us cannot be thin no matter what we do, and that if we try, like Sisyphus we forever and in vain fight an uphill battle. Particularly for those of us with truly chaotic eating patterns, brainwashing ourselves into accepting this thought may be the only way back to behavioral sanity. "The patient's giving up a personally unrealistic body weight," asserts David M. Garner, Ph.D., "is critical in the treatment of bulimia."

Accepting a higher weight may actually be healthier for all of us. The assumption we've all been operating on since the late 1950s, that the healthiest people are underweight, has recently been challenged by a study conducted by the National Institutes of Health. The study indicates that the leanest people are most vulnerable to disease and run the greatest risk of premature death. According to the NIH study, which followed more than 5,000 male and female residents of Framingham, Massachusetts, for twenty-four years, optimum weight (the weight at which we'd live the longest) for most people would be at least 10 pounds more than life-insurance-company weight charts stipulated.[10] These are the same charts that doctors have been referring to since about 1959.

But suppose you simply can't accept yourself 10 or 15 pounds heavier, though you've determined that your setpoint probably demands the extra weight. Is there any way to lower your setting without forever struggling with calorie charts? Apparently there is: by a *sustained increase in physical activity*. In other words: exercise.

"Sustained" means that exercise must become a regular fixture in your life to have a permanent effect on your setpoint. And the exercise itself must be an aerobic one, such as cycling, running, brisk walking, swimming, jumping rope.

The theory that physical activity can lower setpoint over time seems to be validated by the personal experience of both men and women. When Sheila Davidson, 31, heard about setpoint, she related to it instantly: Her stable weight had always been about 122 (she is 5'3"), from about the age of 16. She had manipulated it up and down through dieting and fasting and bingeing, from a low of 98 to a high of 135, but it always returned to 120 or 122 whenever she took a break from dieting. By the time she was 25, she'd given up dieting for good; and as a result, her bingeing stopped as well. Now more or less a normal eater, her weight has stayed at about 120.

At 26, she began the first regular exercise program of her life: She joined a health club and began swimming three times a week in the Olympic-size pool. After a year, she'd worked herself up to a mile of straight crawl, without stopping, which took about forty minutes. Today, five years after beginning her exercise program, which she has maintained religiously, she has a new stable weight: 110. "I don't diet anymore, which also means I'm not as likely to overeat—but when I weighed a hundred and twenty, I didn't eat any more than at a hundred and ten. I can only explain it because of the swimming," she says. Sheila is delighted with her new weight that doesn't require rigid diets to maintain, and exercising is now as much a part of her life as driving to work. "When I think of the effort I used to put into dieting," says Sheila, "the effort of exercising is nothing."

The effect of physical exercise on setpoint makes even more sense if you consider that sustained physical activity has a cumulative effect on your body. It increases the proportion of lean muscle tissue to fat tissue and ups the quantity of fat-burning enzymes in muscle. It may also raise your BMR, for research shows that calories are burned faster for several hours after you work out, even if you are stationary during those hours.

There are, of course, several wrinkles to setpoint theory. How do you explain, for instance, the case of Charlie Landers, product of an obese mother and obese father who themselves had persistent family histories of obesity? Charlie and his two brothers and one sister had inherited the family pattern: All were at least 15 pounds overweight and usually much more at any given point in childhood, adolescence and young adulthood. But when Charlie was 24, he decided to change his way of eating and lost 45 pounds. He is now 35, is a normal eater, doesn't participate in any regular exercise and has never regained the weight.

Does that mean that his natural setting was at the lower weight, but his familial environment, and the eating patterns it spawned, maintained it at an artifically high level until he changed those patterns? If the members of his family changed their eating patterns as well, would they lose weight and keep it off? At the moment, Charlie is still the only normal-weight member of his immediate family, and the jury is still out on the finer details of setpoint.

How to Get Your Eating Back on Track
First, remember three things:

1. The more restrictive your diet, the more likely you are to go off it in a big, bad way.
2. You will be better off (and, quite possibly, thinner in the long run) weighing 10 pounds above your official "ideal" than gaining and losing that same 10 pounds over and over again.
3. Without consistent physical exercise maintained over time, your chances of keeping to a lower weight without great stress are extremely small.

Now: You have to make a choice. Do you want to continue to battle over weight—or do you want to learn how to eat? You can't do both at the same time. Just as it's fruitless to treat the psychological aspects of anorexia nervosa while the patient is at a starvation weight and a slave to the distorted thinking that starvation promotes, it makes no sense to try to regulate your eating if at the same time you insist on continuing to diet, vomit or purge. If you must, you can worry about losing weight after you've stabilized your eating patterns.

Realize that overcontrol is as harmful as undercontrol when it comes to weight maintenance and weight loss. Eating when you're not hungry and not eating when you are hungry are two sides of the same coin. "If you can develop a stance towards fast food that allows you to eat," notes British psychotherapist Susie Orbach, "you will more easily be able to stop when you've had enough. In other words, in giving up dieting and allowing yourself a free range of foods, you are opening yourself up to the possibility of *not* overeating."[11] Throwing away your scale, or at least not getting on it for a month or two, isn't a bad way to start. There are four important guidelines for stabilization:

1. *Make order out of chaos by structuring your eating.*

It is essential that you eat three planned-in-advance meals every day and do not skip any, even if you overeat the day before; even if you binge. Richard B. Stuart, M.D., a prominent behaviorist at the University of Utah and the psychological director of Weight Watchers International, suggests that at first you should schedule your three meals at the most conventional times, starting with an early breakfast. "Even though you may not like the taste of food in the early morning," Dr. Stuart instructs, "you can condition yourself to shift the inner cycle of your food interest and in doing so you can bring your eating under the normal conditions that will help you to limit both what and how much you eat."

Dr. Stuart suggests that snacks be scheduled as precisely as meals in terms of the time they are eaten, the content and the portion size. "You may vary the scheduled times of your meals or snacks by up to 20 minutes or so from day to day, *but greater variations defeat the purpose of the reconditioning program.* Therefore, you will have to be prepared to discipline yourself on weekends as well as on weekdays, having breakfast, lunch, dinner, and any planned snacks at roughly the same time every day," Dr. Stuart adds. His point is that you must learn to reduce your urge to eat before you can change the way you eat. "If freedom from persistent urges to eat is important to you, the effort necessary to retrain yourself to think of food *only at the times that you choose* will be a small price to pay. Once you have reconditioned yourself to think of food at certain times only, you can go back to a more natural flexibility."[12]

2. *Spread calories throughout the day so that you're not starving by night and set up to nosh or binge.*

If you starve yourself during the day, you will end up

with what Dr. Stuart calls a "psychological caloric deficit"—the feeling that you owe yourself extra calories because you declined food at normal mealtime hours.[13] This is yet another reason to stick to that three-meal-a-day rule. Also, if you avoided food all day, your hungriest period— late afternoon or early evening—will possibly coincide with the end of the school- or workday, traditionally a vulnerable period for bingeing unless you've scheduled an activity for this time. If you allow your hunger to coincide with a stretch of unstructured time, you've doubled the chance that you'll binge.

"Most bingers," says Katharine Dixon, M.D., "are high-energy-level, high-achievement people who feel guilt, often experienced as boredom, when they have free time. They feel they should be doing something, and when free time occurs it may contribute to going into the kitchen to look for something to eat. If unstructured time is a vulnerable time, find ways to structure time until you feel in control of your eating."

You must follow your meal schedule, for you are trying to make a new habit—you want to regulate your regular eating in place of regulating irregular eating, as before. The more disordered your eating behavior, the more order you will need. This is particularly true if you have gone beyond dieting and into vomiting, laxative abuse or other purges to compensate for indulgence. At the Cleveland Clinic, bulimic patients are told by Jill Salisbury, R.N.; that if they want to get rid of bingeing and purging, they'll have to accept a 5 percent weight gain as a trade-off.

A small price, when you think about it. If your stable weight was 120, 5 percent means a mere 6-pound gain at the most. Isn't that preferable to all the struggling, the indulgence, the self-hatred? According to the Cleveland Clinic's Elaine Stevens, A.C.S.W., patients who have taken the risk of weight gain, who eat regularly scheduled meals and stop vomiting, haven't gained more than 5 percent, and in many cases have gained nothing at all. But the ones still fighting normalized eating have either gained significantly or continued to vomit.

When one woman determined to give up her twenty-year habit of bingeing and vomiting at least once a day, she found it necessary to stop making up her own rules of eating and not eating. "I had to routinize myself into typical mealtimes. If I wanted to sleep late, I'd still get up at my breakfast time, eat breakfast, then get back to bed. At first I had no idea how much I should be eating, and when you stop vomiting you feel bloated. But I had to determine not to resort to vomiting anymore.

"It's totally experimental at first and you have to expect to make mistakes," she says. "I still have anxiety sometimes over what and how much I've eaten, but it's nothing like the anxiety I get if I fall out of my routine, if I start eating at odd hours, eating unbalanced meals. If you eat too much or too little, it cues a binge. Through trial and error with yourself, you learn about what to eat." This woman did not experience a weight gain when she traded in bingeing and vomiting for regular meals—and so her "fat" terror gradually went away.

Christopher G. Fairburn, of Oxford University, advises a bulimic patient to eat at regular mealtimes even if she doesn't feel hungry, for her hunger sensations are likely to have been disturbed by her irregular eating habits and are therefore an unsatisfactory guide as to when and what she should eat. Dr. Fairburn doesn't tell the patient *what* to eat; instead, he emphasizes the establishment of a controlled and regular eating pattern. He suggests that the patient weigh herself every few weeks to reassure herself that she hasn't gained weight.

Some patients, Dr. Fairburn notes, have such disturbed eating patterns that it would be unreasonable to expect them to be able to confine all their eating to mealtimes. In those cases, therapist and patient determine when the patient's eating is most under control—usually during the day—and she is encouraged to focus on increasing control, by experimenting with eating banned foods, during these safe periods. The intention, he says, is that she should relax control over the content of her diet while continuing to restrict her eating to predetermined mealtimes.[14]

3. *Design your meals from a wide variety of foods.*

The minute you slip into "bad-food/good-food" thinking, you will begin to crave what you have deprived yourself of. Dr. Stuart recommends that you vary the colors, tastes and smells of your preselected foods at every meal, and try not to repeat the same foods in less than three- or four-day intervals. He also recommends that you include foods that require biting and chewing at no less than two of your three daily meals.[15]

Don't avoid food *categories*. If you binge on bread and crackers but deny them at all other times, you need to reconsider them as foods to enjoy in your daily diet. If you don't deprive yourself of them, if you know that you can have some every day, you won't have to indulge in them all at once. However, if you binge only on one particular cracker—say, Cheez-its—then select another kind for your normalization program that doesn't have a direct binge association.

Ellyn Satter, R.D., M.S.W., director of the Nutrition Center at the Jackson Clinic in Madison, Wisconsin, suggests that you learn to eat foods you enjoy. She shows clients how to design a meal from the basic food categories. For example, it's hard to be satisfied without starch and something chewy, such as a bagel, which has both qualities. "You need to practice food selection," Satter says, "and to understand your body signals. Some knowledge of physiology and nutrition is essential to normalize eating; people don't realize that there's no need to fear food, because what they suspect about it is wrong. You can learn to eat when you're hungry to the point of satisfaction and not gain weight."

Satter asks clients to "experiment, to take the risk of eating at times they shouldn't or even gain a little weight in order to find out about their body needs. I try to persuade them not to deprive themselves or allow themselves to be hungry for one week, to deliberately eat the foods they enjoy when their bodies signal hunger and to allow their bodies to eat until satisfied. They need reassurance that it's normal for their belts to feel tighter after a meal; it doesn't mean they've overeaten. But this takes time, because so many of them have lost the ability to read their own body signals. Most patients are able to stabilize their weight automatically once they allow their bodies to regulate their food needs. Part of the process is, of course, psychological: you have to learn to accept your body at its proper weight."

4. *Isolate your trigger foods and learn how to manage them.*

David Garner, Ph.D., of the University of Toronto, insists that his normal-to-low-weight bulimic patients eat at least a small serving daily of the foods they typically binge on but otherwise avoid. "They must do this every day whether they want to or not," says Dr. Garner. "At first in their minds it's equivalent to blowing their diet, but once it becomes part of their diet they think differently about it."

There appear to be physiological as well as psychological reasons for Dr. Garner's approach. Many researchers have observed an abnormal insulin response triggered in some anorexic patients by the ingestion of a small amount of carbohydrates, which compels the patient to continue eating carbohydrates. Since anorexics and bulimics, as well as many rigid dieters, typically restrict their carbohydrate intake severely or avoid them entirely, it's possible that carbohydrate abstinence creates a carbohydrate dependency that comes alive with the slightest intake and fosters a full-fledged binge to satisfy repressed physiological needs. A good reason not to avoid carbohydrates—you may be forcing your greatest fear to come true.

Once you've begun to follow your four golden rules, you can introduce positive-reinforcement techniques. The methods are now traditional in behavioral weight-loss clinics, and they can be applied to eating management as well as weight loss. They include many of the tricks that helped Clare, described in chapter 6.

The food diary is the backbone of most behavioral programs, for it offers its keeper a way to unlock her behavior by giving insight and awareness into her eating patterns and the emotions behind them, the first step toward gaining control. By discovering why you eat at certain times, you are better equipped to help yourself rather than hurt yourself; as the behaviorists say, it's much easier to prevent a binge than to interrupt one. Recording the time of eating is particularly important in terms of prevention, because you'll be able to see what your most difficult and most vulnerable periods are and plan for them in the future.

As we've discussed, most bingers don't eat enough when they're not bingeing. Binge-prone periods tend to be at night, after dieting all day (treatment: Don't let yourself end the day starving); during stretches of unstructured time (figure out when your stretches occur and schedule activities that take you away from food for those periods); or during periods of unusual stress. Most experts suggest you keep a diary for at least the first six weeks of your normalization program. Forewarned is forearmed is the basic idea: If you know when and where the enemy is likely to strike, you can prepare defenses.

Other behavioral techniques are outlined in manuals such as *Habits, Not Diets,* by James M. Ferguson, M.D., which was originally developed for use at Stanford University's Eating Disorders Clinic. Techniques include:

—Eating your meals at the same place each time.
—Ensuring that eating is the only activity pursued at mealtimes, not supplemented by TV or the newspaper.
—Keeping trigger foods out of sight in opaque containers, or, better yet, out of the house entirely, at least until you feel more confident of your control.
—Putting your fork down between bites.

—Introducing a two-minute "interruption" at some point during the meal, after which eating is resumed.
—Learning to identify behavior chains, perhaps just as important as the food-diary technique.[16]

The idea behind behavior chains is that the act of bingeing is the end result of a series of seemingly unconnected events that are actually links in a chain. (They are the behavioral equivalent of the Apparently Irrelevant Decisions mentioned in chapter 8; they set the stage for you to go ahead with the guilt-inducing behavior.) If you can break the chain at any stage preceding the terminal behavior (the binge and its emotional aftermath), the terminal behavior will probably not occur. The earlier you notice a link, the easier it will be to break the chain.

For example: It's 5:00 P.M. You've had a rough day at work. You're starving, because you've only eaten an apple so far. You decide there's no food in the house, so you stop at the market. You buy a bag of Fig Newtons, because they're your husband's favorite. At home, you prepare dinner, tasting and nibbling because you're starving. After dinner, your family settles in front of the TV, but you feel restless. You wander into the kitchen to make a phone call. The bag of Fig Newtons is lying unopened on the counter; you forgot to put them away with the rest of the groceries. You decide that just one won't hurt. You eat one . . . two . . . three. Now you feel guilty. Four . . . five . . . You finish the bag.

You could have made an activity substitution, and probably avoided your binge, at each link of your chain. Obviously, if you'd eaten more than an apple during the day, you wouldn't have felt so deprived of food and set up for indulgence. By going to the market starving and tired, with all your defenses down and self-control teetering, you pushed yourself further into the path of the unwanted behavior. At the very least, you could have protected yourself by buying a different brand of cookies, because if you'd been honest with yourself, you would have known you were buying the Fig Newtons because they were *your* favorite, not your husband's. Once home, you should have put the cookies away, out of sight. After dinner, you could have gone to a movie, read a good book, taken the dog for a walk—anything that would have kept you from being restless. But instead you settled on the easiest solutions to restlessness you know—food and guilt and more food.

A more neutral way to break a chain, suggests Dr. Ferguson, is to add time between the links—in other words, delay the snack by setting a timer or alarm clock for a preset period, starting with a few minutes and working up to ten or fifteen. While you're waiting, do something else. "You will be amazed," says Dr. Ferguson, "at how few snacks you will want if you wait a few minutes between the time you first recognize an urge to eat and the point when you actually open the refrigerator door."[17]

Each time you wait out the cue to eat, according to the behaviorists, you will weaken the effect of the cue; each time you give in to it, you will reinforce it.

Dr. Marlatt and his colleagues at the University of Washington suggest that clients trying to give up a behavior such as smoking, drinking or overeating carry a credit-card-size Emergency Card at all times as a preventive strategy. The card should be read at the moment the urge to indulge hits, but before it is acted upon. The message, according to Dr. Marlatt, might read: "There is no reason why you must give in to the feeling and binge. The feeling will pass shortly. Meanwhile, you can substitute one of the following activities, and soon this high-risk moment will be over." The card would then list some avoidance strategies, such as taking a walk or a drive, or treating yourself to a nonfood pleasure such as a manicure, a new book, a bubble bath.

If you're used to vomiting your food, you should be prepared to feel anxiety at the start of your normalization program when you've eaten a regular meal and must sit with it, stomach full. Try to focus on the fullness as a healthy, rewarding feeling, not one you must get rid of. Remember that you're trying to get used to being normal, and part of being normal is that you are supposed to feel full, satisfied, after a meal. You'll have to teach yourself the difference between feeling satisfied and feeling bloated.

Vomiters must relearn "full" as a signal to put down their forks, sit back and reflect on the pleasures of the meal just eaten—not as a signal to rush into the bathroom and forcibly eject the source of pleasure. You need to practice alternative behaviors in place of vomiting and/or bingeing. Janet, 25, was able to give up her twelve-year habit of bingeing and vomiting after going through the University of Minnesota Hospitals' treatment program for bulimics. She learned in the program to "do absolutely anything to avert the urge to binge and vomit. I'll take a walk, call a friend, even lock myself out of the house or stack furniture against the refrigerator door."

Keep in mind that if you have been bingeing and purging regularly for some time, you should expect a flood of feelings to rush in when you attempt to minimize or stop the behavior. The feelings, painful and intense as they are, are an excellent sign, just as sore muscles are after exercising—a sign that your true feelings are surfacing instead of being swallowed. Now they can be identified and dealt with instead of displaced by your eating cycles.

What can you do about these feelings? Nothing. You can only experience them, which will eventually make them less threatening. Trying to suffocate them with food won't make them go away; it will only intensify them. If you feel overwhelmed by emotions as you give up your behavior, this may be a good time to seek psychotherapy.

Remember:

—Don't try to diet while you're learning to normalize your eating. If you gain a few pounds as a trade-off (and chances are you won't), it's well worth it. But don't weigh yourself for at least a month.
—Never let yourself starve. Eat three meals a day at set times, plan what you'll eat ahead of time, and be sure to vary your foods and include things that you enjoy eating.

—Switch over to regular exercise as your primary means of long-term weight control and well-being.

—Develop alternatives to eating for getting past boredom, anxiety and restlessness, and practice them. In an emergency, at least give yourself a few minutes to reflect before proceeding with a binge. You may decide against it after all.

—Be realistic about your body build and family weight history. If you're 5'2" and curvy, you'll never be 5'9" and lean, no matter how much you starve. Make the most of what you are and stop mooning after the impossible.

You'll also need to introduce more nonfood pleasures into your daily life before you can say a confident goodbye to food abuse. Chances are excellent that your daily life lacks precisely the same quality that your eating behavior lacked: *balance*. And without balance, without pleasure, in your life, you'll make it that much easier to slide back into your old patterns.

10

BALANCING YOUR LIFE-STYLE

Now you've got some ideas about how to rationalize your thinking and how to regulate your eating. You're also developing self-awareness about the situations and emotions that lie behind your urge to eat, possibly through the aid of such techniques as a mood and food journal. Armed with that awareness, you're now able to predict high-risk times and prepare yourself for them.

But maybe you still feel like you're treading water. Maybe, despite your new awareness, you're *longing* for something—for a high. A high that gives you the thrill of anticipation without the agony of waiting. An instant high—that excitement you feel when you decide to go ahead with a binge, when you stop fighting the urge and give in, so close to a drinking high or a drug high or a sexual rush, where you give up all attempts at control and just go for it with abandon. When you go for the high, you don't let yourself think about the aftermath.

You're certainly not alone in the longing itself. As the daily stress of modern life mounts with the increasing hassles and complexities of just getting by, not to mention making it, everyone seems to be seeking some form of instant gratification, some high to compensate for all the scrabbling. If it's not food, it's drink or drugs or sex or buying on credit—anything we can have *right now* while we need it and to hell with the consequences. And that need to counter daily stress with daily indulgence doesn't even take into account individual psychological states such as anxiety, shyness, low self-esteem, perfectionism, guilt, or physiological pressures such as hunger from rigid dieting, fatigue, bad back, headaches, premenstrual tension—all of which may play a part in your drive to gratify yourself in the easiest and quickest way possible.

It would be foolish to deny your need for self-gratification; it's the way you're getting it that's the problem. You need to up the quantity and improve the quality of pleasure in your life. And you also need to *distribute* your pleasures differently. Instead of putting yourself through one chore after another until you're ready to blow, and then rushing to compensate for your burdens in the form of a daylong nibble or a five-hour kitchen-bathroom-kitchen-bathroom session that drains you of energy for anything else and possibly endangers you physically, you need to add some new pleasures to your current one-shot-only repertoire and spread them out over the course of your day. Every day. As with your thinking and your behavior, so with your life-style: You need to move from an all-or-nothing stance to a *balanced* one. If you have a variety of pleasures to choose from, you'll have a built-in protection from having to rely on only one. You know the one.

Chances are excellent that your life is weighted down by trying to fulfill too many "have-to's" and not enough "want-to's." But you don't have to return every phone call. You don't have to come to the aid of every friend. You don't have to accomplish every item on your list. You don't always have to be the one to keep every conversation going and everybody happy. You don't have to feel responsible for everyone else's hurt feelings but assume that your own hurt feelings are only your fault. If you regularly run your life under such rules and take them all seriously, they're exactly what accumulate inside you as anger and guilt and resentment and rejection and explode in a binge.

How do you alter your life-style equation?

Life-style balance is one of the arts that Dr. Marlatt helps clients to achieve. He says that balancing "wants" and "shoulds" is crucial to any permanent behavior change. Without balance, you'll always be prone to swing back and forth between those same old extremes, whether it's dieting/nibbling or bingeing/purging. A life-style too heavily loaded with "shoulds," says Dr.

Marlatt, is "often associated with an increased perception of self-deprivation and a corresponding desire for indulgence and gratification. It is as if the person who spends his or her entire day engaged in activities which are high in external demand—often perceived as 'hassling' events—attempts to balance this disequilibrium by engaging in an excessive 'want' or self-indulgence at the end of the day." To justify the indulgence, Dr. Marlatt continues, "the client may rationalize it by saying, 'I owe myself a drink (dessert, cigarette, etc.) or two—I deserve a break today!' " Dr. Marlatt calls this indulgence drive the "Problem of Immediate Gratification," or the PIG phenomenon.[1]

Dr. Marlatt suggests you do the following things to lessen your own personal PIG and to begin the process of balancing your life:

1. Make two lists, one of everything you do during the course of a typical weekday and the other of everything you do on a typical weekend day.
2. Rate each activity on a seven-point scale relative to how it feels, with a 7 equaling pure "want," a 1 equaling pure obligation, and a 4 equaling half and half (such as a task you do at the office that is required in your job but is also enjoyable or stimulating for you).
3. Identify the run of "shoulds" that might lead to an indulgence desire by the end of the day.
4. Make a third list of all the "wants" you'd do if you didn't have to spend all your time on the "shoulds."
5. Go back into your daily schedule and use the "want" list to break up the pattern of "shoulds." Because you cannot add hours to the day, this will necessitate elimination of some of the "shoulds." That's fine, because many of them have more to do with pleasing other people anyway, *when it's not necessary*, whether it's your husband, children, parents, teachers or boss. Many of the things you do for others they'd do for themselves or just let slide if you weren't

around to do them. Often it's only *you* who feels you need to do these things, not they.
6. Now, follow your plan daily, modifying as you go if necessary.

It's essential that you take a personal time-out for at least a half-hour at the beginning and end of each day to do exactly what you want. If you don't know what you want, you'll need to experiment, as you're doing with your meals. Try listening to music; reading something frivolous and delicious like a suspense novel or romance fiction or a European fashion magazine; taking a long bubble bath; doing stretching exercises or yoga; swimming; meditating—anything that feels like pure pleasure and not like just another chore, and that you do for yourself only.

The importance of taking time for yourself was clearly demonstrated by Dr. Marlatt and colleagues, who conducted an experiment with heavy social drinkers to determine the effects of three types of relaxation techniques: meditation; progressive relaxation involving alternatively tensing and relaxing various muscle groups; and reading restful material chosen by the subject—no newspapers, news magazines, class assignments or accounts of violence or eroticism—in a quiet room. The researchers chose social drinkers (who had no desire to cut down on or quit drinking) instead of alcoholics or problem drinkers, because if regular relaxation periods influenced social drinkers to decrease their drinking without the initial motivation to do so, the technique would be even more effective on alcoholics who were motivated to change.

Results showed that those subjects who were regularly practicing any one of the three relaxation techniques experienced an approximate 50 percent drop in drinking and an increased sense of inner control, as opposed to feeling controlled by something or someone outside themselves. But when subjects discontinued the regular practice of relaxation, their drinking increased.

Why would taking time out for two brief periods a day cause a decrease in drinking, regardless of the relaxation method used?

Dr. Marlatt and his colleagues determined that the methods had two main common denominators: Each involved sitting quietly in a calm and relaxed environment, which gave the subjects an opportunity to reflect on the day's activities and thus possibly desensitized them to whatever anxieties and stress had been experienced in the course of the day; and each method offered a feeling of taking time out for themselves, to be alone for short periods, uninterrupted by the demands and stresses of daily living.

Yet the methods weren't equally effective over the long period. It seemed that the meditation group became more hooked on that technique than did members of the other two groups on theirs. In the end, the researchers decided that "meditation may be a more effective self-control technique because it is easy to do and intrinsically more satisfying, and thus would be practiced over a longer period of time than the other relaxing methods." In addition, "Meditation seemed to offer the drinker a non-drug 'high' which offers none of the drawbacks of excessive drinking."[2]

Meditation may not be for you, but it's certainly one technique to consider as a personal time-out. It's a good example of how some people can and do replace a negative addiction (in the Marlatt experiment, excessive drinking) with a positive one. As outlined by William Glasser, M.D., in his book *Positive Addiction*, a positive addiction is any behavior or activity that is noncompetitive; that you can devote about an hour a day to; that you can do easily and well; that you can do by yourself; that you feel has some personal value; that you'll improve at with practice; that, most importantly, you can do without criticizing yourself.[3]

Positive addictions are crucial to achieving life-style balance, according to Dr. Marlatt. "If a negative addiction can be described as an activity that feels good at first but causes harm in the long run, a positive addiction (e.g., jogging) is an activity which may be experienced negatively at first (especially while one is in the early stages of exercise) but is very beneficial in terms of the long-range effects." Since regular practice of a positive addiction leads to a greater sense of relaxation or improved physical well-being, Dr. Marlatt adds, "Overall coping capacity is increased; high-risk situations may more easily be dealt with, rather than serving as precipitating triggers for excessive behaviors."[4]

In order to become permanent habits, positive activities need reinforcement just as negative ones do. In the Marlatt experiment, for example, once the relaxation procedures were abandoned, the subjects reverted to their former drinking patterns. The point is that you can't simply *stop* a habit; you must replace it with another.

Anyone who's lost weight on a fad diet can vouch for this: If you've achieved your weight-loss goal but haven't substituted new eating habits and new, nonfood, daily pleasures, you have little reinforcement for your achievement and will be in danger of resuming the old patterns. This is even more likely if you're trying to get off the treadmill of a more addictive habit such as bingeing and vomiting. Over time, you've used that pattern not just as self-gratification/self-punishment but also to regulate stress and negative emotions. When you begin the withdrawal process, you'll uncover those emotions, and if you've left yourself naked on a road blocked with stress and anxiety, you'll continually be on the verge of running for cover under the old.

Here's an example of how one 35-year-old woman, a client of Dr. Marlatt's, built a new umbrella by restructuring her daily life-style. By introducing "wants" and eliminating "shoulds," she increased her overall ability to deal with life stress without resorting to her former indulgent behavior. Though hers was alcohol, it might just as well have been food.

The woman, an elementary-school teacher, lived with a man who felt she drank too much. His feeling made her feel guilty, so she rarely drank when he was around. Because she couldn't drink at home and couldn't drink during the school day, she had only the time between leaving work and coming home. She always felt rushed in the morning, because she got up at the last moment possible and had to make lunch for herself and her live-in boyfriend before racing off to a noisy classroom. But instead of taking time out for lunch, she usually monitored the study hall so she could get off work a little earlier. Because she taught drama classes and directed plays, she was often under deadline pressure. By 3:00 P.M., when her workday was over, she was, in her own words, a nervous wreck.

To calm herself down, she kept a half-pint of vodka in her car, which she drank on the way home, a half-hour drive. Naturally, she looked forward to 3:00 P.M. and her only reward for enduring all the hassles of the day. She felt that she owed herself a drunk, explains Dr. Marlatt, since that was almost the only form of self-gratification she allowed herself on a typical workday.

In treatment, Dr. Marlatt and his client first focused on the two key factors in her drinking problem: her boyfriend's attitude and her current life-style. She didn't want to give up drinking altogether, so the goal was to change her drinking pattern. "We agreed," Dr. Marlatt reported, "that a moderate drinking pattern would involve eliminating the afternoon vodka minibinges, replacing this behavior with a moderate drinking pattern at home and in other social situations." After bringing in her boyfriend and discussing with him the role that he played in establishing her drinking patterns, the boyfriend agreed to let her drink wine at home without reacting negatively. Soon the client reported feeling much less guilt and concern over her drinking—which had dropped by about 25 percent. But she still felt a need for some form of release after work.

The next step was to introduce more "wants"—more self-gratifying activities—into her day. First, she chose to get up an hour and a half earlier and let her boyfriend make his own lunch, so that she'd have plenty of time for a Jacuzzi and massage at a health spa on her way to work. At the midmorning break, she practices meditation for twenty minutes in the deserted auditorium. At lunchtime, she no longer monitors study hall (with no more flask, she doesn't need to get off early). Instead, she spends the time with a friend, either eating lunch or jogging together around a nearby lake. At the end of the day, she takes an hour for what Dr. Marlatt calls "body time"—time exclusively reserved for physical exercise or mental relaxation.

To avoid turning body time into another "should" by setting up a rigid pattern ("I must jog every day at 4:00 P.M. no matter what"), she first sits quietly and meditates for a few minutes to sense what her body needs at that particular time. It might be something vigorous like jogging, biking or swimming, or something more relaxed such as meditation.

"To the extent that you feel you must jog each day at a particular time, jogging may become a 'should' instead of a desired form of self-indulgence," says Dr. Marlatt. "If the new behavior becomes a 'should,' you will have difficulty maintaining the behavior over long periods. With the body time concept, you can maintain a sense of freedom of choice, since the activity itself isn't chosen until the designated hour arrives."

Once Dr. Marlatt's client scheduled these changes into her life, her desire for the afternoon vodka declined and eventually died, because she had replaced it with other self-gratifying activities. As for her drinking at other times, she leveled off at two or three glasses of wine each evening.[5]

Substitute a bag of Oreos for a half-pint of vodka and change the boyfriend's complaint to "You're always on a diet" or "Why don't you go on a diet?" or some form of criticism about your eating behavior and you can see how effective a life-style overhaul can be in permanently changing your eating behavior by removing your need for it. If each day holds something other than food that you can look forward to and rely on as a source of immediate pleasure that is in no way related to what someone else wants of you, your need to abuse food will lessen and finally disappear. As we saw in chapter 9, this principle also holds for your meals themselves: As long as you regularly allow yourself the foods you enjoy throughout the day, you won't have to pile them all up in one binge when you hardly even taste anything anyway.

Being able to take your daily time-outs without being nagged by "shoulds"—business calls to return, the laundry to do, the term paper to write—can be difficult at first. For so many of us whose days are filled with lists and responsibilities, relaxation is very low-priority—something you do only when and if everything on your list is checked off. But the more you must get done, the more anxiety you'll feel. And there's an additional problem: Without regular recreation to balance responsibilities, you'll be out of practice in the art of relaxation, which in itself will cause you anxiety when you first try to introduce it into your life.

Professionals who treat bulimics and anorexics include various forms of relaxation training in their treatment; for if a patient can learn to utilize the techniques on her own, she has a tool with which to counter a binge impulse at the moment it occurs. Leslie, a now-abstinent bulimic vomiter, learned about taking time out through the treatment program for bulimics offered at the University of Minnesota Hospitals. She practices meditation daily and reserves at least a half-hour twice a day for reading, contacting other recovering bulimics and occasionally attending an Overeaters Anonymous meeting for the emotional support it provides.

At the Cleveland Clinic, Dr. Gross teaches self-hypnosis to patients with eating disorders by hypnotizing them himself and taping the session so that patients have a guide to follow on their own. He has also included a chapter on hypnosis in his recent book, *Anorexia Nervosa: A Comprehensive Approach*.[6] Dr. Gross believes that self-hypnosis is valuable both as a relaxation technique and as a way to get in touch with your physical sensations and body cues, thus strengthening your ability to perceive the signs of hunger and fullness. If you would like to try hypnosis, you can locate a qualified hypnotherapist in your area by contacting the American Society of Clinical Hypnosis, 2250 E. Devon Avenue, Suite 336, Des Plaines, Illinois 60018.

At the Austin Stress Clinic, Dr. Hawkins uses biofeedback therapy combined with imagery to get his patients to work through their emotions without turning to food. Often, Dr. Hawkins uses temperature biofeedback: He hooks a sensor to the patient's fingertip and has her picture herself experiencing rejection, anxiety or another binge-trigger emotion. He tells her to imagine that hollow feeling that precedes a binge, and then to focus on the warm, pleasant feeling coursing through her body from the sensor. The warming sensation comes to be associated with getting over the emotional distress that would otherwise lead to a binge, and the temperature trainer is used because it's a portable device—the patient can take it home with her. When and if she experiences a binge urge, she can pull out the trainer and reenter that state of pleasant warmth. Thus, she has a new ritual to follow that she can substitute for a binge when trigger situations arise.

You can use imagery on yourself either as an emergency measure to avert a binge or as a daily pleasuring tool during your time-outs. As a further aid to letting yourself relax, stress specialists often recommend that you acquire some relaxation tapes, such as the stress-management series offered by Thomas Budzynski, Ph.D., director of the Biofeedback Institute in Denver. Also effective is participating in movement or dance therapy. Many food-control programs, such as Feeding Ourselves (Arlington, Massachusetts), routinely include it as a part of treatment.

You will also benefit by working on the way you interact with other people. As we've discussed, food is often used as a substitute for dealing directly with the real problem, which frequently has to do with not getting what you want from others. One reason you don't get what you want is that you don't let people know what you want clearly enough. You turn anger into hurt and resentment and guilt and depression, and then you try to swallow it all down. For most of your life, particularly if you're female, you've tried to be popular, to please others, to smooth over touchy situations, to be easy to get along with. In a social or business situation, you'll give the benefit of the doubt to anyone but yourself. You're quick to assume blame, less quick to take credit. You find it no easier to accept compliments than you do criticism.

At some point in your early life, you decided that anything else was being selfish and unlikable. So instead of playing the warrior or the winner, you play the martyr and the loser. Getting what you want from others becomes a matter of covertly manipulating them under the shield of selflessness, because speaking up is too demanding and too risky. When you can't figure out how to maneuver things your way, you might just give up and feel sorry for yourself. Another excuse to swallow and swallow again.

Some of us have never known the feeling of inner freedom that comes with not swallowing, with recognizing and expressing active emotions such as anger. But the more indirectly you try to take care of yourself by eating, the more frustrated and ineffective you'll feel in relationships with others. You need to be the actor in your life instead of just the reactor. You must speak up to others instead of keeping quiet and accommodating their needs and demands in place of your own. You must stop worrying about being nice and start getting what you need. You're the only one who can really be relied upon to take care of yourself.

If your typical role in relationships has been a passive one, you'll need to learn new skills before you can change it to an active one. Because most people who rely on food as a solace and punishment for their lives and emotions do tend to be passive, professionals are increasingly aware of the need to teach clients how to express themselves directly. The most effective treatment programs for eating and weight disorders now include some form of assertiveness training (sometimes called "personal-effectiveness" or "social-skills training") along with relaxation techniques, nutritional guidance and psychotherapy.

Social-skills therapists distinguish the assertive person as someone who respects the rights of others but actively defends his own, as opposed to the passive person (who allows himself to be taken advantage of and his rights to be violated) and the aggressive person (the one who does the violating.) As you learn to become more assertive, your self-confidence and self-esteem will increase along with the quality of your relationships.[7]

Keep close tabs on what you're feeling in situations with others. If you feel anxious, it may be that you sense you're being taken advantage of or forced to do something you don't want to do. *Experiment*. Take the risk of coming to your own defense or saying no instead of just letting it happen. Speaking up on your own behalf can be frightening at first, but you'll become more comfortable with it as you continue to do it and see that others tend to respect instead of reject you for it.

Practicing your expressiveness with others is another area in which you can put journal-keeping to good use, especially if you have trouble identifying your specific feelings at the moment they occur in interpersonal situations. Instead of mentally beating yourself for having blown it, for saying the wrong thing, for letting the other person get the best (or worst) of you, and then heading out the door in search of edible solace, take some paper and a pen and record the dialogue and action of the encounter as soon as possible after it occurs, while it's still fresh in your mind. Think of the situation just past as an *emotional*-behavior chain (see chapter 9) from which you can learn how to do it differently next time. At what point could you have said or done something to cause a more satisfying outcome for yourself? Was the role you took in the situation—passive? resentful? accommodating? guiltridden?—a familiar one? If so, you're probably looking at a long-established pattern of dead-end interaction that you'll want to revise to one that gets you somewhere.

Though you may have been too stressed or unprepared to deal with the situation at that time, you will be better able to do so when and if it recurs, as long as you act on your new awareness. At least once a day, try to replace a passive stance with an active one. For example: Instead of waiting for your boyfriend to call and feeling increasingly depressed and desperate as the minutes click by, make plans with a friend and follow through before you have a chance to start forging that passive emotional chain. Instead of attending a cocktail party and feeling uncomfortable because no one is talking to you, force yourself to initiate a conversation with a stranger. Instead of giving in to your teenage son and lending him your car when you need it yourself and then resenting him for it, tell him he'll have to wait. If he tries to manipulate you by getting angry, ignore him. Instead of wishing that your boss would give you a raise, ask for one. If your request is refused, ask when you might expect one.

Each time you let yourself risk one of these seemingly small assertions, compliment yourself for taking action no matter what the outcome. In the short run, you will have delayed and possibly removed the urge to turn to food by taking direct and appropriate action instead of getting stuck with bad feelings. In the long run, you will have added another inch to your sense of self-efficacy, your confidence that you can and will take care of yourself in a self-supportive way. If possible, consider taking an assertiveness-training course. It may sound like 1970s cliché to you, but not to the professionals.

If you're actively bulimic or anorexic, your interpersonal problems may involve more than a lack of assertiveness. The longer you've maintained your behavior, the more you've probably cut yourself off from former relationships, whether with friends, family or lovers. As your chaotic eating patterns became more and more entrenched, you began to seek isolation to keep the behavior secret. This is yet another vicious cycle. You isolate yourself so you can binge; the isolation makes you feel lonely and depressed, causing you to continue to binge as a poor substitute for people. And with the growing absence of others from your life, you become increasingly focused on yourself instead of reaching outward.

Social isolation was a clear pattern among young bulimic women, aged 19 to 33, studied by Craig Johnson, Ph.D., and Reed Larson, Ph.D., of the Michael Reese Medical Center in Chicago. Using beepers to monitor the circumstances of the subjects' daily lives, the researchers established that these women were alone an average of half of the time signaled, while a comparison group of normal women in the same age range were alone only one-third of the time. Though the bulimic women may have originally chosen to be alone more in order to pursue their food addiction, that choice works to their great disadvantage by reinforcing the need for the addiction. Several of the bulimic women said angrily and somewhat despairingly that over the years food had become their closest companion, and they would often choose to stay home and binge rather than be with friends or family.[8]

Anne, a college senior, is an honors student, 5'5", weighing anywhere from 115 to 125. She appears very normal on the outside, but says she has been bulimic since freshman year. "I have very few friends, none close, and do not go out often. I avoid people when I am in the scarfing mood, because, of course, you cannot scarf in public because people will think you are gross. After the scarf, I also avoid people because I feel terrible, look awful, absolutely hate myself so much that I would like to pack up and move out of my body, and I do not dare to let anyone see me when I am fat! Next, I go on a very strict diet. Of course, when I'm dieting, I also avoid people because I'm afraid they will try and make me eat."

But Anne also complains of being alone too much. She thinks her eating behavior would get better if she had more of a social life. Clearly, she needs to take one step out of the cycle she's locked herself into, to start the reverse domino effect going. One step in the right direction brings with it other positive effects: By asserting herself and asking a friend to see a movie, or by accepting someone else's invitation (which normally she would reject), she'll also: (1) not feel lonely for at least one night; (2) not binge, at least while she's out; (3) have the opportunity to feel involved with something other than food and her own self-deprecation.

To try to break the isolating component of bulimia, Sandy Perlo, M.D., of Tarzana, California, has used response-prevention strategies in the bulimic-group-therapy sessions he leads. For example, patients have to make a monetary contribution each time they fail to use a social intervention, such as phoning a friend, to counteract the impulse to binge. This buddy-system approach is mentioned by members as one of the more effective self-help techniques taught by organizations such as Overeaters Anonymous. The point is clear: Turning to friends rather than shutting them out, on any level you can manage, is one of the best ways to reduce stress and anxiety, emptiness and loneliness—the factors that may trigger a binge, or any indulgent behavior.

The extent of your ability and willingness to seek and maintain mutually gratifying relationships has a direct bearing on your ability to banish food and weight preoccupation from your life. Women who have maintained at least some degree of openness and honesty about their food-control problems and who have not cut themselves off entirely from their support systems have found it easier to give up their behavior and get on with their lives once they made the decision to do so. They'd kept at least one alternative coping strategy around: their friends.

Friends, in fact, may be one of your most valuable tools in increasing not just the quality but even the quantity of your life. When researchers A. D. Weisman and J. W. Worden compared two groups of patients with advanced cancer, they found that those who survived longer than expected had actively maintained satisfying relationships, while those whose deaths occurred earlier than expected lacked such relationships.[9] Close relationships are among your best allies in combatting life stress and improving physical and emotional health.

Remember:

—Develop a range of activities that give you pleasure, and sample freely and frequently from your Pleasure Roster. Include at least one relaxing activity daily that you do for yourself only.

—Make room for your pleasures by eliminating some of your pains. Chores don't all have to get done exactly on schedule, and phone calls don't have to be returned the same day.

—Stop saying yes to everyone else and no to yourself. If you're always the one who seems to be worrying, ask yourself if it's necessary. Learn to be selfish.

—Speak your mind to people whenever possible. Practice on someone safe, like your sister or your son. It will give you confidence to go out and speak your mind to the world. Keep in mind that assertiveness and anxiety don't coexist comfortably: Which would you rather have?

—Friends and a sense of humor will get you through almost anything.

As you begin to replace the old, boring, passive patterns with new ones, as you experiment with fresh ways of thinking and behaving and living, be sure to take a good look around you. While you've been stuck inside your head fretting about fat and thin and eating and not eating and what would you *do*, dear God, if you gained 3 pounds, there have been people waiting for you, people who couldn't care less about any of that. All they know is that they've *missed* you and they want you back— imperfections and all.

MEDICAL NOTES

Hypertension and high blood pressure. Painful sore throats. Swelling of body tissue. Cardiovascular problems. Stomach cramping. Hardening of the arteries. Amenorrhea. Fainting and dizziness. Dental erosion. Dehydration. Loss of essential body chemicals. Urinary infection. Diabetes. Rupture of the esophagus. Musculoskeletal difficulties. Kidney failure. Seizures. Death.

Depending on just how abnormal your eating and purging patterns have become, you may be in danger of one or more of the above. At the very least, continual stuffing and starving—even if you are not vomiting or using drugs—will stress your body's ability to maintain its natural state of *homeostasis*, or balance, because you are continually giving your body mixed signals and not allowing it to moderate intake and output. Do you starve yourself when hungry and stuff yourself when full? Tune out your bodily signals long enough and you'll be lost without a life jacket in an increasingly turbulent sea. If you binge and vomit, over time you will come to experience the process as one behavior, and your only cue to stop may be exhaustion. "Satiety, our ability to appease and satisfy hunger, is altered radically by overeating followed by vomiting," notes anorexia-nervosa specialist Steven Levenkron. "The individual finds that hunger is abated only after larger and larger meals. Conversely, even if small meals are eaten, a feeling of incompleteness and discomfort intensifies until the individual vomits."[1]

Severe medical consequences can result from prolonged vomiting, laxative, or diuretic abuse. There are no statistics on the death rate from bulimia without anorexia nervosa (in anorexia, the rate is a frightening 5 to 15 percent), but cardiac arrest and death have been known to occur in bulimic patients who were not at an abnormally low weight but who maintained extreme vomiting and/or purging patterns. Signs of physical abnormality resulting from frequent purges can include swelling of the salivary glands, muscle spasms and tetany, dryness of the mouth, irritation and pain in the throat, and scars on the back of the hand from constant efforts to induce vomiting.

"Those who abuse laxatives may take 50 to 100 tablets a day, and amounts of up to 600 milligrams per day of diuretics are not uncommon," says Arnold Andersen, M.D., of The Johns Hopkins Hospital in Baltimore. "These doses would produce fatal consequences in persons who had not gradually adapted to their usage."[2]

Such self-imposed physiological chaos creates psychological chaos as well. The chaos created in your head is expressed in rapidly shifting emotional states. Rigid dieting or fasting also creates a drop in blood sugar; though not as dramatic as vomiting, the process is similar, for your body struggles against the low level of blood sugar by seeking carbohydrates to restore the proper level, thus triggering a binge.

By vomiting and by abusing laxatives or diuretics, you are depleting your body of certain chemicals and fluids necessary to the proper functioning of the heart, muscles and other essential organs. For your body to function, substances in your body fluids called "electrolytes"—sodium, chloride, bicarbonate and potassium—must be present in the proper concentrations in proportion to body fluids. If the levels of these electrolytes, particularly potassium, drop too low, you can suffer muscle fatigue, cardiac irregularities and possibly death. Marked fluid and electrolyte shifts may also provoke seizures.

The occurrence of seizures, incidentally, is another of those chicken-and-egg controversies so commonly posed by the study of eating disorders. Some researchers speculate that in a few patients the need to binge stems from a neurological condition—an electrical abnormality in the brain, similar to epilepsy, that can be treated with anticonvulsant drugs. Other researchers say that the brain abnormalities, which show up on an electroencephalogram (EEG) that records brain waves, are a result of the altered fluid and electrolyte balance in the blood caused by constant self-induced vomiting or laxative or diuretic abuse.

In a study of thirty patients—twenty-seven of whom vomited, at least sixteen vomited *and* took laxatives, and all of whom binged at least once a day and had established these patterns over long periods—British researcher Gerald Russell found that thirteen had abnormally low levels of potassium, one developed kidney failure and hypertension (after eight years of vomiting and laxative abuse), three had urinary infections, four had occasional epileptic seizures, one had tetany, and one had constant swelling of her salivary glands.[3]

Self-induced vomiting and, to a somewhat lesser degree, laxatives and diuretics literally washed out the body's supply of potassium, which can and will lead to a medically dangerous condition. The loss of potassium and other chemicals creates, at the very least, fatigue and loss of energy, a medical condition often experienced by the victim as a psychological state of depression.

Laxatives and diuretics cause a loss of fluid from the body, but not a loss of fat, which is why such drugs have no permanent effect on weight loss. You have to keep taking them, and in increasing amounts, to cause the same fluid loss, and sooner or later you will deplete your body's natural ability to get rid of fluids—meaning that the longer you take the drugs, the harder it will be for your body to resume normal functioning. Abuse of diuretics impairs the kidneys' ability to regulate the flow of sodium and water. The dehydration and electrolyte problems caused by excessive loss of fluids, through diarrhea via laxatives or urination via diuretics, can lead to feelings of weakness, dizziness, mental confusion and, in extreme cases, to shock and death.

Repeated use of laxatives may cause chronic constipation that makes you increasingly dependent on them for excretion. Laxative abuse can also lead to a condition similar to spastic colitis—irritation and changes in the physiological functioning of the bowel. The colon may lose its normal pattern on X-ray.

The binge itself causes stomach distension, which in the extreme can lead to a gastric rupture. Constant vomiting can result in laceration of the esophagus and possibly hemorrhage.

If you regularly take laxatives, diuretics, enemas, or make yourself vomit, it's important that you see a medical internist as soon as possible to be sure that you are not in danger. If you vomit frequently, you should also see a dentist, for the acid continually accumulating in your mouth can cause serious decay in your enamel and gums.

The following are the official diagnostic criteria for anorexia nervosa and bulimia, according to the American Psychiatric Association:[4]

Anorexia Nervosa

1. Intense fear of becoming obese, which does not diminish as weight loss progresses.
2. Disturbance of body image: for example, claiming to "feel fat" even when emaciated.
3. Weight loss of at least 25 percent of original body weight or, if under 18, weight loss from original body weight plus projected weight gain expected from growth charts may be combined to make the 25 percent. (Many experts will diagnose anorexia nervosa at only 15 percent weight loss.)
4. Refusal to maintain body weight over a minimal normal weight for age and height.
5. No known physical illness that would account for the weight loss.

Bulimia

1. Recurrent episodes of binge eating (rapid consumption of a large amount of food in a discrete period of time, usually less than two hours).

2. At least three of the following:
   a) Consumption of high-caloric, easily ingested food during a binge.
   b) Inconspicuous eating during a binge.
   c) Termination of such eating episodes by abdominal pain, sleep, social interruption, or self-induced vomiting.
   d) Repeated attempts to lose weight by severely restrictive diets, self-induced vomiting, or use of cathartics or diuretics.
   e) Frequent weight fluctuations greater than 10 pounds due to alternating binges and fasts.
3. Awareness that the eating pattern is abnormal and fear of not being able to stop eating voluntarily.
4. Depressed mood and self-deprecating thoughts following eating binges.
5. The bulimic episodes are not due to anorexia nervosa or any known physical disorder. (*Note:* Most informed psychiatrists ignore this criterion, because experience tells them that bulimia can certainly be present, up to 50 percent of the time, in anorexia nervosa.)

WHERE TO GO FOR FURTHER HELP

Support Groups

American Anorexia Nervosa Association, Inc. (AANA), 133 Cedar Lane, Teaneck, New Jersey 07666. (201) 836-1800. Estelle Miller, M.S.W., executive manager.

Membership is $15 a year for an individual, $25 for a family. You receive five newsletters per year. Self-help groups meet on the first Saturday of every month if you live in a chapter city: Philadelphia, Atlanta and New York City. The groups are led by recovered anorexics and bulimics and by mental-health professionals, but the organization stresses that the groups are not meant to substitute for psychotherapy. AANA also provides a list of referrals to therapists and psychiatrists in this country, Canada and the United Kingdom, and will send information on eating disorders as well. Be sure to enclose a legal-size, self-addressed, stamped envelope (SASE).

Anorexia Nervosa and Related Eating Disorders, Inc. (ANRED), P.O. Box 5102, Eugene, Oregon 97405. (503) 344-1144. Jean A. Rubel, director.

ANRED's primary function is to collect and distribute information about eating disorders. If you send a legal-size SASE, Rubel will send an extensive bibliography of eating-disorder literature, a speaker's bureau list and national psychiatric referral list at no charge. ANRED also publishes a monthly newsletter; it's $5 for a year's subscription.

Help Anorexia, Inc., 5143 Overland Avenue, Culver City, California 90230. (213) 558-0444. Steve Simon, director.

This organization offers free self-help groups twice a month and family groups once a month, sometimes with guest speakers. The emphasis is on getting anorexics "out of the closet" and into a supportive environment. A brochure, local referral list and printed information will be sent to you if you provide a SASE.

Maryland Association for Anorexia Nervosa and Bulimia, 222 Gateswood Road, Lutherville, Maryland 21093. (301) 252-7407. Ann Boyer, A.C.S.W., president.

Membership is $10 for an individual, $25 for a family, and includes a subscription to a newsletter. Area residents can take advantage of the organization's varied programs, which currently include a ten-week group-therapy program at a sliding fee scale based on ability to pay. Referrals are provided, and Boyer stresses the need for individual psychotherapy for anorexics and bulimics to supplement the group programs.

National Anorexic Aid Society, Inc. (NAAS), P.O. Box 29461, Columbus, Ohio 43229. (614) 846-6810. Leah Melick, program administrator.

This educational-oriented organization is affiliated with the Bridge Counseling Center of Columbus, which offers individual psychotherapy for bulimics and anorexics at $50 an hour and group therapy at $25 an hour. For $12 a year, you'll receive NAAS's quarterly newsletter, plus information on support groups throughout the country that are organized by NAAS. A national referral list for treatment and support is also available if you provide a legal-size SASE.

National Association of Anorexia Nervosa and Associated Disorders (ANAD), Box 271, Highland Park, Illinois 60035. (312) 831-3438. Vivian Meehan, president.

This is a nonprofit, volunteer, educational and self-help association of individuals with disorders, their families, and professionals; it stresses early awareness and treatment of eating disorders. ANAD sponsors support groups throughout the country, run by recovered or recovering anorexics and bulimics, often with health professionals acting as sponsors. The organization also offers international referral lists, bibliographies and educational information on eating disorders. All services and information are free, including the support groups; send a SASE.

New York Anorexia and Bulimia Aid, 1 West 91st Street, New York, New York 10024. (212) 595-3449. Stephen Zimmer, M.S.W., director.

This is the support group for the Center for the Study of Anorexia and Bulimia, listed under "Clinics." It offers multifamily anorexic and bulimic groups. Multifamily sessions are given once a month, $5 per family; groups for bulimics or anorexics themselves are limited to eight people and are held weekly. Cost is $25 per month, plus $10 for initial interview

Overeaters Anonymous, P.O. Box 92870, Los Angeles, California 90009. (213) 320-7941.

OA, which follows the basic program of Alcoholics Anonymous, is geared to compulsive eaters, not specifically to anorexics or bulimics. There are no fees (although voluntary contributions are welcome), no referrals and no medical authorities involved; emphasis is on the shared experiences of compulsive eaters and the fostering of mutual support in the group goal of "abstinence" from compulsive eating. Founded in 1960, OA's strength as a support system is vouched for by over 100,000 members in 33 countries. For information and a listing of chapters in your area, send a SASE.

Weight Watchers International, 800 Community Drive, Manhasset, New York 11030. (516) 627-9200, ext. 240.

Though Weight Watchers is designed for overweight people and not for anorexics or bulimics, it does offer a support system as well as a balanced, if highly regimented, diet plan, behavior-modification instruction and a weigh-in program. You must be at least 10 pounds overweight in order to join. The fee for registration ranges from $4 to $7, and the weekly meeting ranges from $4 to $6. Check your phone directory for local chapters.

Clinics

CALIFORNIA

Los Angeles

Eating Disorders Clinic, UCLA Neuropsychiatric Institute, 760 Westwood Boulevard, 90024. (213) 825-0173. Joel Yager, M.D., director.

This is an outpatient service for anorexic and bulimic patients. Initial evaluation is $250, which includes a psychiatric interview, three hours of psychiatric testing and a follow-up appointment with a staff psychologist. Following the evaluation, you can join one of the bulimia or anorexia groups, each run by two therapists. Cost is $25 per session, and you must be willing to attend regularly for one year. Additional services include a medication clinic (Carole Edelstein, M.D., is medical director); family evaluations and family therapy; support groups for the patient's "significant others." Individual psychotherapy is not available, but the clinic will make referrals to private practitioners experienced in the treatment of eating disorders.

Eating Disorders Unit, Care Unit Hospital, 5035 Coliseum Street, 90016. (213) 295-6441. Judy Hollis, Ph.D., clinical director.

Inpatient program of four to six weeks, with a four-to-six-week posthospital outpatient follow-up, for anorexics and bulimics. The daily rate is about $277 and includes the initial evaluation. The entire program includes individual, group and family therapy sessions; nutritional consultation; lectures; and self-help and exercise programs. Eating disorders are viewed as both a physical addiction and a psychological obsession, requiring treatment of the entire family.

Palo Alto

Children's Hospital at Stanford, Psychosomatic Unit, 520 Willow Road, 94304 2-99. (415) 327-4800. Hans Steiner, M.D., director.

This is an inpatient unit for anorexics and bulimics under 18. Initial two-hour evaluation involves patient and family. Individualized treatment includes family therapy (one to two sessions per week) and individualized psychotherapy (three to four per week). The patient also must take part in various group activities and attend the hospital school. Cost varies widely.

Pasadena

Las Encinas Hospital, 2900 East Del Mar Boulevard, 91107. (213) 681-2301. Robert Morgan, Ph.D., coordinator.

Inpatient and outpatient treatment for bulimics and anorexics, though not exclusively for them. Inpatient rate is $225 a day for initial medical and psychiatric evaluation, semiprivate room, individual and group therapy sessions, and "specialty" groups, including the topics of substance abuse, chemical dependency, eating disorders, "spiritual integration," relaxation, transactional analysis and psychodrama. Outpatient group therapy is limited to four to eight members per group, and each ninety-minute session costs $55. Individual outpatient psychotherapy is $45 a half-hour and $80 an hour. Outpatients occasionally participate in the "specialty" groups, and nonprofessional self-help groups are encouraged

Stanford

N.O.A. Psychiatric Ward, Stanford University Hospital. (415) 497-5636. Dennis Clegg, M.D., director.

Emphasis is on a medical approach to anorexia and bulimia as psychosomatic illnesses. Inpatient program lasts three months. Fee is based on hospital room rate, plus cost of physician, psychotherapist and internist. Group, family, occupational and physical therapy. Psychological testing. Follow-up programs vary.

N.O.B. Psychiatric Ward, Stanford University Hospital, 211 Quarry Road, 94305. (415) 497-5001. Jo Ellen Werne, M.D., medical consultant.

The emphasis here is on behavioral treatment. Three-month inpatient program for anorexics and some bulimics. Fee of $350-plus per day includes initial evaluation; group, individual and usually family therapy; and ward-centered support groups. The average "contract" for anorexics requires a .2-kilogram daily weight gain. Follow-up programs after the three-month stay vary.

Tarzana

Eating Disorders Medical Group, 18370 Burbank Boulevard, Suite 710, 91356. (213) 345-2577. Solomon ("Sandy") Perlo, M.D., director.

Outpatient treatment for anorexics and bulimics. Group and individual psychotherapy, nutritional and psychological support. Multidisciplinary team of professionals includes a dietician. If hospitalization is necessary, Dr. Perlo is also clinical director of Woodview-Calabasas Psychiatric Hospital's inpatient eating-disorders program, and can arrange for inpatient care.

Life Management Center, 6047 Tampa Avenue, Suite 309, 91356. (213) 788-1292. Shari Schiff, Ph.D., director.

Outpatient psychotherapy program for anorexics and bulimics. Fees are based on ability to pay. The one-to-two-hour initial evaluation consists of a questionnaire and a series of psychological tests and interviews. Individual and group therapy available, along with self-help support groups. The center supplies local medical referrals if needed.

CONNECTICUT

New Haven

Dana Psychiatric Outpatient Clinic, Yale/New Haven Hospital, 20 York Street, 06504. (203) 785-4628. Daniel Moore, M.D., director.

Outpatient program for anorexics and bulimics includes individual, group and family therapy. Medical and psychiatric evaluation takes one to two hours, at $60 an hour; sliding fee scale available for some patients. Hospitalization is also available.

ILLINOIS

Chicago

Eating Disorders Project, Michael Reese Medical Center, 29th and Ellis Avenues, 60616. (312) 791-3878. Craig Johnson, Ph.D., director.

A research and treatment facility with inpatient and outpatient services for anorexics and bulimics. Outpatient group and individual therapy available through the Wexler Clinic. The initial ninety-minute evaluation costs $70; all other fees are based on ability to pay. There is a twelve-week short-term group and another, long-term group that lasts up to a year and requires a minimum commitment of three months. The project has a twin focus: teaching techniques of eating management and offering psychotherapy for self-awareness.

Eating Disorders Research Program, Illinois State Psychiatric Institute, 1601 W. Taylor Street, 60612. Regina C. Casper, M.D., director.

Research-oriented facility, with some inpatient and outpatient treatment for anorexics and bulimics. The treatment program is small and there is a long waiting list. They offer national and international psychiatric referrals.

MARYLAND

Baltimore

The Eating and Weight Disorders Clinic, Johns Hopkins Hospital Medical Institutions, Meyer Building 3-181, 21205. (301) 955-3863. Arnold E. Andersen, M.D., director.

Inpatient and outpatient programs, though the emphasis is on inpatient treatment. Inpatient treatment includes nutritional rehabilitation, twenty-four-hour inpatient supervision, individual and family psychotherapy at $237 a day for room and board; doctors' fees and initial evaluation are additional. Outpatient services operate on a sliding fee scale.

MASSACHUSETTS

Arlington

Feeding Ourselves, 30 Bartlett Avenue, 02174. (617) 661-3727. Emily Fox Kales, director.

Comprehensive outpatient program for bulimics and chronic dieters, focusing on techniques of behavioral change, psychological counseling, movement therapy and some individual therapy. The staff of psychiatrists, endocrinologists and social workers lead workshops and intensive weekend-long sessions as well as ongoing groups. There are also self-help support groups. Fees based on ability to pay. Call for an initial consultation.

Boston

Anorexia Nervosa and Associated Disorders Clinic, Children's Hospital Medical Center, 300 Longwood Avenue, 02115. (617) 735-6728. Eugene Piazza, M.D., director (outpatient); Gordon Harper, M.D., director (inpatient).

Inpatient psychosomatic treatment for anorexics 18 and under includes group, family and individual therapy, plus art and dance therapy on a sliding fee scale. Outpatient therapy offers individual or family sessions on a sliding fee scale. Medical and psychiatric evaluations and referrals to self-help groups also available.

Eating Disorders Unit, Massachusetts General Hospital, Parkman Street, 02114. (617) 726-2700. David Herzog, M.D., director.

Outpatient clinic for anorexics and bulimics offers a multidisciplinary approach, including nutritional, psychiatric and medical treatment. Fee for all-day initial evaluation varies. Group and individual therapy are recommended. Hospitalization for anorexics can be arranged if necessary.

MINNESOTA

Minneapolis

Center for Behavior Therapy, 606 24th Avenue South, Suite 602, 55454. (612) 332-1503. Frank Quale, M.A., director.

Outpatient group and individual treatment for anorexics and bulimics conducted by social workers, with a psychiatrist on staff. Hospitalization available. Initial evaluation costs $35; individual therapy from $45 to $85; two-hour group sessions are $45. Discounts of 10 percent if you pay in cash.

Eating Disorders Clinic, University of Minnesota Hospitals, 420 Delaware Street S.E., Box 301 Mayo, 55455. (612) 376-9166. Richard Pyle, M.D., director; Gretchen Goff, coordinator of bulimia treatment.

Intensive outpatient program for bulimics (hospitalization available if needed). The eight-week, group-oriented program costs $800 for professional fees plus $90 for clinic fees. There are five four-hour evening meetings the first week, four sessions the second week, three sessions the third and fourth weeks, and two sessions each week for the fifth through eighth weeks. Individual and family sessions are included in the program, as are meals and course materials. Additional fees for initial evaluation and lab work. About ten people are accepted into the program each month. Weekly support groups are also offered at a fee of $25 per session.

Rochester

Family Consultation Center, 1312 7th Street, N.W., 55901. (507) 289-4509. Glenn Van Laningham, M.S.W., A.C.S.W., director.

Outpatient program, primarily for bulimics, offers group and individual therapy with fees based on ability to pay. Each patient writes his/her own "contract" and presents it to the group, and people are encouraged to plan meals and keep food journals. Local medical and psychiatric referrals are also offered.

NEW YORK

Freeville

Marlene Boskind-White, Ph.D., and William C. White, Ph.D., 67 W. Malloryville Road, 13067. (607) 838-3067.

The Whites, a husband-and-wife psychotherapy team, coined the term "bulimarexia" in the mid-Seventies to refer to the binge-vomit cycle. They run three-day feminist-oriented intensive group workshops nationally for bulimics only, with a trained professional staff. The Whites work with women individually for two months before they can enter a workshop. Fee is $25 an hour for group treatment.

Hyde Park

Long Island–Jewish Hillside Medical Center, Hillside Division, Box 38, 11042. (212) 470-2756. I. Ronald Shenker, M.D., director, chief of adolescent medicine.

A comprehensive adolescent-care program (not specifically for bulimics and anorexics), both inpatient and outpatient. Family, individual and group therapy by referral; fees based on ability to pay. Initial evaluation is $125, scaled down according to need. Psychiatric consultation, social-worker counseling and some group therapy available.

New York City

Associates for Bulimia and Related Disorders, 31 W. 10th Street, 10011. (212) 254-3866 or 254-2809. Ellen Schor, Ph.D., and Judith Brisman, Ph.D., codirectors.

Three-day intensive group program for bulimics, twelve people per group. Medical work-up required before acceptance into group. Price is $400 for the three-day workshop and includes one three-hour evening session during the week following the workshop. Additional three-hour sessions are offered every two weeks at a charge of $25 per session. Development of ongoing support groups is encouraged so that patients "can turn to each other instead of to food." If you're from out of the area and want to attend the workshop, the directors will refer you to a therapist in your area beforehand. The program is modeled after that of William C. White and Marlene Boskind-White (see above), with whom Dr. Schor worked.

Center for the Study of Anorexia and Bulimia, 1 W. 91st Street, 10024. (212) 595-3449. William N. Davis, Ph.D., executive director.

Nonprofit outpatient center for bulimics and anorexics. Individual and group therapy offered at $15 to $60 per session, depending on ability to pay. For information, send $2 check or money order.

Eating Disorders Clinic, New York State Psychiatric Institute, 722 W. 168th Street, 10032. (212) 960-5752 or 960-5754. Timothy Walsh, M.D., director.

Outpatient research program currently testing the use of antidepressant medication in the treatment of bulimia. There is a long waiting list. Limited inpatient facilities available for anorexics and bulimics. Referrals are made to other clinics. Treatment is free.

Rochester

University Health Service, University of Rochester School of Medicine and Dentistry, 250 Crittenden Boulevard, Box 617, 14642. (716) 275-3113. Linda Barnett, Ph.D.

Outpatient service for bulimics, compulsive overeaters and recovering anorexics. Group ($25 an hour and a half, in twelve-week program) and individual ($50 an hour) therapy; fee can be negotiated if you're unable to pay. Medical work-up required before entering the service; they'll make medical referrals to internists in the community. Cognitive-behavioral approach with a feminist orientation; work on body-image concepts, nutritional rehabilitation, relapse prevention.

White Plains

Eating Disorders Clinic, New York Hospital (Westchester Division), Cornell University Medical Center, 21 Bloomingdale Road, 10605. (914) 682-9100, ext. 2452. Katherine A. Halmi, M.D., unit chief.

Inpatient program for anorexics and bulimics. Behavioral approach, with individual, group and family therapy. Basic cost is $373 a day; private consultation with Dr. Halmi is extra unless admitted the same day. Average stay ranges from two to eight months.

OHIO

Cincinnati

Clinic for Eating Disorders, University of Cincinnati College of Medicine, Department of Psychiatry, 231 Bethesda Avenue, Mail Location 559, 45267. (513) 872-5118. Susan C. Wooley, Ph.D., and O. Wayne Wooley, Ph.D., codirectors.

Outpatient treatment for anorexia, bulimia and obesity. Individual and group therapy at $55 per one-hour individual session or two-hour group session. Three-week intensive program for bulimics. Self-acceptance and improvement of body image is stressed. For program information, send SASE or request by telephone.

Cleveland

Cleveland Clinic Foundation, 9500 Euclid Avenue, 44106. (216) 444-5822. Meir Gross, M.D., director of the adolescent unit.

Inpatient and outpatient treatment for anorexics and bulimics. Treatment includes individual, group and family therapy; assertiveness training; biofeedback and hypnosis therapy; nutritional guidance; and behavioral therapy. Comprehensive initial psychiatric evaluation is

$150 for one and a half hours; medical evaluation is additional. Other fees vary, depending on lab charges.

Columbus

Ohio State University, Child Psychiatry Division, 473 W. 12th Avenue, Upham Hall 2-West, 43210. (614) 421-8235. Katharine Dixon, M.D., assistant professor of psychiatry.

An outpatient program for anorexics and bulimics, with inpatient facilities available at Ohio State University Hospital. Individual and group therapy, behavioral techniques and relaxation/stress-reduction training. Fees based on ability to pay. Local referrals provided.

PENNSYLVANIA

Philadelphia

Philadelphia Child Guidance Clinic, No. 2 Children's Center, 34th Street and Civic Center Boulevard, 19104. (215) 243-2600. Ronald Liebman, M.D., director.

Inpatient and outpatient treatment for anorexics and bulimics (age 24 and under for inpatient care; outpatient can be any age). Primarily oriented around family therapy. Group therapy is available, and self-help referrals are provided. The first visit to the center is with an individual therapist, who then refers the patient for testing or directly to a specific group. Complete physical necessary prior to treatment. Other services include biofeedback training and local referrals. For local residents, fees are based on ability to pay.

TEXAS

Austin

Austin Stress Clinic, 512 E. 11th Street, Suite 201, 78701. (512) 472-5780. Raymond C. Hawkins II, Ph.D., psychological consultant.

Outpatient habit-control program; Dr. Hawkins specializes in food control. Initial evaluation is $25. Individual therapy is $50 per session, group therapy $25 per session. Biofeedback therapy is $50 an hour, recommended for bulimics as relaxation training. The program generally involves ten visits over a three-month period and is extended as needed. Local medical referrals available.

WASHINGTON

Seattle

Addictive Behaviors Research Center, Department of Psychology, University of Washington, 98195. (206) 545-1395. G. Alan Marlatt, Ph.D., director; Sue Goldstein, research associate.

Outpatient clinic with a cognitive-behavioral approach to the treatment of "indulgent behaviors"—smoking, drinking, gambling and overeating. Consultations, individual psychotherapy and relapse-control training for long-term maintenance of behavioral change. Self-help literature available on request; send SASE.

WISCONSIN

Madison

Jackson Clinic, Department of Psychiatry, 345 W. Washington Avenue, 53703. (608) 252-8661. Ellyn Satter, R.D., M.S.W., director.

Outpatient program for bulimics, chronic dieters and other individuals for whom eating and weight is a major life preoccupation. (There is a referral list for anorexics.) Treatment includes individual, group, family and nutritional therapy. Individual sessions are $45 an hour; group sessions $20 for two hours. Short-term program is aimed at changing eating behavior and lasts ten to fifteen weeks; long-term treatment to change the "diet mentality" lasts about one year. Initial evaluation is $45. Ellyn Satter, author of *Child of Mine: Feeding with Love and Good Sense*, also works with overweight children and their parents to develop sensible eating patterns.

Note: Most state universities and many private colleges offer counseling, treatment or referrals for eating disorders. Check with your local campus mental-health center.

NOTES

CHAPTER ONE
The Eating Arc

1. For a discussion of the general behavior patterns and personality characteristics of bulimics, see Richard L. Pyle, James E. Mitchell, and Elke D. Eckert, "Bulimia: A Report of 34 Cases," *Journal of Clinical Psychiatry,* vol. 42, no. 2 (February 1981): 60–64; and Craig L. Johnson, Marilyn K. Stuckey, Linda D. Lewis, and Donald M. Schwartz, "Bulimia: A Descriptive Survey of 316 Cases," *International Journal of Eating Disorders* 2, no. 1 (Autumn 1982).
2. Michael G. Thompson and Donald M. Schwartz, "Life Adjustment of Women with Anorexia Nervosa and Anorexic-Like Behavior," *International Journal of Eating Disorders* 1, no. 2 (Winter 1982): 49.

CHAPTER TWO
Leaving Childhood

1. Hilde Bruch, *Eating Disorders: Obesity, Anorexia, and the Person Within* (New York: Basic Books, 1973). Cited in David M. Garner and Paul E. Garfinkel, *Anorexia Nervosa: A Multidimensional Perspective* (New York: Brunner/Mazel, 1982).
2. David M. Garner and Paul E. Garfinkel, *Anorexia Nervosa: A Multidimensional Perspective.*
3. Hilde Bruch, "Psychological Antecedents of Anorexia Nervosa," in *Anorexia Nervosa,* ed. R. A. Vigersky (New York: Raven Press, 1977).
4. A. H. Crisp, "Some Psychobiological Aspects of Adolescent Growth and Their Relevance for the Fat/Thin Syndrome (Anorexia Nervosa)," *International Journal of Obesity* 1, (1977): 236.
5. R. E. Frisch and J. W. McArthur, "Menstrual Cycles: Fatness as a Determinant of Minimum Weight for Height Necessary for Their Maintenance or Onset," *Science* 185 (1974): 949–51.
6. A. H. Crisp, "Anorexia Nervosa: 'Feeding Disorder,' 'Nervous Malnutrition,' or 'Weight Phobia'?" *World Review of Nutrition and Dietetics,* vol. 12 (1970): 452–504.
7. Ibid., p. 494.
8. P. J. V. Beumont, Suzanne F. Abraham, and Kathleen G. Simson, "The Psychosexual Histories of Adolescent Girls and Young Women with Anorexia Nervosa," *Psychological Medicine* 11 (1981): 136.

9. A. Keys, J. Brozek, A. Henschel, O. Mickelsen, and H. L. Taylor, *The Biology of Human Starvation,* vol. 1 (Minneapolis: University of Minnesota Press, 1950).

10. Steven Levenkron, *Treating and Overcoming Anorexia Nervosa* (New York: Charles Scribner's Sons, 1982).

11. A. H. Crisp, L. K. G. Hsu, and Britta Harding, "The Starving Hoarder and Voracious Spender: Stealing in Anorexia Nervosa," *Journal of Psychosomatic Research* 24 (Great Britain, 1980): 225.

12. Two of the most important sources on anorexia nervosa families are: Salvador Minuchin, Bernice L. Rosman, and Lester Baker, *Psychosomatic Families: Anorexia Nervosa in Context* (Cambridge: Harvard University Press, 1978) and Mara Selvini Palazzoli, *Self-Starvation* (New York: Jason Aronson, 1978).

13. Janice E. Hedblom, Felicity A. Hubbard, and Arnold E. Andersen, "Anorexia Nervosa: A Multidisciplinary Treatment Program for Patient and Family," *Social Work in Health Care* 7, no. 1 (Fall 1981): 67–83.

14. Michael Strober, "The Significance of Bulimia in Juvenile Anorexia Nervosa: An Exploration of Possible Etiologic Factors," *International Journal of Eating Disorders* 1, no. 1 (Autumn 1981): 28–43.

15. Bruch, "Psychological Antecedents of Anorexia Nervosa."

16. Bruch, "Psychological Antecedents of Anorexia Nervosa."

17. Hedblom, Hubbard, Andersen, "A Multidisciplinary Treatment Program."

18. Crisp, R. L. Palmer, and R. S. Kalucy, "How Common is Anorexia Nervosa? A Prevalence Study," *British Journal of Psychiatry* 128 (1976): 549–54.

19. Ruth L. Huenemann, Leona R. Shapiro, Mary C. Hampton, and Barbara W. Mitchell, "A Longitudinal Study of Gross Body Composition and Body Conformation and Their Association with Food and Activity in a Teenage Population," *American Journal of Clinical Nutrition* 18 (May 1966): 325–38.

20. Ingvar Nylander, "The Feeling of Being Fat and Dieting in a School Population," *Acta socio-medica Scandinavica* 1, (1971): 17–26.

21. David M. Garner, Paul E. Garfinkel, Donald M. Schwartz, and Michael G. Thompson, "Cultural Expectations of Thinness in Women," *Psychological Reports* 47 (1980): 483–91.

22. Richard G. Druss and Joseph A. Silverman, "Body Image and Perfectionism of Ballerinas," *General Hospital Psychiatry,* vol. 1, no. 2 (July 1979): 115–21.

23. L. M. Vincent, *Competing with the Sylph* (New York: Andrews and McMeel, 1979).

24. Crisp, "Anorexia Nervosa at Normal Body Weight!—The Abnormal Weight Control Syndrome," *International Journal of Psychiatry in Medicine* 11, no. 3 (1981–82): 203–33.

CHAPTER THREE
Entering Adulthood

1. Regina C. Casper, "Some Provisional Ideas Concerning the Psychologic Structure in Anorexia Nervosa and Bulimia" (Paper presented at the conference on Anorexia Nervosa, Toronto, September 1981). To be published in *Anorexia Nervosa*, P. L. Darby, P. E. Garfinkel, D. M. Garner, and D. V. Coscina, eds. (New York: Alan Liss, in press).

2. Katherine A. Halmi, Regina C. Casper, Elke D. Eckert, Solomon C. Goldberg, and John M. Davis, "Unique Features Associated with Age of Onset of Anorexia Nervosa," *Psychiatry Research* 1 (1979): 209–15.

3. Raymond C. Hawkins II and Pamelia F. Clement, "Development and Construct Validation of a Self-Report Measure of Binge-Eating Tendencies," *Addictive Behaviors* 5 (1980): 219–26.

4. Howard J. Osofsky and Seymour Fisher, "Psychological Correlates of the Development of Amenorrhea in a Stress Situation," *Psychosomatic Medicine* 29 (1967): 15–23.

5. Mary Ellen Donovan, "Hard Times in the Pressure Cooker," *Dartmouth Alumni* (December 1981): 30–34.

6. Garner and Garfinkel, "The Eating Attitudes Test: An Index of the Symptoms of Anorexia Nervosa," *Psychological Medicine* 9 (1979): 273–79.

7. Garner, Marion Olmstead, and Janet Polivy, "The Development and Validation of a Multidimensional Eating Disorders Inventory for Anorexia Nervosa and Bulimia," *International Journal of Eating Disorders* 2, no. 2 (Winter 1983, in press).

8. Garner, Polivy, Olmstead, and Garfinkel, "A Comparison Between Weight-Preoccupied Women and Anorexia Nervosa," submitted for publication.

9. Thompson and Schwartz, "Life Adjustment of Women with Anorexia Nervosa."

10. Hawkins and Clement, "Binge-Eating Syndrome: The Measurement Problem and a Conceptual Model," *Binge Eating. Theory, Research and Treatment* (New York: Springer, in press).

11. Chris Dufresne, "The Hidden Danger in Gymnastics," *Los Angeles Times*, part 3, 5 May 1982.

12. Hawkins and Clement, "Binge-Eating Syndrome."

CHAPTER FOUR
Fear of Fat: Just a Woman's Problem?

1. Richard Morton, *Phthisiologica—or a Treatise of Consumptions* (1689). Cited in Bruch, *Eating Disorders*.

2. Crisp, "Anorexia Nervosa: 'Feeding Disorder,' 'Nervous Malnutrition' or 'Weight Phobia'?", 494.

3. P. J. Dally and J. Gomez, *Obesity and Anorexia Nervosa: A Question of Shape* (London: Faber and Faber, 1980).

4. John A. Sours, *Starving to Death in a Sea of Objects: The Anorexia Nervosa Syndrome* (New York: Jason Aronson, 1980).

5. Bruch, *Eating Disorders*.

6. Sours, *Starving to Death*.

7. Crisp, Kalucy, J. H. Lacey, and Britta Harding, "The Long-Term Prognosis in Anorexia Nervosa: Some Factors Predictive of Outcome," in *Anorexia Nervosa*, ed. R. A. Vigersky.

8. Sours, *Starving to Death*.

9. Levenkron, *Treating and Overcoming Anorexia*.

10. Orland W. Wooley, Susan C. Wooley, and Sue R. Dyrenforth, "Obesity and Women—II. A Neglected Feminist Topic," *Women's Studies International Quarterly* 2 (Great Britain, 1979): 81–92.

11. K. Krumbacher and J. E. Meyer, "Das Appetitverhalten des Gesunden unter Emotionalem Stress," *Zeitschrift fur psychosomantische Medizin* 9 (1963): 89–94. Cited in J. E. Meyer, "Anorexia Nervosa of Adolescence," *British Journal of Psychiatry* 118 (1971): 541.

12. Eugene L. Lowenkopf, "Bulimia: Concept and Therapy" (Paper presented at the 135th Annual Meeting of the American Psychiatric Association, Toronto, 18 May 1982.

13. Vincent, *Competing with the Sylph*.

CHAPTER FIVE
On Their Own

1. Michael R. Liebowitz and Donald F. Klein, "Hysteroid Dysphoria," *Psychiatric Clinics of North America* 2, no. 3 (December 1979): 555–75.

2. Levenkron, *Treating and Overcoming Anorexia*.

3. Betty Rollin, "Hers," *New York Times*, section C, 19 August 1982, p. 2.

4. Craig Johnson and Reed Larson, manuscript in preparation.

5. Selvini Palazzoli, *Self-Starvation*.

6. "Bulimia: The New Danger in Dieting," *Harper's Bazaar* (March 1982): 148.

7. William C. White, Jr., and Marlene Boskind-White, "An Experiential-Behavioral Approach to the Treatment of Bulimarexia," *Psychotherapy: Theory, Research and Practice* 18, no. 4 (Winter 1981): 501–507.

CHAPTER SIX
At Home

1. Levenkron, *Treating and Overcoming Anorexia*.

2. Betty Friedan, *The Feminine Mystique* (New York: Dell paperback, 1981)

3. Levenkron, *Treating and Overcoming Anorexia*.

4. Soo Borson and Wayne Katon, "Chronic Anorexia Nervosa: Medical Mimic," *Western Journal of Medicine* 135 (October 1981): 257–65.

5. Bruch, *Eating Disorders*.

CHAPTER EIGHT
Changing Your Attitude

1. Based on a study by William Hunt and Joseph Matarazzo, cited in Stanley Schacter, "Don't Sell Habit Breakers Short," *Psychology Today* (August 1982): 27–33.

2. Schacter, Ibid.

3. William Gerin, "(No) Accounting for Results," *Psychology Today* (August 1982): 32.

4. G. Alan Marlatt and Damaris J. Rohsenow, "The Think-Drink Effect," *Psychology Today* (December 1981): 61–69.

5. Janet Polivy, "Perception of Calories and Regulation of Intake in Restrained and Unrestrained Subjects," *Addictive Behaviors*, vol. 1 (1975) 237–43.

6. G. A. Marlatt and J. R. Gordon, *Relapse Prevention* (New York: Guilford Press), in press.

7. Ethel Roskies and Richard S. Lazarus, "Coping Theory and the Teaching of Coping Skills," *Behavioral Medicine,* Park O. Davidson and Sheena M. Davidson, eds. (New York: Brunner/Mazel, 1980), pp. 38–69.

8. Cited in Richard B. Stuart, "Weight Loss and Beyond: Are They Taking It Off and Keeping It Off?" *Behavioral Medicine,* Ibid., pp. 151–94.

9. Halmi, James R. Falk, and Estelle Schwartz, "Binge-eating and Vomiting: A Survey of a College Population," *Psychological Medicine* 11 (1981): 697–706.

10. Marlatt, *Relapse Prevention,* 44.

11. Ibid., pp. 87–88.

12. Garner, Garfinkel, and Kelly M. Bemis, "A Multidimensional Psychotherapy for Anorexia Nervosa," *International Journal of Eating Disorders* 1, no. 2 (Winter 1982): 3–46.

13. Ibid.

CHAPTER NINE
Learning How to Eat

1. Wooley and Wooley, "The Beverly Hills Eating Disorder: The Mass Marketing of Anorexia Nervosa," *International Journal of Eating Disorders* 1, no. 3 (Spring 1982): 57–69.

2. Jane Wardle and Helen Beinart, "Binge Eating: A Theoretical Review," *British Journal of Clinical Psychology* 20 (1981): 97–109.

3. C. Peter Herman and Janet Polivy, "Anxiety, Restraint and Eating Behavior," *Journal of Abnormal Psychology* 84, no. 6 (1975): 666–72.

4. Wooley and Wooley, "Obesity and Women—I. A Closer Look at the Facts," *Women's Studies International Quarterly* 2 (Great Britain, 1979): 69–79.

5. Wooley and Wooley, "Eating Disorders: Obesity and Anorexia," *Women and Psychotherapy*, Annette M. Brodsky and Rachel Hare-Mustin, eds. (New York: Guilford Press, 1980), pp. 135–158.

6. R. E. Nisbett, "Hunger, Obesity, and the Ventromedial Hypothalamus," *Psychological Review* 79 (1972): 433–54.

7. William Bennett and Joel Gurin, *The Dieter's Dilemma* (New York: Basic Books, 1982).

8. Bruch, *Eating Disorders*.

9. Gerald Russell, "Bulimia Nervosa: An Ominous Variant of Anorexia Nervosa," *Psychological Medicine* 9 (1979): 429–48.

10. National Institutes of Health study, cited in "Yes, You Can Be Too Thin," *New York* magazine (June 22, 1981): 43.

11. Susie Orbach, "Emotional Hunger," British *Cosmopolitan* (May 1982): 179.

12. Stuart, *Act Thin, Stay Thin* (New York: W. W. Norton, 1978).

13. Ibid.

14. Christopher G. Fairburn, "The Place of a Cognitive Behavioral Approach in the Management of Bulimia" (Paper presented at the Conference on Anorexia Nervosa, Toronto, September 1981).

15. Stuart, *Act Thin, Stay Thin*.

16. James M. Ferguson, *Habits Not Diets: The Real Way to Weight Control* (Palo Alto: Bull Publishing, 1976).

17. Ibid.

CHAPTER TEN
Balancing Your Life-style

1. Marlatt, *Relapse Prevention*.

2. Marlatt and Janice K. Marques, "Meditation, Self-Control and Alcohol Use," *Behavioral Self-Management: Strategies, Techniques and Outcomes*, ed. Richard B. Stuart (New York: Brunner/Mazel, 1977).

3. William Glasser, *Positive Addiction* (New York: Harper and Row, 1976).

4. Marlatt, *Relapse Prevention*.

5. Ibid.

6. Meir Gross, *Anorexia Nervosa: A Comprehensive Approach* (Indianapolis: D. C. Heath & Co./Collamore Press, 1982).

7. Robert Paul Liberman, Larry W. King, William J. DeRisi, and Michael McCann, *Personal Effectiveness* (Champaign, Illinois: Research Press, 1975).

8. Johnson and Larson, "Bulimia: An Analysis of Moods and Behavior," *Psychosomatic Medicine* 44, no. 4 (September 1982): 341–52.

9. A. D. Weisman and J. W. Worden, "Psychosocial Analysis of Cancer Deaths," *Omega: Journal of Death and Dying* 6 (1975): 61–75.

CHAPTER ELEVEN
Medical Notes

1. Levenkron, *Treating and Overcoming Anorexia*, p. 69.

2. Arnold E. Andersen, "Psychiatric Aspects of Bulimia," *Directions in Psychiatry* (New York: Hatherleigh, 1981).

3. Russell, "Bulimia Nervosa."

4. *Diagnostic and Statistical Manual of Mental Disorders*, 3d ed. (Washington D.C.: American Psychiatric Association, 1980): 67–71.